JOE,
you coulda made
us proud

by Joe Pepitone
with Berry Stainback

ꟼ❦P

A Playboy Press Book

ACKNOWLEDGMENTS

Excerpt from the poem "All Clowns Are Masked and All Personae" by Delmore
Schwartz from *In Dreams Begin Responsibilities,* originally published in *Summer
Knowledge: Selected Poems.* Copyright © 1938 by New Directions Publishing Corporation, © 1966 by Delmore Schwartz. Reprinted by permission of New Directions Publishing Corporation.

Published simultaneously in the United States and Canada by Playboy Press, Chicago,
Illinois. Printed in the United States of America. Library of Congress Catalog Card
Number: 74-33557. ISBN 87223-428-2. First edition.

PLAYBOY and Rabbit Head design are trademarks of Playboy, 919 North Michigan
Avenue, Chicago, Illinois 60611 (U.S.A.), Reg. U.S. Pat. Off., marca registrada, marque
déposée.

In memory of Willie Pepitone, who left too soon,
And for Ann Pepitone, who endured.

All men are masked,
And we are clowns who think to choose our faces.
—DELMORE SCHWARTZ
from the poem
All Clowns Are Masked and All Personae

Contents

Joe, you coulda made us proud

Introduction

When an editor at Playboy Press called me in July 1974 and asked if I would be interested in writing a book with Joe Pepitone, I was intrigued. I had written a long article about Pepi for *Sport* magazine in 1963. That was his first full season in the majors, and during it Joe earned the starting job at first base for the American League All-Star team, was a key man in bringing the New York Yankees another pennant, and revealed that he had all the talent to become the new Mickey Mantle. It didn't work out that way. When I next saw Joe, eleven years later, he had suffered through two divorces, had lost three children, and had blown his baseball career. Why?

That, Joe said, was what he wanted to find out. After all these years, he felt he finally had some perspective on his bizarre behavior, some insights into why he had followed a crazed muse toward self-destruction. But he still had some heavy questions, and he thought that in laying out his entire story, examining it in sequence, he might uncover those missing answers.

It wasn't easy for Joe Pepitone to thrash through his past, relive old pain. In doing so, as he digs deeper and deeper into his head and heart, he offers a rare look at the human condition, at a very talented young man to whom too much came too soon —too much praise that told him he was special, and too much guilt over the sudden death of a larger-than-life father. It is a measure of just how far Joe Pepitone has come that he holds nothing back, because his entire existence had been an act devoted to *not* revealing what lay beneath his mask of perpetual wackiness and fun. Joe Pep, he'd always announced to the world, was having an unrelieved ball.

There was fun, a lot of fun. And Joe Pepitone is as honest in relating some of the funniest, most startling inside baseball stories that anyone ever admitted participating in, as he is in baring the most personal kind of truths. He is a genuinely funny man who can laugh at himself. Many of his early problems stemmed from his willingness to break rules if he thought he'd get a laugh. Often he would get caught. He is still paying for certain indiscretions. One afternoon in the mid-Sixties when he was with the Yankees, Joe was late leaving for the stadium. A cop pulled him over for speeding through the Brooklyn Battery Tunnel.

"Officer, I'm Joe Pepitone of the Yankees," he said. "Maybe you'd like a couple of tickets to a game?"

"I'm not a Yankee fan," said the policeman. "I don't even like baseball."

"Oh, you don't like baseball."

"No. But I love the football Giants."

"Hey! Well, I'll get you a couple of Giant tickets. Give me your name and address and I'll mail them to you."

The policeman did so, closing his traffic violation book. Joe drove on, throwing the policeman's name and address out the window. Recently Joe got stopped for speeding on the West Side Highway in Manhattan.

"Officer, I'm Joe Pepitone," he said. "I used to play with the Yankees. Maybe you'd like a couple of tickets to a Yankee game or a Met game?"

"Never mind that shit, Pepitone. I'm still waiting for those Giant tickets you promised me eight years ago. Here, I've got a ticket for you."

BERRY STAINBACK
North Tarrytown, N.Y.
January 1975

I

To Willie: "Bless you, damn you. Love, Joe."

My father was a god in my eyes when I was growing up. His name was William Pepitone, and he was called Willie Pep after the fighter, but my father was bigger and a helluva lot tougher than the former featherweight champion of the world. My father was six feet, one inch tall, he weighed about 190 pounds, and his muscular shoulders and chest sloped down to a thirty-inch waist from working construction all his life. He had been a Golden Gloves fighter, not a boxer, as a kid. He was a puncher who kept coming, and he did that all his life, too. He was the toughest guy in my neighborhood. I saw him fight, in the street, at least fifty times. He never lost. *Never.* And this was in a very tough neighborhood, the Park Slope section of Brooklyn, a semislum that was populated almost entirely by Italian and Irish hard-noses. He had a furious temper and, when he wasn't spoiling the shit out of me, he was beating the shit out of me.

Willie's main thing was family, the Pepitones and Caiazzos. Nobody could mess with any of them without having to deal with my father. He took care of the physical problems in this very physical neighborhood, and my grandfather, Vincent Caiazzo, took care of the housing problems. Vincent Caiazzo was a shoemaker who did very well for all of us, even though he so disbelieved in banks that he saved his money in a water pipe in his shop. At the close of business every day, he rolled up his bills and with a long pole rammed them into a forty-foot pipe. To make a withdrawal, he rammed farther until cash flowed out the other end. "Who ever think anyone putta their money in a water pipe?" he would say, and he was right.

When I was very young, Vincent owned two three-story apartment buildings that he filled with members of the Caiazzo and Pepitone families. Later he sold them to buy two bigger, five-story apartment buildings that housed more of the family. The older Italians were all heavily into family togetherness, all looking out for one another, genuinely caring for one another —a particularly warm and lovely thing it seems to me these days. My family, the Pepitones and Caiazzos, has had Sunday dinner en masse at Vincent's for as long as I can remember. A couple of dozen Italians sitting around eating, talking loudly, throwing bread at one another, and laughing. My father, who enjoyed kidding, would lead the laughter. But it ended abruptly if I got out of line.

I remember one Sunday when I was eight years old going to my grandfather's with Willie. My mother had gone over earlier with my younger brothers and my dog. My grandfather kept telling me every time I'd go there that he was going to kill my dog because it peed on his tomato plants out back and damaged them. "One day I kill that dog, Joe," he'd say. "I cook him." This day my dog wasn't there when I arrived. I got scared and went right to the oven. I opened the door and inside, staring at me, was a head, with two shining eyes and a tongue hanging out like a dog . . . cooking.

"My dog!" I screamed, bursting into tears. "Look what Grandpa did to my dog!" I grabbed the head and yanked it out of the oven, but it burned my hands and I dropped it on the floor.

My grandfather came running in from the living room. "That's my *capozell* on the floor!" he yelled.

I started punching him and kicking him. "You killed my dog!"

"That's my *capozell!* Sheep head!"

My father rushed in, saw me kicking my grandfather, and knocked me to the floor, yanked me up, and knocked me down again. It was a sheep head, one of my grandfather's favorite meals, eyes and all. Just then my mother, Angelina, who is called Ann, came in with my dog on a leash. She'd been walking it.

"Willie, that's enough!" she yelled at my father, who was still beating me. But she didn't step in to stop him. She was as afraid of Willie as anyone, fearing he'd turn his terrible temper on her. He never pulled his punches, left me black-and-blue and bloody, particularly as I got older. My mother, who never raised a hand to me, could do nothing about it. Some of the blood that was spilled out of me by Willie was her fault. She was always a very nervous person, and she had a hysterectomy when I was ten, had to live on tranquilizers after that. If I was two minutes late getting home at night, she would put a pillow on the windowsill and lean out, looking for me, worrying. Anything could happen on the streets in that neighborhood. If you stepped out of your area into another neighborhood you'd get beaten up. So she had reason to worry. But the more she worried, the angrier my father got. I'd come home five minutes late, and Willie would punch the shit out of me.

When I look back, I don't know how my mother was able to get through it with my father and me, all the crap we brought down on her. My father was such a jealous person that my mother could never really relax, be comfortable, enjoy herself in any kind of social situation. Even with her sisters' husbands she had to avert her eyes if Willie was present. She'd just glance at a guy at a party, and if that guy's eyes paused on her, Willie would jump up and scream at him, challenge him, embarrass him . . . and Ann.

My mother worked most of her life in a clothing factory in Brooklyn. Willie always picked her up after work because his construction job ended earlier. One evening he was about thirty minutes late. My mother's boss was nice enough to give her a ride home. When he dropped her off, Willie pulled up, leaped out of his car, and screamed at this man, threatened to punch him out if he ever drove my mother home again. My mother ran into the house crying.

I don't see how she was able to push aside all the pain, all the fears through all those years. She is truly an amazing human being, with a great, all-giving heart and super strengths, resources. She loved my father because he worked hard and was a good family man, because he would do anything, as she would, for anyone in our family. Like me, she had to be proud of a guy who would physically stand up to anyone, *anyone,* if his family had been threatened, had reason to be afraid.

My Uncle Red, Louie Caiazzo, is my mother's younger brother, and he was also like a kid brother to Willie. My parents took him every place they went. One day when I was about eight and Louie was about eighteen, he walked into our apartment all beat up. There was dried blood under his nose, a bruise on his cheek, a mouse under one eye. Willie's jaw got very tight, like the skin on a drum, and his eyes kind of clenched, as they always did when he got mad. "What in the hell happened to you?" Willie said. Louie's eyes filled up, he was so ashamed of having Willie see him in that condition. But he was more ashamed of going home like that, so he'd come to Willie. I guess he also came to Willie because he knew my father would straighten out whoever had beaten him. Willie always took care of such things promptly. Louie sucked in the tears and told Willie he'd gotten into an argument with the guy who owned the hardware store in the area, a big guy who'd just beaten the shit out of him over nothing.

"Come on," Willie said, and stormed out of the apartment, followed by Louie, who could barely keep up. I knew my father wouldn't allow me to go along, but I didn't want to miss the action. I waited a couple of minutes, then ran to the hardware store. Willie and Louie were standing outside the window, Louie was pointing through the glass, and then Willie nodded. "Okay. Wait here," I heard Willie say; then he went inside. I walked right up beside Louie by the doorway, knowing he wouldn't care if I was there.

"Listen, I need a piece of copper pipe," Willie was saying to the guy. "One-inch pipe about five inches long."

The guy turned to a bin behind the counter and handed him a length of pipe. "How's this?"

Willie hefted it in his hand, staring at it, then closed his fingers around it. "Yeah," he said, "that's just right." Then *bing!* he hit the guy in the jaw and, as the guy went down, Willie yelled, "You beat up *my* brother-in-law? Get up, you bastard!" Stupidly, the guy got up; Willie hit him again and busted his nose. He was lying on the floor bleeding, half conscious, when Willie tossed the piece of pipe on his chest. "You're not worth a shit, but your pipe does the job."

He came outside and said, "Let's go, Louie. That guy ever messes with you again, it'll be the last—" Then he noticed me. "What the hell are you doing here?"

"I was just walking by, looking for a stickball game, Dad."

"You little wise-ass!" He raised his hand to me, then lowered it with a smile. "Come on, we're all going home."

Willie took on everyone, even racket guys who could and did lay very heavy beatings or worse on people who gave them trouble. It wasn't long after the hardware store problem had been corrected that my father heard that this guy I'll call Valonni was badmouthing someone in our family all over the neighborhood. Valonni owned a clothing store, but he was also large in the rackets. Willie went to see him at his store and got there just as the guy was rolling up his awning, closing for the day. "What's this shit I hear you're saying about my family?"

"Get lost," the guy said, pulling out the awning rod.

Willie hit him on the point of the chin, and Valonni lifted off his feet and did a back dive right through his plate-glass window. "Don't *ever* badmouth *my* family again, you bastard!" He left the guy lying among the broken glass in the window, trying to shake some light back into his head.

Within hours, bad guys all over Brooklyn were out looking for my father. Luckily the word got to Jimmy the Bug right away. Jimmy the Bug lived in our building and was a good friend of our family. He was in the numbers business. As soon as he heard what had happened, he came right in to see my father. "Look, Willie," he said, "stay in this apartment. Don't go out until I talk to some people. I'll straighten this thing out." He did. It only took him a month of steady negotiations to keep Willie alive. But after the first couple of days at home, Willie said, "Fuck them." My mother ran and got Jimmy the Bug, who told Willie to be patient, that he'd work it out. But that Willie had to think of his family, and if he cared about them at all he wouldn't leave the apartment. Every day or so he had to come and convince Willie again. But he kept at it, with Willie and the racket guys, and finally negotiated a pardon. When it was over, Willie said, "They still better not badmouth my family unless they like sleeping in windows." Jimmy the Bug threw his hands up in the air.

Jimmy the Bug had solid juice with both sides of the law. He saved my father from getting arrested for assault one day—after the police had started writing the report. My friend Lemon was the cause of it. We called him Lemon because he was shaped like one: short and round, very fat. He was two years older than I, and Willie had appointed him as my protector against the big guys. "Lemon, anyone hits Joe, you hit them—or I hit *you,*" my father had told him. Anyway, on this day Lemon, who was about thirteen, and I went to the movie across the street from our apartment: The National Theater, which we called The Itch, because that's what you did the moment you sat in the place. We were sitting way down front and there was some kind of collection between shows, March of Dimes or something. While the cardboard collection cups were being passed, we saw this little boy, five or six years old, wandering around by us, crying. He was lost. So we got up and walked up the aisle with him, yelling, "Anybody lose a kid? We've got a lost kid here!"

The movie came on and we were still yelling, which brought the manager running down to us. He took us in back and threw us out. "We were just trying to help this kid!" I yelled.

"At the top of your lungs!" he said angrily. "You're ruining the show for everyone."

"I'm not leaving!" I yelled, and Lemon yelled, "Me neither!"

"Get outta here!" he said, and pushed us out the door. As he did so he kicked me in the ass.

Lemon, who loved to see my father fight, said, "Let's go tell your dad." I was so upset, on the verge of tears, I didn't want to. But Lemon dragged me along and told Willie. The story came out like a hyphenated word: "The-theater-owner-kicked-Joe-in-the-ass-for-us-helping-a-lost-kid!" By then the tears were rolling down my cheeks.

My father grabbed our hands and said, "Come on. Show me the guy." He was always very careful to go after the right guy. The manager was in the ticket booth when we got back to the theater. "There he is!" cried Lemon. "There he is!"

"*You!*" my father said, pushing his face against the bars of the booth. "Come out of there. I want to talk to you." The manager saw the anger on my father's face and decided the last place he wanted to be was out of that booth. He latched the screen door behind him, then started to close the metal door. But my father stepped behind the booth, punched his hand through the screen, grabbed the guy by the front of his shirt, and dragged him through the split screen. "You kick *my* son in the ass, huh?" Willie hit him in the face. "For helping a little lost kid, huh?" He hit him again, holding him up with his other hand. "You are a no-good sonofabitch!" He hit him and let him go this time, and the manager sailed backward, his head banging off the sidewalk.

Just then, two policemen ran over from the Eightieth Precinct, which was a few doors up the block across the street. "That's assault, Pepitone," one said. "You're under arrest."

"What arrest—for smacking a grown man who kicked a kid?"

Each cop grabbed an arm and started marching him across the street. My father turned his head over his shoulder. "Joe, go get Jimmy."

I ran over to our building and up the two flights of stairs to Jimmy the Bug's apartment. I told him what had happened and he shook his head, buttoning on his shirt. I followed him into the station house where my father was being booked. Jimmy reached his hand behind him and touched my chest for me to wait there. He walked right up to the desk and leaned in to the officer on duty, who leaned his head close to the numbers baron. Jimmy the Bug whispered something to the policeman, who nodded, signaled one of the arresting officers to come over, whispered something to him, and then said, "All right, Pepitone, get your ass out of here." Case closed. That was how important Jimmy the Bug was in my neighborhood, a big man and a good man.

Jimmy the Bug was also a very tough man, too. I saw him, not once but several times, tell a cop on the street who was giving him trouble about his business: "You come at me with that kinda shit? Take off that badge and I'll kick your ass right now! Right here in the fucking street! I'll destroy you!" And every time, the cop walked away from Jimmy.

He was tough, but my father was the champion. I used to wait for him to come home every evening when I was young. He parked his car in the garage at the end of our street at this time, and every day around five I'd run down there and wait for him, see if he'd brought me anything—which he often did —and walk back to our house with him. One day I went down a little late and my father was already coming down the street —with both of his arms in casts. The plaster ran from his hands all the way up his forearms.

"Dad, Dad! What happened?"

"Just an accident on the job."

The accident, it turned out, had happened on the head of Willie's foreman. My father was the number one man on his construction crew because he was the hardest worker. And the guy who owned the construction company loved Willie. He was always doing Willie favors: lending him big cars, giving him extra jobs that brought in good money for little labor—like setting out fresh "bombs," those round black pots full of fuel oil that were lit around construction sites, on weekends at double-time rates. The foreman was very jealous of Willie, and on this day he tried to give him some crap to do, just to harass him. Willie did not find it amusing. The foreman told him he wanted some heavy piece of equipment moved, and Willie said, fine, he'd get some of the guys to take care of it. The foreman said, No, I want you to move it. Willie suggested what he might do to himself with the shovel handle lying nearby. "I'm the foreman here, Pepitone, and you move that thing or I'm docking you!" He was a large man and he grabbed Willie's arm. "Now get to it!"

Willie slapped his hand away and yelled, "You can dock me —but I'm decking you, you big fat sonofabitch!" And he punched this guy from one side of the job to the other. Guys ran over to pull him off; he tossed them away and kept hitting the guy in the head until both his hands were broken. They took six weeks to heal, and by that time the foreman was out of the hospital. He never bugged Willie again.

If my father was hard on people who crossed him, he was even harder on me, it often seemed. I have two brothers— Jimmy, who is a year and a half younger than I am, and Billy, who is six years younger than I am. My father would tell me that I was responsible for them, that I had to look out for them all the time. "They come home hurt," he'd tell me, "you're gonna get a beating. Understand?"

So Jimmy would get in a fight and come home with a bloody nose, and my father would be waiting for me. "I told you to look out for your brother!" he'd yell, and without another word, no explanation, nothing, he'd beat the hell out of me with his fists, bloody my nose, leave bruises all over my face. Little Billy would fall off his bike, come home with a scraped-up knee, and my father would just whale the shit out of me. "But it wasn't my fault! I wasn't there!" "You shoulda been there!" *Rap, bang, crack.* One time Billy hit a fire hydrant on his bike, flipped over the handlebars, smacked his head. "I was there, Dad! I was right there, I just couldn't catch him!" "You shoulda caught him!" *Rap, bang, crack.*

He had a flare temper and he was very strict. He said do something, I had better do it—or duck. Whatever time he said I had to be home, eight o'clock, nine o'clock, I better not be a minute late.

I remember the evening he brought me home a new bicycle. It was a Schwinn with chrome fenders, a chrome headlight, a chrome horn, a chrome basket, a fancy reflector on the back. It was beautiful! I was so excited I almost cried. "Thanks, Dad! Wait'll Lemon and the guys see this!"

"All right, Joe. But watch the time. It's five-fifteen. We eat at six. You be back here to eat at six. No later."

I rode off down the block on my new bike, met the guys, and they all went what we then called apeshit. I let them have a couple of rides each, I had a couple. Then I pedaled home. My father was waiting on the front stoop. He was looking at his watch. It was three minutes after six.

"Get off that goddamn bike, you little bastard!"

He jumped down the steps, grabbed my shiny new bike, raised it over his head, and smashed it down the steps to the basement. The headlight flew off and all kinds of other pieces. But it wasn't enough. He leaped down the basement steps, kicked in the spokes, lifted the bike again, and smashed it against the wall, just kept smashing it and smashing it against that concrete wall until there was nothing left in his hands except twisted metal.

I ran up to my room crying, thinking, *Three minutes late, three minutes!* I was lying on the bed crying when he came in and beat me. But I didn't feel that beating. All I could think of was that mutilated bike. I'll never forget it. The next day he bought me a new bike.

Usually, right after he'd beaten me, my father would cool down and apologize to me, saying he was sorry, that he didn't mean to hit me so hard. Almost every time he'd beat me, he'd come back minutes later and apologize. Finally I told him, "Dad, don't apologize to me—just stop beating me, or at least make sure I deserve it." But he couldn't control that temper. It would just *explode!*

He had no patience whatsoever. NONE. I liked to be with him, do things with him, I admired him so much, respected him so much as a man. He'd take me fishing, crabbing, to ball games, and for a long time I enjoyed it. But as the years went on, it got harder and harder.

He wanted to do things with me, to teach me, but so many times he'd just blow it. I remember when I was fourteen or fifteen he let me drive the car, and I did okay, just steering it around. So he decided to teach me to drive. He had a "fluid drive" Chrysler. You could use the clutch or put it in automatic and it would shift itself. You let up on the gas, waited for the click, then you shifted and you pressed the gas again. I wasn't too sharp with the clutch, but I was all right in automatic.

So we went out in the car and I was driving along very nervously, very tense. My father said, "Relax, Joe, relax." He was making me more nervous, and the next thing I knew I'd gone through a stop sign. Luckily nothing had been coming in either direction, so there had been no real problem. But Willie blew up, smacking me in the shoulder as hard as he could.

"Get the hell out from behind that wheel!"

I hit the brake, stopped dead. "Why, Dad, we're okay—"

He grabbed me and yanked me right across his lap, out of the driver's seat. "You ain't driving no more till you get some sense!"

"Aw, Dad . . . what the hell." Shit, it tore me up. I just couldn't understand why he couldn't relax, why he couldn't have patience, couldn't give me a chance to show him. I wanted so badly to do well when I was with him.

A year or so later, he had the car parked on the block and he gave me the keys because there was a guy coming to charge the battery and Willie himself had to go see his mother. "You wait for the guy to do the charge, let him start it, then put the keys in the house. I'll be back in a couple of hours."

About ten seconds after my father left, the guy came and charged the battery. Then my friend Lemon showed up and we decided to sit in the car and play "driving." I started it up, and every time a girl would stroll by, I'd race the gas and say, "Hey, how ya doin'? Wanna go for a ride?"

We didn't get any calls, but finally Lemon said, "Why don't we take it around the block, Joe?"

"Are you shitting me, man? Take Willie's car around the block? He'd kill our asses."

"Hell, he won't be back for an hour. We'll just go around the block and be back here in ten minutes. C'mon."

I put it in third and let the clutch out very, very easy and we pulled out. I knew I didn't have to shift, but I forgot I had to put in the clutch when we stopped. We putted up to the corner, stopped, and stalled. I restarted, turned the corner, putted up to the next one, and stalled again. I made the third corner without stalling and I was feeling pretty good. I speeded on up to about ten miles per hour, and cruised right back to our parking space. But it was gone.

"Lemon—someone's taken the spot! There's no place to park!" I looked around frantically, and every space on the street was occupied. "Goddamn! My father'll come back and find his car in the middle of the street!"

I thought I knew the owner of the car that was in our spot, and I ran to his apartment and asked him to please move. He said it wasn't his car. I ran back to Lemon. "What the hell are we gonna *do,* man? Willie will kill us."

"Uh, Joe," Lemon said, "I better be getting home. It's getting late."

"Lemon—it's eight fucking o'clock! Going around the block was your idea! You stay with me!"

I turned on the engine and started backing down the street, looking for a space, when all of a sudden Willie came running over, screaming, "Turn off that goddamn engine!" He grabbed me by the throat through the open window and dragged me out of the car, plopping me on the sidewalk. He leaned down and rapped me twice. From where I was lying I could see Lemon's fat ass running up the street. He was in a crouch, as if to keep Willie from seeing him. Willie saw him.

"You ever hang around with my son again, I'll kick your ass, you sonofabitch. Make him drive my car!"

"Dad," I said, "I just pulled out to give a guy a space. I figured you'd want to test the battery."

"You lying sonofabitch!" He punched me again.

"You're right, Dad. It was Lemon's idea. He made me—" He punched me again.

I deserved it that time, and a lot of other times. But there were still others, too many others, when there was no way I should have been beaten. And those times really hurt, when I hadn't earned the whacks. What hurt even more was when my father didn't keep his word, when he would tell me we'd do something together, and then change his mind.

Next to playing ball, crabbing was my favorite thing as a kid. So many times on a Saturday my father would tell me we were going crabbing the next morning. We'd take our nets to the Cross Bay Bridge at daylight and catch baskets of crabs. But the night before, I'd be so excited I couldn't sleep. I'd go to bed early to get up at five o'clock in the morning and I'd just lie there all night praying, *Don't rain, don't let it rain!*

Then at five in the morning I'd go into my Dad's room and shake him. "Come on, Dad. Get up. It's time to go."

And he'd roll over. "No, I decided we're not going today."

He did that to me quite a bit, and I *hated* it. This would hurt me more than anything. I know now he didn't mean it, that when he said we would go crabbing he fully planned to do so . . . but that when I'd waken him in those dark mornings, the fatigue from a week's construction labor would hit him, or perhaps the residues from that extra glass of wine the night before, and he'd cancel. He didn't intentionally disappoint me. He did the best he could for me in all things. He wanted only good for me, wanted me to do right, wanted to teach me about obligations, responsibilities. It took me years and years to understand, to realize that the beatings were a reflex, his way of teaching me, the only way he knew. The constant beatings followed by apologies were not the best way, not for me. Willie didn't know that. I think he loved me too much, wanted too much for me, expected too much from me.

I know I loved him too much. As a little kid I always wanted to be with him. I remember sitting next to him at the dinner table and looking up at him like a puppy. He'd look down at me, and that small warm smile would tingle me, my whole body. He was so alive, such a vibrant man, always kidding, putting people on. Every Sunday, when twenty to twenty-five members of the family would assemble for dinner at my grand-father's, Willie would lead the conviviality, the laughter, keep everyone loose, happy. They all looked up to him, had so much respect for him, and I bathed in the glow around him. I wonder if ever a father has been such a god to his son? I know now, though, why being alternately praised and put down by a god was so painfully confusing, disorienting. Bless you, Willie; damn you. I miss you.

II

"You give? You give up?"

When you are born and raised in the slums, you don't know any different until you get away from them, live other places for a while. I remember my early years away from Brooklyn, looking back on living conditions there from the vantage point of a nice, plush residence, and saying to myself, How the hell did I ever live there as a kid, grow up in such a place? How did I ever manage to get through it? How did I ever get out of there? I think back on three friends who as kids wanted to be priests, who instead got into the racket business and, ultimately, into prison. It could have happened to any of us and, I realize in retrospect, we all had to work out our escapes in our own ways.

But it wasn't all that bad, either, growing up in Park Slope. I didn't know anybody there who went hungry, anybody who was truly short of clothes, anybody who didn't have the money to get into a movie or go to Coney Island when the rest of the guys had decided to. Yes, the Park Slope section of Brooklyn, viewed in perspective, was more good vibes than bad, more fun than fury.

The biggest problem for me growing up in this neighborhood was that you had to act like a tough guy to get by. I had a very hard time getting that act together. I was anything but tough. I was always very tall for my age and stickball-bat skinny. I had short, wire-curly hair that gripped my head like a stocking mask and emphasized my beaklike nose and turn-signal ears. I looked a great deal like a baby robin.

And I was always scared as a kid. I was always being challenged physically, because that's the way it was for everyone until you proved yourself. I didn't like to fight. I didn't like to fight simply because I was always getting my ass beat. I mean, consistently, without ever any change in the outcome. I was quick on my feet and I'd dance around very skillfully for a while, but I always ended up on the ground with someone pounding me. Then I'd go home with bumps and bruises, and my father would enlarge them because I hadn't done better.

"Dad, you shoulda seen the other guy!"

"Shit!" *Rap, bang, crack.*

I think this is why I became such a fast runner. "You wanna fight, Pepitone—you skinny sonofabitch!" "No!" *Zoom,* sprint away. If Lemon, who was shorter and wider and two years older, was around, and the challenger wasn't too big, he'd look out for me. He was tough, and he also preferred taking a rap from a tougher guy to getting one from my father. But when Lemon wasn't around, it was strictly, *feet, do your thing.*

I remember when I was about twelve or thirteen, there was this kid Johnny O'Hara, a little Irish kid, who would beat the shit out of me regularly. I was twice his size, but every time he saw me he'd kick my ass. Whenever I spotted Johnny O'Hara, I'd duck behind a car, slip into an alley, get out of sight till he passed. There were times I crouched for forty-five minutes waiting for him to leave the area. One day he got me in a headlock and had about seven or eight of his friends kick me in the ass. One after the other. I couldn't sit down comfortably for three days.

It wasn't until I was fifteen years old that I finally stood up to anyone. My friend Jimmy Cunningham—Mokey—coerced me into it. At this time there was a kid called Knucks who was beating the shit out of me every other day. This guy was really beating on me—huge bruises, bloody noses, swollen lips, black eyes. It seemed like I was always holding ice on my face to take the swelling down so that my father wouldn't see the losses all over my face. Finally Mokey said to me, "Pep, I'm sick of this shit."

"Mokey," I said, "you think *you're* sick of it. . . ."

"Yeah, well you can take him, Pep. You got to stand up to him, fight him back. You can kick his ass."

"I don't know, Mokey."

"I'm telling you, you can kick his ass. You just gotta do it once. He won't bother you again."

"You know, Mokey, you're right, goddamnit. I'm gonna do it!"

So the next day we were at school and classes were over. But the shop class stayed open an extra hour for anyone who wanted to work on a project. You could make boats, lamps, tie racks for your mother. Mokey and I were passing the shop and Knucks was in there all alone.

"Now's your chance, Pep," said Mokey. "You can get him!"

"Jeez, I don't know. . . ."

Mokey got furious. "Go get him, goddamnit! You don't hit that sonofabitch, I'm gonna hit you!"

"Aw, shit, Mokey. Why don't we go play some ball?"

He hit me a helluva shot in the arm. "Ouch! Christ, Mokey!"

"You hit him, or I hit you!"

I walked to the shop door rubbing my arm and yelled, "Knucks—come out here!"

He looked up from the bench he was working at, saw it was me, and said, "What the fuck do you want, jerk?"

"Knucks—I'm gonna *fight* you. I'm gonna beat the shit out of you!"

He put down his project and walked straight toward me, and I was scared. I was so frightened I didn't think I could throw a punch. But he walked right up to me, about eighteen inches from my face, and my fist just shot out, as if Mokey were controlling it with a string, and caught Knucks flush on the jaw. I didn't think I hit him that hard, but he went down! He flopped right down on the floor! Holy shit! I jumped on him, grabbed him in a headlock, and squeezed. "You give?" I said. "You give up?"

"Yeah, yeah!"

"No, you don't!" I squeezed harder, loving it. He was giving up to *me!* After all those beatings, I had him on the ground, choking the shit out of him! I wasn't scared any more! I was winning! I was tough! I let him go, and when he staggered to his feet, I started pounding the hell out of him, hitting him as hard as I could: lefts, rights, in the gut, in the face, just whaling away.

Then, a few days later, I'll be damned if I didn't win *another* fight. Two in a row! I *was* tough. I started going around looking for fights. Tall, skinny Joe Pepitone was not a guy to mess with. I beat up two of my good friends. Another friend, my cousin Paddy Boy, gave me some lip one day, wised off about something, and I punched him in the stomach so hard that he lay on the sidewalk gasping for breath for five minutes. When he got up, I said, "Don't fuck with Joe Pep!" I felt mean, like I was the toughest sonofabitch in the world. I even started getting cocky with my uncles. And suddenly I had won five fights in a row—*five!* Me! Willie wasn't going to have to worry about me coming home beat up any more. Shit, man, I couldn't lose!

If anybody said anything that seemed out of line to me, I came right back at them for the first time in my life. About three weeks after my victory streak began, a bunch of us were in the school yard playing stickball and this Irish kid was bugging me, acting kind of big. He was about my size, tall and skinny. I picked a fight with him. He grabbed the stickball bat and smacked me with it.

"You wanna fight, huh?" he said, holding the bat.

I danced around him, throwing punches, but I couldn't get close enough to him to land anything. Every time I swung, he cracked me with the bat. Finally I started covering up, and he chased me around the school yard, leaving welts all over my body.

I ran home and my mother saw I was bruised and bleeding. "Mom," I said, "I tried to hit him, but he had a stickball bat!"

"Get a baseball bat and get him," my mother said.

I got a baseball bat out of the closet, went back to the school yard, and ran right up to that Irish kid. He yanked the baseball bat out of my hands and beat the shit out of me with that.

I went home and told my mother, "Mom, don't tell me to get a gun, 'cause he'll take it away from me and *shoot* me." That was enough of that fighting shit for me. I lost that one twice, maybe the next fight would be even worse. Five in a row wasn't bad, after all. Why push it?

In my neighborhood you had to belong to a gang or you'd get your ass whipped every day. You couldn't go to Prospect Park, to a church dance, to the roller rink, even to school if you weren't in a gang. I didn't much like gangs, but I did like protection. I *needed* protection.

We'd had a gang of twenty to twenty-five guys for years: The Washington Avenue Boys. All of a sudden one day Joe Fortunato, the leader, came over to me with a bunch of the other guys and said, "Joe, we're gonna have to initiate you into the gang."

"What the hell do you mean 'initiate into the gang'? I've been with you guys all my life!"

"No, this is a new thing we're starting, Joe. Make it official. The older guys have to initiate the young guys."

"Who initiated you guys?"

"We initiated each other," said Fortunato, who was a couple of years older than me and looked like Muggs McGinnis of the East Side Kids. He wore an old fedora hat pushed up in front just like Muggs in the movies.

"Joe, it won't be bad, it's just a little test we're putting all the young guys through. You won't have any problem."

"What do I have to do?"

"We're just gonna tie you to a tree in Prospect Park tonight for four hours, then come back and set you free."

"*Four hours! Me* tied to a tree in Prospect Park for four hours! At night! No way."

Fortunato and the other older guys huddled a minute, then he said, "Okay, Joe, if you don't wanna do that, there's another test you can do to be initiated. All you have to do is swim halfway across the park lake."

"Halfway? Then what do I do when I'm out in the middle? How do I get back? You guys are nuts. I'm not gonna do any of this shit."

They huddled again. "Joe, you want to be in the gang or don't you?"

"Yeah, shit, you know I want to be with you guys."

"Okay, this is your last chance. Come on. The initiation will be held right in my house."

We all went over to Fortunato's and they put a blindfold over my eyes in the living room. They told me to wait there, that they were all going into the bathroom for a conference. A conference? I thought. What the hell are they up to? As soon as I heard the door close, I lifted up my blindfold and saw that they were all gone. Then I heard them all coughing up phlegm and spitting in the bathroom. They went on for about five minutes, hacking and coughing and spitting. Then the door started to open, so I pulled the blindfold back down.

Fortunato walked over to me and put a glass in my hand. "Okay, Joe, drink this," he said.

"Man, I'm not gonna drink that."

"Joe, you wanna be in the club, you gotta drink it."

"I wanna be in the club, man, but I can't drink that shit." I felt the glass in my hand, thinking about what was in it. "C'mon, man . . ."

"Joe, it's up to you, if you don't wanna hang out with us any more."

"Aw, shit . . ." I thought about what it would be like, not having the guys to hang around with, not having any protection out on those mean streets. I lifted the glass toward my mouth and something sticking out of it jabbed me in the nose. "What the hell—?"

"That's a straw, Joe. You gotta drink through a straw."

I put the straw in my mouth and tried to hold my breath, but I couldn't draw anything in at the same time. Fuck it! I thought, and sucked hard—and this thick, slimy gook filled my mouth and stuck in my throat. Then it came out, along with everything else in my stomach, all over Fortunato's living-room floor. I ripped off my blindfold.

"You no-good bastards! Making me drink lungers!"

They were all laughing and slapping one another, and I looked at the glass in my hand and saw that the end of the straw was buried in a raw egg.

"Hey, you're a member, Joe! You're a member!" Fortunato was yelling.

I was always a follower, never a leader. Not just because I was one of the younger guys, but because that was my nature. I went along with everything, not because I liked everything that went on, but simply because I had to in order to be one of the guys. I remember a couple of gang wars we had around the Fourth of July that were really crazy, I mean where guys got some really bad injuries.

The wars started when one of our guys went to buy fireworks

and got ripped off. We'd all chipped in a few bucks apiece for the fireworks, and they were sold in another neighborhood in which we had trouble with the guys who lived there. We had trouble with gangs every place around us, that's the way it was. But our guy was careful, we thought: he took a taxi to the store that sold the fireworks, bought about forty dollars' worth of stuff, and was carrying it out to the taxi he'd had wait for him —when six guys jumped him and stole the entire buy. Were we pissed off!

So we scraped together over fifty dollars, and one of the guys got his uncle and a couple of other adults to drive him to the fireworks store. Then we challenged the guys who'd ripped us off to come into our neighborhood. We caught a couple of them alone, kicked their asses, and dared them to come back with all their guys. They did and we were ready. We had guys on the roofs with cherry bombs that you lit and torpedoes that exploded on impact. We also had filled garbage cans with the loose gravel that covered the tar on all our roofs. We had guys in alleys on the street with Roman candles. And we posted one guy on the roof of the building where our territory began, two blocks away, who as soon as he saw them coming fired a Roman candle to signal us. It was like a war.

When they marched down the street where we were waiting, we threw down cherry bombs, torpedoes, and gravel. Our guys in the alleys jumped out and fired Roman candles at them from twenty yards away. They hit a couple of guys right in the chest and their shirts caught on fire. Shoes were blown off, pieces of fingers. You never saw anything like it. It scared the shit out of me and repelled me when I saw those guys running with their shirts on fire. But I had to be part of it, had to act tough, like I didn't give a shit. If you didn't throw your bombs or fire your Roman candles at the enemy, another guy in your gang would see you and tell everyone, and you'd be ostracized. It was a wild, crazy scene. I heard that one guy was blinded in one eye. I know we destroyed them. They dared us to come into their neighborhood for a rematch, and we told them to fuck off. We said, you guys want to get even, come on back—and those stupid bastards did. It was just as bad the second time.

I was lucky in the gang fights we had. I managed to stay out of the heavy brawling, pick out another skinny guy to wrestle with, just run around a lot. Until one night when I was about fifteen and a half. The trouble started at the Empire Roller Skating Rink. We were all there skating and laughing it up. A lot of the guys were fooling with the girls from our neighborhood, which was something I wasn't into much at all. Not only did I look like a baby robin and didn't get a whole lot of calls from the girls, but playing ball was my thing. Besides, my father made me be home every night at ten o'clock, and the girls stayed out later than that.

This night at the Empire Roller Skating Rink there was a whole crowd of Puerto Rican guys who started coming on with our girls. There was almost a big fight right then. Instead the decision was to have a gang fight the following night in Prospect Park. If a fight had started at the rink, the police would have been there in minutes. Well, it turned out to be my last gang fight.

They had a lot of guys, way more than we did, and four of them got me, held me up against a wall, and beat the living shit out of me. They broke my nose and I was a bloody mess, my white T-shirt was solid crimson in front. Even here I was lucky, because the brawl only lasted about two minutes. Somebody had tipped the police and about four squad cars came screaming in and everyone took off. If they hadn't shown up so fast, I might have ended up crippled. Those Puerto Ricans were small, but mean as hell.

We all ran in different directions but ended up back at the luncheonette we hung around, Eddie G's. I went right into the bathroom in back to try to clean up. I soaked my T-shirt in the sink and wiped the blood off my face. My nose was blown up twice its normally considerable size, and I was having a helluva time breathing. I was standing there sucking in air through my mouth when I heard a door slam and a shout:

"Where the hell's Joe?"

Jesus Christ! It was my father—who'd told me to stay out of gang fights or he'd kill me.

"I don't know where he is," my friend Okie said.

I heard a scuffling sound and found out later that Willie had grabbed my friend by the front of his shirt. "If you don't tell me where Joe is, I'm going to punch you right in the goddamn face, you little bastard!" my father said.

"He's in the bathroom!" my friend yelled. "In the bath-room!"

I turned and put the little hook through the eye on the door and stopped sucking in air, stopped breathing entirely. I wrapped my hands around the knob and braced my feet on the floor, leaning backward. The next thing I knew, I was flying out of the bathroom, sailing past my father—who had yanked the door so hard he'd ripped the hook out of the door—onto the floor. He grabbed me by the back of my T-shirt and twisted as he lifted me up. The neckband was cutting into my neck, chok-ing me.

My father pushed me toward the front door like that, where he stopped by my friend Okie and stuck a fist in his face. "And you're tomorrow, you sonofabitch Irish bastard!" he said. "This is your friend and you're supposed to watch out for your friends." He pointed at my nose, which was bleeding again, the blood trickling down my cheek. "You're dead when I catch you tomorrow."

He shoved me outside where my Uncle Tony was sitting in a car with the door open at the curb. My father spun me around and hit me a shot in the jaw that knocked me right into the car. Uncle Tony drove us around to our building, and the instant we got there my father threw me out on the curb. I scrambled to my feet and headed up the stairs as fast as I could. My father was right behind me, rapping me all the way. We had an old Bendix washing machine with the little window in front sitting at the top of the stairs. I stumbled on the next-to-last step. When I got up, my father punched me in the back of the head as hard as he could. I was half conscious when my head smashed through that Bendix window, shattering it but some-how not cutting me.

That was the end of my gang fights. I swore that night as I cried myself to sleep that I'd never get into another gang war, never. And I didn't. When the next one came up, I told the guys what had happened to me in the last one and said no thanks. It wasn't worth it. I'd gotten destroyed in a gang fight in Pros-pect Park, then gotten double-destroyed at home. My father taught some hard lessons, but this one paid off for me. Hell, I'd been birthed with a big enough nose.

III

"What comes out is your essence."

My good friend Lemon, being older and wiser, taught me some very important things, too. When I was eleven he taught me how to jerk off. When we finished, I said, "Hey, what's wrong? Why did that stuff come out of you? Nothin' came out of me."

"Don't worry," he explained. "You're too young to shoot. That stuff's 'come' and you'll 'come' when you get a little older."

"When, Lemon, when?"

"I don't know . . . a few more months, a year."

"Shit."

When I was about twelve and had finally started to dribble a bit jerking off, Lemon had what we called "the hots" for a girl named Pat with great big breasts and a saucy mouth. Lemon was always fooling around with her: "I'm gonna get you." "Yeah," she'd say, "it might be fun."

One day he and I were coming out of The Itch and he spotted Pat leaving in front of us. "Hey," he said to me, "my mom's not home. I'm gonna ask Pat to come over to my house. I bet we'll get a hand job." We were always talking about getting a girl to give us a hand job then. We didn't know how to fuck.

Pat said sure, she'd go along with us to Lemon's apartment. Lemon's eyes got all watery, as if he couldn't wait. We went into the hall in his building, and Lemon *couldn't* wait. He reached over and put one of Pat's hands on his dick and the other on mine. She smiled and started rubbing and squeezing.

"Hey, Lemon, don't you think we better go upstairs," I said. "Somebody might see us."

We hadn't even closed the door to his apartment when Lemon was unbuttoning the back of Pat's blouse. She finished undressing herself and sat back on the sofa, smiling at our expressions—which were a mutually bug-eyed gape. What tits! I looked down at her thing, the first I'd seen with hair, and I thought, Wow, is that ugly! No part of me is going near *that!* I'd get a disease or something.

Lemon was anything but put off and moved toward the sofa. Then we heard *clomp, clomp, clomp* on the stairs. "Oh, Christ," he said, "my mother's coming!" He ran over and locked the door, scooped up Pat's clothes and threw them under the sofa, grabbed Pat's arm, and said, "C'mon, quick—out on the fire escape!"

"Are you crazy? I can't go out there like this!"

"Lemon, why the hell have you locked this door?" his mother yelled, knocking very hard.

"Be right there, Mom!" he yelled, shoving Pat toward the window. I took her other arm and helped her up on the sill.

"Lemon, what the hell are you doing?" His mother kicked the door. "Open this door!"

"Hurry, get out there!" Lemon whispered.

"People will see me!" Pat whispered as we pushed her out on the fire escape.

"It's better than gettin' killed by my mom—*you and me!*" Lemon slammed the window down.

"Lemon, open this goddamn door right now!"

Lemon raced to the door and unsnapped the bolt. His mother barged in, a large bag of groceries in her arms, and almost knocked over Lemon. She screamed at him for five minutes, then went into the kitchen. We looked out the window. One of Pat's eyes was peering in around the frame, and water was streaming down her face. It was pouring outside—a cloudburst. She was out there for over forty-five minutes—Lemon and I sitting there whistling, talking about nothing—before his mother said she was going upstairs to a neighbor's for a minute. "And don't lock this door, you two!"

We opened the window and Pat poured in, her hair plastered to her head, the water puddling off her on the floor. Lemon went for a towel, but Pat was half dressed when he got back.

"Shove that!" she said, putting on the rest of her clothes and hurrying to the door. "Next time," she yelled as she left, "you guys can go fuck yourselves!"

There was a very pretty, very sexy woman in the neighborhood who used to turn us on all the time. She was married, and was a mature woman when I was thirteen. Lucy, I'll call her, had huge breasts and she used to lean them out her windowsill and tease us. We would hang around outside the grocery store across the street, and when Lucy would come by she'd grab the thigh or tap the crotch of whoever was sitting on the box by the door. Lemon would go crazy, like spittle would slide out the corners of his mouth. We were all semi in love with Lucy, as I think half the men in the neighborhood were. She was very good-looking. I thought sure Willie had something going with her. Willie was a solid family man who couldn't have fooled around much because he never went out. But he was a sexy-looking man, Sicilian sexy, tall and dark with his hair slicked back and a kind of impish smile. I know my mother always kept an eye on him when they were around Lucy.

One day Lemon and I saw Lucy coming out of The Itch with a man who was not her husband. "Now's our chance to get some from her!" Lemon said.

"Yeah!" I said, realizing his plot.

We went right to her apartment and knocked on the door. "What do you two want?"

"We saw you comin' out of the theater with a man who wasn't your husband," Lemon said.

"We don't think you'd want your husband to know," I said.

"Shhh! Come in here," she said, tugging us into her apartment and closing the door. "What, are you two gonna start trouble?"

"Not if you give us a kiss," said Lemon.

"I give you each a kiss, you're not going to say anything?"

"You give us each a kiss," I said, "we'll *think* about it."

She gave me a quick kiss and grabbed my cock, after she searched around to find it. Then she did the same to Lemon and laughed. She opened the door and pushed us out into the hall. "I'm gonna tell your father!" she said to me, laughing.

"You do and I'll tell your husband!"

That night when I went up for dinner, my father grabbed me by the back of the neck and marched me into my room. He turned me around and there was a small smile on his face. "You little sonofabitch," he said, "I don't believe you! You tried to blackmail Lucy?"

"No, Dad—uh—I just like her husband, and—"

"You do that again and I'll beat your ass," he said, shaking his fist. But he couldn't keep himself from smiling as he walked away.

Two days later Lemon and I were hanging around the grocery store when someone grabbed us by the back of our shirts. It was the guy we'd seen with Lucy, and he said he was going to beat the shit out of us. He shook us and walked away, so I didn't figure he was serious, that he had just tried to scare us. Lemon insisted we tell my father. He ran as fast as he could waddle to my house. "Lucy's boyfriend says he's gonna kick the shit out of me and Joe!" Lemon told my father.

Willie clamped one hand on one of my shoulders and the other on Lemon's and marched us off. "Let's go see this guy."

My father knew who it was and where he lived. We reached the guy's building and rang the outside bell. The guy stepped out in the corridor to see who was there before opening the hall door.

"Open up," Willie said. "I want to talk to you."

"Bullshit!" said the guy, who obviously knew Willie's reputation.

Willie kicked in the door, shattering one of the little rectangles of glass. He dragged me in to the guy and said to him, "All right, hit 'im!"

"No, Willie, I—"

"You said you were gonna kick the shit out of this kid, now hit 'im!" He was holding me by the neck in front of him and I was trying to bob and duck.

"Willie, I'm not gonna hit your kid," the guy said. "I was just trying to scare him because—"

"*You* were trying to scare *my* son?" He pushed me aside and knocked the guy all the way to the staircase. He turned and was up three steps when my father's left hand grabbed his belt, yanked him around. The right-hand punch dropped him to the tile floor, unconscious.

Then my father took me home and dialed the telephone. "I just knocked your goddamn boyfriend on his ass for trying to intimidate my son, Lucy! Don't *ever* try that shit again!" He slammed down the receiver.

To this day when I go to my mother's house in Brooklyn—she bought a two-family house in the Canarsie section after my grandfather sold his apartment buildings several years ago—I love to look through drawers to find old pictures, old things that bring back memories. I remember, when I was thirteen or so, sitting on my parents' bed one day looking through a bureau drawer that was full of old albums. I was really getting a kick out of staring at pictures of my parents when they were kids, all neatly dressed and pressed for the photographer. My mother was so pretty—fine, smooth features, long dark hair, and large eyes.

Then I got down to the bottom of the drawer and found a stack of about fifty pictures I'd never seen before—of people screwing. I had never imagined there were so many ways to do it, all those positions. I sat there studying them and holding my breath to listen for the sound of feet coming up the steps. I got all excited and picked out the ten pictures I liked best. I took them, after putting the rest back in their place, into the bathroom and did what I had to do. Just as I finished, I heard my mother come into the apartment. So I pulled the medicine chest away from the wall and stuck the pictures behind it.

Every couple of days after that, I'd go in the bathroom, pull the medicine chest out, grab the pictures, and play with myself. What a turn-on! But after a while my mother began to wonder why I was spending so much time in the bathroom. She began hurrying me up, knocking on the door and saying, "Joe, come on out of there, somebody else wants to use the bathroom."

Then one day she really got angry. My little brother Billy, who was seven, had to go, and my mother started screaming and banging on the door. "He's going to wet his pants, Joe! Now come out of there, damnit!"

"Mom, I'll be right out! Tell him to wait a second!" I

smacked my cock to get rid of my hard-on and quickly shoved the pictures up behind the medicine cabinet. My brother Billy went in, and while he was going to the bathroom he noticed the corner of one of the pictures sticking out from behind the bottom of the medicine cabinet. He reached up, pulled it, and all ten dropped to the floor. He walked out with them in his hand.

"Look what I found in the bathroom, Mom."

"Joe," my mother yelled, snatching them away from Billy, "what were you doing in there with these?"

"What?" I said. "Those aren't mine, Mom. They must be Billy's."

My face was absolutely scarlet, I mean burning up. My mother turned on her heel and took the pictures into her bedroom without another word. Obviously she didn't say anything about this to Willie, because I didn't hear from him. But it was the most embarrassing thing that ever happened to me, to be caught with those dirty pictures by my mother, who I was sure knew damn well what I'd been doing in the bathroom. I couldn't look her in the eyes for weeks, I just couldn't.

It was at about this time that all the guys in the gang started going to the Majestic Ballroom, a fifty-cents-a-dance hall near Times Square in Manhattan. I could never go with them because I had to be home at nine—ten o'clock at the latest—every night. All of us had phony draft cards that said we were eighteen, but mine didn't do me any good. One Friday, though, I told my father there was this movie Lemon and I really wanted to see at Times Square that didn't get out till almost eleven. I told him we'd come right home afterward if he'd let me go.

"All right, just this once," he said to me, then turned to Lemon. "But you don't bring him right home, your ass is *mine.*"

I was so excited on the subway ride there. All the guys were talking about Carmen, this Puerto Rican girl who rubbed up against them and talked dirty. "She made me come in my pants last time!" Lemon said, and several of the other guys claimed they'd gotten off dry-hump dancing with her.

When we got there, we bought five dollars' worth of tickets

apiece. "There's Carmen," said Lemon, waving to her. "Go dance with her, Joe. See what we mean."

I walked over and asked her to dance and she said, "Lovely," and took all of my tickets.

"Hey, why are you taking all of them?"

"You get ten dances," she said, "and I know you'll want to dance all of them with me."

We went out on the floor and I held her close. She held me closer, moving against me. Right away she started talking, her lips on my ear: "Oh, I want to take you home with me tonight. I'm going to teach you everything. I'm going to teach you how to make love to a woman. I can feel you already. You're going to be so good. Very good."

Within thirty minutes my ten tickets were gone. "Thank you," said Carmen, walking away from me toward a table.

"Wait," I said, "I want to dance some more."

"Get some more tickets, lover."

I ran to the table where the guys who weren't dancing were sitting. "Lend me a few bucks, you guys. I gotta dance with Carmen some more. She's gonna take me home tonight."

"Joe, she won't take you home," one of the guys said. "She just says that. All she does is show you a nice time on the dance floor. Nice, ain't it?"

"No, no. She wants to take me home. She said so. Lend me a few bucks."

I got some more tickets, but Carmen was then dancing with an older guy. I didn't dance with anyone else. I just sat there watching Carmen rub against that old guy on the floor. They danced for almost an hour. I kept looking at the clock, waiting. Finally she went and sat at a table, but the guy sat with her. Shit! I thought, staring at them, waiting for him to leave. Then I just stood up and walked over to her.

"Carmen, you wanna dance? I got more tickets." I held them out to her, semipleading I guess.

"Later," she said.

"I can't stay too late," I said.

"I'll see you later," she said, not even looking up at me.

"Where are you gonna take me? I gotta be home before twelve."

"Go on back to your table."

"Hey, what's the matter? Don't you like me any more?"

"Go back to your table."

"You said you were gonna take me home . . . teach—"

"Look, kid," the man said, "get your ass away from here."

"But she said—"

He stood up and pushed me. "I said get the hell outta here." Two bouncers hustled over and one of them grabbed my arm. The next thing I knew my seven friends came running over and pushed the bouncers off me. What a fight! Chairs over, tables over, people yelling, girls screaming. They rapped us around a bit and we ran toward the stairs. When we got to the door— they didn't even bother to chase us—I turned and yelled to Carmen, "You fucking cunt!"

That was one of the biggest things you could do then, tell a girl she was a fucking cunt. All the way home on the subway I was bragging to my friends, "You hear me call her a fucking cunt? Right to her face."

"Yeah, Joe, you really told her off."

Growing up in Brooklyn was a lot like an East Side Comedy. All the guys were crazy, came on like big shots. I remember when the oldest guy in our gang got a car, all we did for weeks was drive around and yell at girls. When we'd see a girl walking along, the big thing was to pull up next to her and stop and say, "Hey. You. Get over here." Then, if they paused and came toward you: "Can I get into your pants, or what?"

Of course, 98.2 percent of the girls would just walk away, or say, "Get away from me, you fucking pigs!"

But I'll never forget this one chick. There were six of us in the car. "Can I get into your pants, or what?"

The chick put her hand on her hip and said, "Okay. How many of you do I have to take on?"

The guy who was driving threw the car in gear and shot away. "Jesus Christ!" he said. "There must be somethin' wrong with her!"

I was a terrible hypochondriac as a kid. For some reason, I'd worry about every cough, every sneeze, thinking I was coming down with a fatal disease. Along about the age of fifteen, I started having wet dreams, enormous noctural emissions. I didn't know what the hell was going on. Was I jerking off too much? It was impossible to jerk off in your sleep. There had to be something wrong with me. Then I started having two, three, four in a night. There had to be something *seriously* wrong with me, I thought. Would I die in my sleep?

My mother noticed how stiff the front of my pajamas and sheets were getting and called it to my attention without actually saying anything. I told her something was happening in my sleep, that I didn't know why, that I was really worried. I was examining my face in the mirror every morning and swore I looked drawn, that I was dwindling away.

"I'll have your father talk to you about this," my mother told me.

That evening my father sat down with me in my room, closed the door, and said, "Look, Joe, you don't have to worry about this thing that happens in your sleep, it's natural. It happens to everybody. It won't hurt you. But listen, now, don't ever play with yourself and make that happen. That is unnatural, it's bad for your body. When you play with yourself and that happens, what comes out is your essence . . . it's a . . . it's like white blood, and it's very bad."

I didn't jerk off for three months after that. I was really afraid it would kill me. But what my father told me, that was the way Italian families explained things to their sons in those days. I still can't figure out why.

IV

"He's not playing any more goddamn baseball!"

My Uncle Red, Louie Caiazzo, was the person who got me started playing ball. He started catching with me when I was seven or eight. As I got older, nine or ten, he'd throw harder and get angry when I missed one. If I missed easy ones, he'd smack me. One day my father came around just as Louie smacked me, and Willie smacked him. But I played baseball, catching and picking up grounders, only with Louie.

Stickball was my first love. We played every day on our street. I was the guy who cut the brooms off the handles for bats. If we had a game scheduled for ten in the morning, I'd be out in the street at eight-thirty. I'd call for guys, and they'd come to the door wiping sleep from their eyes. "What the hell you out so early for?" "C'mon, let's practice." I loved it. When I was ten I was a one-sewer hitter—I could drive a Spaldeen from one sewer to the next. When I was eleven I was a two-sewer hitter. When I was twelve I was a three-sewer hitter. When I was thirteen I could hit one of those little pink rubber balls with a broom handle and knock it past four sewers into the next block. I was a superstar.

When my brother Jimmy was about twelve and a half he started playing baseball with a team in the neighborhood, and he came home after the first practice with a nice uniform. I'd never played baseball and asked Jimmy if I could try out. He said he'd see. The next day he told me the team could have only one fourteen-year-old player on it, and they'd have to vote me in, or out. A lot of them knew how I could hit a Spaldeen. I started the next game, at the Madison High School field, and there happened to be a bird dog for a Yankee scout in the stands, a guy called John King. A bird dog tips off a scout on a prospect, and John King was at the field to watch the second game that afternoon between sixteen- and seventeen-year-olds. But he got there early and saw me hit three home runs out of the ball park. After the game he came down to talk to the tall, skinny left-handed hitter who'd driven three balls over the fence. He started showing up at just about every game I played after that, a rumpled man in a cap, sitting there watching me.

I got hooked on baseball. When we didn't have a game or a practice, I'd go to Prospect Park by myself carrying my bat, ball, and glove. There would always be a few guys playing there. "Hey, can I join you?" We'd shag flies, hit grounders to one another, play one-a-cat where you batted until you made three outs. Gee, I loved it. Baseball was really my thing; something I could do well right from the start. I could run, I could throw, I had an unusual instinct for getting under fly balls—moving with the crack of the bat to be where they came down—and I had a quick bat. I couldn't get enough of the game. I played from the moment I could get another guy out in the morning until balls were caroming off me in the dark.

My father encouraged me, coming to every game he could make, even if he didn't get there till the last inning. The following year, when I started playing for Manual Training High School, my father would quit work early to see me play. He never made me work like most of the other guys had to. Just play baseball.

According to my mother, that's what my father wanted most to do as a kid—be a baseball player. But my father's father was from Sicily and he said baseball was a sissy's game, that if Willie played he'd beat him good. I remember my grandfather Pepitone, even though he died young, at age forty-two. He was a silent, grim-faced man who, like my father, demanded instant obedience. My grandfather owned several trucks which he used to peddle vegetables around the neighborhood and, my mother says, my father had to start working for him almost as soon as he was big enough to walk. But my father always wanted to play baseball. And when he'd finish work, he would sneak off to play ball. Usually my grandfather caught him, and then he'd beat him with a razor strop. My father kept sneaking off to the ball field and kept getting beaten with that strop—until the welts became too much for him to take any more. He gave up baseball, but he never forgot how much he had cared for it as a kid, how much he'd wanted to become an outstanding player himself.

John King, the bird dog for the Yankee scout, became like a second father to me. He looked after me, helped me tremendously in a nice patient way. He gave me all kinds of advice that improved me as a ballplayer every year. That first season he taught me how to run better, stay up on my toes, and how, on throws from the outfield, to keep the ball low by releasing it with a downward snap. He was always working with me.

John King also became very close to my mother and father. We all respected him and trusted him. Too much as it turned out. When I was fifteen, in my second season of playing baseball, he had me sign an agreement which gave him exclusive rights to represent me, act as my agent. He would receive something like fifteen percent of everything I earned until I was about forty-four years old. My mother and father, not knowing any better, not realizing the ramifications of this "contract," signed it, too. It seemed like a fine arrangement then. After all, John King was going to help me become a major league ballplayer eventually.

When I was sixteen, I'd grown to about five feet, ten inches tall, weighed about 135, 140 pounds, and I really started to get my strength, to power the ball. We played a game at Hamilton High School, which is 320 feet down the right-field line. Beyond the fence is a handball court, and beyond that is a lawn. I put a ball, on a fly, on that lawn. Somebody measured it at 410 feet, and they set a bronze plaque in cement where the ball landed that says, "SCHOOLBOY JOE PEPITONE HIT A BALL IN THIS SPOT IN 1957." I was also doing some pitching that season, and that same day I threw a one-hitter. It blew my mind.

I batted about .600 in high school ball in 1957, and a dozen other scouts started coming to see me play. Then I tried out for one of the best semipro teams in Brooklyn, Nathan's Famous

Hot Dogs, and made it. Nathan's played in five different leagues, about a hundred games a season. The Nathan's players ranged in age from twenty to twenty-five, and all of them had some minor-league experience and received a little pay for playing. I couldn't take any money because I wanted to play another year of high-school ball, but I didn't care about money anyway. All I cared about was playing.

I batted .390 with Nathan's. I was proud as hell. My friends were proud of me: skinny Joe Pep was a baseball star. He knocked the shit out of that ball. John King said I was going to earn myself a nice bonus, that with thirteen bird dogs or scouts constantly in the stands at my games there would be terrific competition among them to sign me, which would push the numbers up. Somebody said I'd get $25,000; another said $35,000; another said $45,000. I couldn't believe $25,000, couldn't imagine just how much money that was. I knew my father, breaking his ass on construction, brought home in a good year, working a bunch of Sundays and a lot of overtime . . . about $7000.

My father was also proud as hell of me. But, given his nature and his early frustrated desire to be a baseball player, my performance was almost never enough. He couldn't relax, be patient. He couldn't abide any mistakes. I guess he tried to relive his strop-welted lost youth through me, and he wanted so agonizingly badly for me—us—not merely to succeed, to excel, but to be perfect. I felt the pressure.

He started coming to every game, and I always felt his presence. If I made an error in the field, if I made a mistake running the bases, if I struck out, I'd look over at him and he'd have his face in his hands in embarrassment, or he'd be shaking his head in disgust. After the game, we'd be walking home and he'd yell at me, "Jesus Christ, why didn't you hit that guy? I moved behind home plate, and he had nothin'! *Nothin'!* You should've hit him *easy!* You weren't concentratin'!"

I wasn't concentrating because of him, a piece of my head was always fixed on Willie. And if his friends were at a game and I fouled up, it was even worse . . . he had so much pride, so much ego, so much desire for me. He'd really get pissed off, scream, even smack me. I'd yell back, and he'd punch me.

Then, two minutes later he'd come in my room and hold me in his arms and hug me, and we'd both cry together and he'd apologize. "Joe, I didn't mean it. I'm sorry."

"If you're gonna hit me—don't apologize!" I'd tell him. "Either don't hit me, or don't apologize afterward. It's driving me nuts!" It didn't help; he couldn't control himself.

And if anyone put me down or tried to hurt me in any way in a ball game, my father would go over and beat the shit out of the guy. No matter who it was or where it was, he wouldn't allow anyone to put any crap on his son. If a pitcher would throw at my head, my father would run behind the screen in back of home plate and yell, "You sonofabitch! You throw at him once more, I'll come out there and kick your ass! You hear me? One more—just one more pitch at his head—I'm coming out there to get you, you bastard!"

Everybody in the stands would stare at the crazy man yelling. He'd go back to his seat, and if he'd come alone, if none of his friends were there, people sitting near him would slide away, leave him sitting there with a big space all around him. I don't think he even noticed, he was so intent on the game, on me.

I remember we played an all-black team called the Vikings at their field on Myrtle Avenue one day. I was playing first base and there was a very close play. I stretched as far as I could with my foot on the inside edge of the bag, just my cleats and the sole of my shoe touching. This big black guy came down the line and purposely jumped on my foot. The spike went through my shoe and almost chopped off my toe. I screamed and fell back on the ground holding my foot. The blood was running out the gash in my shoe.

"Hey, you!" I heard someone yell. I looked up and saw Willie running out onto the field. He met the guy who'd spiked me as he trotted across the infield toward his dugout. Willie didn't say another word. He just hit that guy and knocked him out with one punch. The Vikings leaped out of their dugout. Willie set his feet and motioned them on. Unfortunately for the first three guys, they came one behind the other. My father flattened each of them with a single punch. Bang, bang, bang: they went down like tenpins. None of them got up. I just lay there watching as half the men in the stands poured onto the field. My teammates, the Vikings, and scores of fans ran around slugging one another. I finally got up and limped circuitously toward the stands. I saw the scouts all leaving and I thought, I wonder what they think of this shit? Is my father driving them away from me? The game was suspended.

A week or so later we were playing at the Shore Parkway field and there were six scouts in the stands. I was in a little slump, and I was feeling unbelievable pressure at this time. The presence of the scouts, the presence of my father . . . I felt at times like I couldn't breathe. And I couldn't shake it, couldn't clear my head. I struck out my first three times at bat in this game.

There was a guy in the stands, a huge man with one of those deep, booming voices that carries all over the ball park. He started getting on me after the second strikeout, yelling, "Oh, you're some hitter. Way to make contact, Pepitone."

When I stepped to the plate in the ninth, the game tied, I was so tight, so tense, I thought I'd burst. This guy started on me. "You're overrated, Pepitone. Why the hell would the Yankees consider signing *you?* You're a big whiff."

On the first pitch, a fast ball inside, I connected. The ball carried about 350 feet, a helluva shot. Home run. As I trotted home, I saw my father, who had been sitting up behind this guy, walk down in front of him.

"He's overrated, huh, bigmouth?" my father shouted into the guy's face. "That ball went over 350 feet, you asshole." The guy stood up and my father knocked him down. He stood up again, and my father knocked him out.

He was an incredible man. But it wasn't easy for me, every time I heard a commotion in the stands, seeing my father beating hell out of somebody, fighting and destroying three grown men at once. It wasn't easy with all those scouts watching me. They wanted to see the long ball, to see if I had consistent power. So I had to go up there swinging away, and when I didn't make contact it crushed me. I felt I was blowing my chance, and I really didn't think it was fair, all that pressure from the scouts plus my father. I just kept getting tighter and tighter.

It reached the point where all the bird dogs and scouts were saying, "Joe Pepitone's old man is gonna ruin that kid." John

King kept hearing this, and he knew they had a point, knew it was getting harder and harder for me with my father at the games.

The night following that game at Shore Parkway field, we'd just finished dinner and I was getting ready to go out when the phone rang. I was standing right next to my father when he answered it. "Hello, John, what's up?" He listened for a minute, and I stood there watching the anger clench his face into a blazing scowl that could kill.

"What do you mean—*I'm* hurting his performance? Are you crazy, you sonofabitch?"

He listened a moment.

"I do take it personally, goddamnit. And I don't give a shit what you say or what any of the scouts say. Nobody's telling me I can't go and watch my own son play baseball."

He listened again and his hand started trembling, and the tears swam into my eyes. I stepped back by the china closet and leaned against it.

"I'm not making him nervous, goddamnit!"

He was making me nervous, I thought. Shit, he *was!*

Then my father exploded. "Who the fuck are you talking to? If I can't go to his games any more, my son's not going. You got that? And you're not his agent any more. In fact, I don't ever—I mean *ever*—want to catch you around my son any more. He's not playing any more fucking baseball!" He crashed the receiver into the phone.

I couldn't believe it. My own father had just killed my dream. I looked him right in the eyes and yelled, "I *hate* you!"

He snatched up a thick glass ashtray sitting by the phone, whirled around, and threw it at me. Instinctively, my head turned away, toward the china closet. The ashtray hit the closet and smashed into a hundred pieces, and a dozen shards richocheted into my eyes and face. I had searing pains in my eyes and I couldn't open them. I thought I was blind, and I could feel the blood running down my face and dripping off my chin.

My father let out a cry like a dog that had been run over. I felt him hug me, lift me up, sobbing, his body shaking, and felt him carry me down the stairs to the street. He gently eased me into the car, then raced to the hospital, his hand clamped on the horn, never stopping once. "You're gonna be all right, Joe. Hang on. You're gonna be all right!"

I was scared to death. I thought I'd be blind, that I'd never be able to open my eyes again. When we got to the emergency room, I didn't think I could stand the pain when they forced me to open my eyes, when they peeled back the lids and picked out those shards of glass. My father held my hand, knelt next to me, and let me squeeze his hand as hard as I could against the pain.

"Go ahead, Joe, squeeze! He's getting all the pieces out. You're gonna be all right!"

He was right. They got the glass out and I could see again, there was no permanent damage. They cleaned and dressed all the cuts on my face and we drove home. On the way, my father said, "Joe. Joe, I'm sorry." He didn't have to say any more. I knew he had been as frightened as I was, knew that if I had been blinded, he would have never forgiven himself, knew that he would have spent the rest of his life trying to make it up to me. But I also felt some bitterness, because I really didn't want the fanciest tapping cane and tin cup in New York. I wanted to play baseball.

My father never hit me again, though, after this incident. I think the glass in my eyes scared him so much that he finally forced himself to stop punching me. Whenever he lost his temper with me after that, he'd ball up his fist as if he were going to bash me, then he'd turn and put his hand through a wall, a window, whatever was there when he blew up. That's how he was. He ended up with a lot of cut and bone-bruised hands, but he never left another mark on me.

Sometimes I wished he would hit me, because once he stopped hitting, he yelled at me more. He'd get angry and scream at me at the top of his lungs, call me everything he could think of. And that hurt me more, really hurt me. I finally told him, "Stop yelling! Please! I'd rather you hit me, get it over with! Just don't yell at me, Dad—don't *do* this to me!"

He couldn't stop yelling at me any more than he could stop beating me all those years. I knew he didn't mean it, that all he wanted was for me to do well. But the yelling really got to me because it stuck with me longer than a punch, the words crouching in my head and repeating themselves, the things he called me. I guess this kind of put-down, when it comes from a god—and I had so much respect for my father in spite of everything—becomes heavier and heavier to bear. Because the put-downs came from my father, because I couldn't live up to his expectations, I began to feel incompetent even though I knew damn well I wasn't. It wobbled my head, affected my play.

Fortunately, for almost two months after the glass was picked out of my eyes my father didn't appear at my ball games. John King's words must have finally reached him, given him some realization that his presence at the games wasn't helping me. He stopped coming, and I started hitting the hell out of the ball. I still felt tremendous pressure from the scouts who were always there, still felt I couldn't afford to make mistakes, that I had to show them the long ball, display my power. But I was able to handle it. I loved my father so much and I knew he hated not being at the games, and there were so many times when I'd look over and see he wasn't there . . . and I wished he were. Yet I knew I was better off, knew it was better for both of us.

He often pulled up just as a game was ending, driving a Caddy or some other big car the owner of his construction company, Tony Gull, had lent him for the evening. He'd pick me up, ask me how I did, and smile that smile of his that was as wide as a keyboard when I'd had a strong game. It was nice.

Of course, it couldn't last. Willie couldn't stay away from my games forever. When he started coming back, he was a bit more subdued at first. He'd yell at any opposing player who seemed to be threatening to hurt me, but at least he didn't slug anyone for weeks. And when he finally lost control of his fists again, I don't know as I could blame him.

The flare-up occurred at the Kings Park Hospital field where there was a section of the stands enclosed by a wire fence for the resident psychiatric patients. My father was sitting on a seat down below them, and for some reason one of the inmates started yelling at him.

"You. *You.* The one with the twenty-dollar socks. Who the hell you think you are?"

I was playing first base for Nathan's this game, and I saw my father look around at the guy, who was making funny faces at him. The next thing I knew the nut was throwing pebbles down on my father's head.

"Hey, you crazy bastard," my father yelled. "One more pebble hits me, I'm gonna come up there and kick your crazy ass!"

The nut kept it up, but my father didn't go after him. He went down to our dugout and borrowed a batting helmet, walked back and took his seat again. Then: pling, pling, pling. The pebbles started bouncing off the helmet. My father went berserk. He jumped up and plowed through people in the stands to get to the gate leading into the enclosed area. Enraged, he locked his fingers in the wire and tried to pull the gate open. It didn't give, but the wire did, tearing out and sending him spinning backward. The nut was sitting there laughing, and still tossing pebbles at my father. But Willie scrambled through the hole in the fence, shoved an old guard out of the way, and punched the nut. My father was so upset, it was a glancing blow, and the nut kept laughing and saying, "You with the twenty-dollar socks—sit here. You with the twenty-dollar socks—sit here."

My father threw his arms in the air. Then he crawled out through the hole in the wire. He walked to the far end of the stands shaking his head. I laughed. I didn't feel any pressure that day, none at all.

I often wonder, looking back, how Willie would have treated my brother Jimmy if he'd lived with us. Jimmy and I shared a bedroom in our two-bedroom apartment until my youngest brother, Billy, was born. At age four and a half, Jimmy went to stay with our Aunt Fifi, my mother's sister, and her husband for a few weeks. He stayed over eight years. Aunt Fifi lived only a block away and I ate lunch at her house daily during the week when my mother was working. Fifi was childless, and when Billy was several weeks old and my mother went to bring Jimmy home, Aunt Fifi started crying and hid under a table. She made such a scene that my parents let Jimmy stay on with her a little longer, and a little longer, until he became more like Fifi's son.

It's interesting to note how different Jimmy—who wasn't

constantly around my father—turned out from Billy and me. Jimmy, a New York City detective who also works two days a week as a bank teller, is a much more responsible, dependable guy, careful with his money. When we were kids, I got a job delivering for the local grocery store. After one week, I gave the job to Jimmy and went back to spending most of my time playing ball. Jimmy liked earning money more than playing ball. He delivered groceries for six years. There was never any evidence of rebellion in him, that I was later to exhibit so graphically. Billy, who was also a good ballplayer and signed with the Giants, quit after one season because his wife didn't like the baseball life. He's a New York City policeman, a guy who doesn't worry all that much about tomorrow. He was Willie's baby son, his pride and joy, and never got rapped around. Jimmy was Willie's responsible son, who wasn't present to get rapped. I was the eldest son and took the abuse. It just happened that way.

I remember, when Jimmy had been gone about a month, asking my mother to bring him home. I was six years old, and I said, "I want my brother Jimmy back, Mamma."

"Soon," she said. "He'll be home soon."

And as the years rolled along and the brother I'd been so close to stayed away, stayed on and on and on with my aunt . . . I began to think my whole goddamn family was fucked up.

V

"Mom—I wish he'd die!"

Just before the start of my last season of high-school ball, my father had a heart attack. He was thirty-nine years old, had worked hard all his life, was in fantastic shape, drank very little. Yet one day he was in the peak of health, and the next day he was almost dead. They had to rush him to the hospital to save his life.

I couldn't believe how close we'd come to losing him. I was a seventeen-year-old kid, and there were some thirteen scouts for major-league baseball teams following me around. This was the season in which they would come at me with a contract if I hit the ball even as well as I had the year before—and the man I counted on most at this time, needed most despite our problems, was critically ill. He was so sick, this superman, the toughest man in a very tough neighborhood, that I couldn't even go to visit him.

Two days later I was in another hospital, on the critical list. There was a lot of trouble at Manual Training High in the spring of 1958, a lot of violence. On this day, when school ended, I went to my locker to get my jacket and go home. A guy I knew named O'Dell was standing by the lockers with a group of people. All of a sudden he came over to me and said, in a put-on gangster voice, "Stick 'em up." I looked down and there was a gun in his hand, a .38, its muzzle inches from my belly.

"Hey," I said, staring into the cylinder and seeing bullets in them, "that thing's loaded!"

Bang! it went off, the sound echoing through the corridor. I didn't even know I was shot, didn't feel a thing. I just stood there looking down, and I saw the hole in my shirt near the lower edge of my rib cage. I picked up my shirt and there was a hole in my skin, circled by what looked like a bruise, but there was no blood. I reached my hand behind me and felt my back, sliding it over the flesh in search of a hole. Then I felt it, my fingers meeting the slippery wetness all around the aperture. I looked at my hand and it was smeared with blood. I fell to my knees, still not feeling pain, only a queasiness in my stomach, like I was going to throw up.

Just then a woman teacher ran up behind me and tugged at the back of my collar. "All right, you," she said sternly, "give me those firecrackers!"

O'Dell had run off crying, but one of the other guys said, "He's been shot."

"Oh my God," said the woman, seeing the hole in my shirt. "Lie down—you'd better lie down."

I was on my knees, in shock, but I didn't think lying down in this corridor was going to do a whole lot of good for a gunshot wound.

Then the teacher said, "No, we've got to get you to the nurse. Can you walk?"

Someone helped me to my feet, and I found I could walk slowly if I bent over slightly. She led me to the elevator of the four-story building and pressed the Down button, leaned on it till the door opened. The elevator operator was a guy who had a well-deserved reputation for playing with a quarter deck. We were on the second floor, and when the elevator door opened, the teacher said, "Hurry up, get us down to the nurse's office. This boy's been shot."

The elevator man said, "Okay, I just gotta pick up somebody on the fourth floor that rang a while ago." The door closed in our faces.

The teacher screamed after him, then turned to me with a worried look. "The stairs are right here," she said. "Do you think you can walk down?"

With help, I made it down to the nurse's office. She took one look at me, helped me lie on the table with the long sheet of white paper covering it, and called for an ambulance. She placed her hand on my forehead and asked, "How do you feel?"

"I don't feel any pain," I told her—and the minute I said it I remembered something I'd heard one of my aunts say when a member of the family was very sick: "If you don't feel no pain, that's when it's bad. I tell you, that's when it's *very bad.*" That was when I got *very scared.*

A few minutes later there was a priest at my side with a purple stole draped around his neck. He had come to administer the last rites. "Are you sorry for all your sins of your past life, my son?"

"I'm sorry! I'm sorry!" I said, panicking and beginning my confession. "Father, I didn't go to the store for my mother like I told her I would; Father, I played with myself—" Then I broke it off, wondering out loud, "What if I don't get it all out, Father?"

The priest reassured me and finished giving me last rites. Now I was really afraid, and I lay there thinking all kinds of weird things. I remembered having heard my mother and other women in my family say—as all Italians seemed to then—that just before you die you see the face of Christ. I put my hand over my eyes.

The ambulance took me to Methodist Hospital and they operated to close up everything the bullet had torn inside me. I was in surgery for nine hours. I had been lucky, the doctor told me afterward. The bullet had struck a rib and caromed out my lower back . . . missing three vital organs by inches. I was on the critical list for six days, in the hospital for twelve.

Perhaps the most amazing thing was that the day I was shot, my father—who was in Jewish Hospital some distance away—suddenly asked his nurse what had happened to me. "Something's wrong with my son Joe," he told her. He had an instinct, like a second sense, about me that seemed to tell him every time I had a real problem. The nurse told him he was mistaken, to relax. With his heart condition, he was not supposed to get upset. But he kept insisting that something bad had happened to me, that they were keeping it from him—until finally the nurse gave him a sedative, put him to sleep. Of course, my mother had informed them about me, and that night they removed the television set and radio from his room. In the morning, their absence confirmed his fears. My father started screaming, and his doctor decided he had to tell Willie. My father tried to get out of bed, saying he had to go see me. The doctor gave him a shot to calm him, but it didn't do much good. The only thing that could be done to take the strain off his damaged heart was to lift him into a wheelchair and take him to see me.

When they rolled him into the doorway of my room and I saw him sitting there in that chair, looking small, haggard, the tears just spewed out of my eyes. I almost ripped out the tubes snaking from my body as I reached for him. They pushed him next to my bed and he leaned over and hugged me and kissed me and then lay his head on my chest sobbing, our tears intermingling on the front of my hospital gown. We stayed like that, holding onto each other and crying, for about ten minutes.

My father got out of the hospital a week before I did. He had to stay home and take it easy. His doctors couldn't say when he could go back to work—they didn't know whether Willie would ever be able to do heavy construction labor again. Probably not. My father couldn't stand it—being sick, being confined to the apartment, unable to do anything except shuffle around, lie around all day long. I guess he must have felt as if someone had stolen his manhood . . . had crept in one night and made off with his muscles, snipped off his balls.

He was awful to be around, constantly grouchy, yelling about something every minute—particularly at my mother. She was an angel through all of this, as she had been through all the shit Willie and I had brought down on her over the years, all the tension and fear and pain. Now she had both of us to care for in beds across a hall from one another, two semiinvalids to wait on, comfort, abide. And my father kept yelling at her.

I remember the second day I was home from the hospital, when it became too goddamn much for me. My father and I had had an argument, and minutes later he started screaming at my mother, who was in my room. I got angry, absolutely furious, and I said, "Mom—I wish he'd die. I really wish he'd *die!*"

"Joe, you don't know what you're saying!" she said to me. "Don't say that about your father!"

The next night, it was Good Friday morning, I woke up with

a start at 3:20 A.M. I heard three loud, grating snores. They had come from my father's room. I got out of bed and hurried into his room, with my mother coming in right behind me. My father's head was down on his shoulder, his eyes wide open, unblinking, staring right into my eyes.

"Willie!" my mother yelled. "Willie!"

I started crying. My aunts and uncles came in from next door, and one of them held a mirror under my father's nose. The glass didn't fog. My face fell into my hands, the sobs ripping at me, and an uncle took me across the hallway to his apartment. About fifteen minutes later the doctor got there, and my uncle came in and told me what I already knew but had refused to admit to myself: "Willie is dead."

Then I went crazy, completely lost control of myself in my guilt over what I'd said the day before. I wanted to hurt myself, to pay myself back for those words about my father. I dove at a second-floor window, trying to throw myself out into the street below. I cracked two panes and bounced off the framing, and my uncle and aunt dragged me sobbing into bed. My aunt sat with me, tried to comfort me, but she only made it worse . . . much worse.

"Your mother told me you said you wished your father would die, but that doesn't mean anything," said my aunt. "God took your father and gave you back your life, because you were supposed to die when you were shot, Joey. It's God's will."

That statement destroyed me. I couldn't get it out of my mind, and the guilt feelings tracked me in my subconscious for years, until a psychiatrist helped me. All that time I actually thought I'd willed my father dead, that I had killed him.

After that I went into a heavy depression and cried myself to sleep every night. My mother, who had gone back to work, would sit on my bed for hours every night and rub my back until I went to sleep. I was a big boy, almost six feet tall, seventeen years old, and I managed to go to school and to play ball again, finish the high-school season. In fact I hit damn well: ten home runs in fourteen games. Yet every night I cried, every night I had trouble sleeping. My mother got me the most powerful sleeping pills and they didn't work.

Then one day in typing class, toward the end of the semester, I suddenly began getting these hot and cold flashes. They sent me home and my mother took me to the doctor, who said it wasn't dangerous but that my heart was skipping beats. I stopped going to school, just stayed home, never left the apartment. I became a real hypochondriac, certain that every twitch was going to kill me. My nerves went and my eyes blurred; for a week I saw everything through double vision. I lost almost fifteen pounds, went down to 125 on a six-foot frame. I looked like death.

Finally, after I hadn't left the apartment for over a month, my mother went to my friends and told them they had to get me out of there. She told them to drag me out if they had to, but that I had to get out. The guys came up, four of them, and literally picked me up and carried me out to a car, threw me in it, and took off to Coney Island. When we got there, everyone but me jumped out. "C'mon, Joe," they said, "let's get something to eat." I didn't answer, just sat there in my depression. Then the smells of all that great-tasting Coney Island food wafted into the car, filled my nostrils. I must've eaten ten hamburgers and fifteen franks that day. I was ambulatory again.

I started playing ball with Nathan's again and regaining the weight I'd lost. But there were no longer thirteen scouts following me. That bullet wound caused ten of them to drop off. Only the Philadelphia Phillies, Los Angeles Dodgers, and New York Yankees were still interested in me. When the bidding got up to $25,000, the Phillies withdrew. And although I'd grown up only a little over a mile from Ebbets Field and had gone to a lot of Dodger games before they moved to the West Coast, I'd always been a Yankee fan. My father had been a Yankee fan and my uncle Louie who'd started me playing ball was a Yankee fan. If I hadn't picked them, Louie would have given me a shot in the head. The Yankees put me through a thorough physical examination, I was judged fit, and on August 13, 1958, I signed with them for a $25,000 bonus.

I'm sure that in the years since then the Yankees have wished they'd examined my head, been able to see the terrifying guilt, the compulsive rebellion against authority, the need to be loved that led me down so many bizarre and painful tracks.

My father's death was a traumatic experience, but secretly after it I think I felt, good, *good,* I'm free now. *Free.* When he died I was crying on the outside, but inside I think I was happy, actually happy not having to worry about him rapping me or yelling at me any more. It was a relief to get that pressure off my head. Now I was on my own, and I could do whatever I wanted to because my mother couldn't stop me, and it felt wonderful. Yet mixed in with this elation was the guilt from the belief that I'd not only willed my father's death but that I was *happy* about it. God, it was so sick, so hateful to me.

And then I went through a year of tremendous highs and abyssmal lows that wrenched my mind, shattered my sleep, and came very close to producing a nervous breakdown. I still have nightmares about that depression. To this day I don't know how I got through it. I guess I was finally able to shove it aside, never totally dispelling it, but never permitting it to overwhelm me thereafter. Or so I thought.

I remember the day I got through the depression, and that day I swore—*swore*—that I would never again allow myself to get that depressed. I was never again going to allow myself to feel that bad, feel that kind of excruciating pain, no matter what happened. I was going to be happy, have fun from then on. Fuck misery. Live it up, Joe Pepitone. The past is past and the world is yours.

VI

When fucking couldn't compare with playing baseball.

When I signed with the Yankees I was told I wouldn't play until after the 1958 season at the Florida instructional school. I was disappointed. But about ten days later I got a call from the front office saying the Yankee Class D farm team in Auburn, New York, needed an outfielder for the last few weeks of the season. Would I like to be that outfielder? It was like asking a dog with weak kidneys if he'd like a tree.

I went right out and bought myself a new Thunderbird, in my mother's name, of course, because I wouldn't be eighteen until October and didn't have a driver's license. I talked her into it, and she went along with me after all I'd been through. She was probably tired of rubbing my back to help me get to sleep. I also bought several 250-dollar silk suits, sleek, very tightly cut like the younger, sharper racket guys wore then. I never gave a thought to the fact that I'd spent some five-thousand dollars in one day. Hell, as far as I could tell, I was rich.

I rubbed neat's-foot oil on my gloves, packed my bags, and the next day was off to join the Auburn club of the New York-Pennsylvania League. Joe Pepitone, age seventeen, from the Park Slope section of Brooklyn, property of the New York Yankees, perennial World Champions, sitting tall behind the wheel of a sparkling new T-Bird . . . was on his way.

I joined the club on the road, in Corning, New York. I went into the clubhouse at the end of the game, and Tommy Gott, the manager, said, "You're rooming with the shortstop, Phil Linz." He pointed at a guy a year or two older than me with an open, smiling face. He was wearing thick glasses that made him look like a scholar, and he seemed quiet, very serious. He was obviously the ideal person for me to hang out with breaking into professional baseball. Phil Linz turned out to be one of the flakiest, wildest people I ever met, my kind of guy.

That very first night we roomed together, we were lying around on our beds in the hotel talking, when I heard someone in the corridor yell, "The shit's on!"

"The shit?" I said to Phil. "What shit?"

"We're having a water fight," he said, jumping up and going to his bureau. "Want to join me?" He pulled out about a dozen large balloons and ran into the bathroom. "Come on!"

We filled them with water and stepped out into the corridor. We heard someone coming toward us from around the corner. I got excited and dropped my balloon, which broke on the floor. "Shit, Joe, they're coming—grab something!" Phil whispered.

There was a fire extinguisher hanging on the wall near the corner. I grabbed it and pressed myself against the wall as the approaching footsteps grew louder. When they were almost to the corner, I jumped out, tipped the extinguisher over, and started firing. Yellow foam shot out all over the suit of the guy approaching. The problem was that the guy inside that suit was Tommy Gott, my manager.

"Hey, Phil—uh—" The corridor behind me was empty, the door to our room closed. It was just me and my manager, whom I hadn't even played a game for, but whom I'd thoughtfully bathed with chemical foam. He was not pleased. Not only was his suit ruined, but also the wallpaper and rug around him. The hotel was not real happy, either—throwing the entire team out within the hour. The damages and fine I had to pay came to 250 dollars—two and a half weeks' salary. Linz thought it was very funny.

Tommy Gott didn't hold it against me on the ball field. He put me right in the starting lineup, and I hit the shit out of the ball—14 runs batted in 16 games, and a .321 average. Professional baseball was not only fun, it was a cinch.

All I cared about then was playing the game and having a

little fun. I did both. The day we got back home to Auburn I went to the ball park early, as I always did then. I pulled up in my big T-Bird, parked, and started walking to the players' entrance. A girl about my age was standing there.

"You're new, aren't you?" she said.

"Yeah. Joe Pepitone, from Brooklyn, future New York Yankee."

She smiled, a bright laughing smile. "Can I have your autograph?"

Autograph? I smiled. "Sure, if I can have a date after the game tonight."

"Okay, sign here."

I got a hit and made a nice running catch in the outfield, which she commented on afterward as I led her to the T-Bird. We made out in the front seat until the parking lot emptied. Then I suggested we get in back, she agreed and—wow! Right in! Wet and warm! My first piece of ass was so easy! So sweet! I'd never been all that interested in sex before—beyond my five fingers—and suddenly I was kinda interested. As I drove her home afterward, I thought, yeah, that was nice, really nice, but, shit, playing baseball's just as nice, even nicer. In fact, fucking couldn't compare with playing baseball.

The only bad things about Auburn were: (1) I got homesick in about forty-eight hours and took to calling my mother every day or so thereafter; and (2) the haunted house where I lived. Linz and another player, Russ Serzen, had rented this place that had about seventeen rooms for sixty dollars a month. The price was right, but the squeaks and groans and strange noises that rang through that place were unnerving. The house was out in the sticks where it was dark as hell, and the front door was jammed, so we had to stumble around to the back every night. The back door wouldn't lock. We never knew who we might find inside.

"There's a prowler around, Joe," Linz told me, "but don't worry. He'll get Russ and me before he gets to you, because we sleep in the two downstairs bedrooms. You have your choice of any of the upstairs rooms."

Phil, who was from Maryland, showed me the switchblade

knife he kept under his pillow. I had come from Brooklyn completely unprepared. But after my first night in that spook house, I slept with a bat beside my bed. My third night there I jumped out of bed and grabbed it. Either someone was in my room or he was trying to get in the window from the porch roof outside. A scratching, banging noise had wakened me. I squeezed the bat in my hand and tiptoed to the light, which was above the string hanging in the center of the room. It was an overcast night, pitch dark outside, and I couldn't see a thing until I managed to grab the string. I flicked on the light and saw a stick dangling inside my window from a line that went down the outside of the house. Then I got it—that line ran down to Phil Linz's hand.

"You no good sonofabitch!" I yelled, running down the stairs waving the bat over my head. They started roaring.

After the Auburn season, I went home until the instructional school began, then I drove off to St. Petersburg. On the way, I kept passing these boat dealers. I began slowing down when I saw one coming up so I could look at the neat-looking speed boats. I started imagining myself behind the wheel of one. I started imagining myself skiing behind one. I stopped at the next dealer and bought one. Hell, I was on my way to Florida, which has water around most of it. The dealer attached a trailer hitch to my T-Bird, and I told him to just stow the water skis, life preservers, and the rest of the gear I'd bought in the boat.

Needless to say, when I pulled up to the Yankees' headquarters, management didn't waste a great deal of time informing me that they'd never had a ballplayer—much less a rookie with all of sixteen games' experience—report to them towing a boat. They gave me twenty-four hours to sell my virgin craft, but I didn't understand why they had to get so excited about it. Damn landlubbers.

There was no faulting my performance on the field, my desire to do well. Steve Souchock, who ran the instructional school and who became a good friend, liked my arm, my speed afoot, my quick bat, and the fact that I never stopped hustling. He didn't like some of the foolishness I got involved in. But we'd always done a lot of fooling around in my neighborhood, and

I was hyper, I had so much nervous energy to burn up.

After about a week of working out, another young guy named Rich Barry—who was a helluva pitcher and half crazed—and I stayed late to have a catch. There was a huge water tower by Miller Huggins Field, with a catwalk running around it about three hundred feet from the ground. We started arguing about who had the stronger arm, Rich or I, so we got a bucket of baseballs and went out to see who could throw a ball up onto the catwalk. Each of us threw eight or ten balls and they all landed on the catwalk. In the midst of this, Steve Souchock walked up behind us.

"You guys having fun?" he yelled. "Maybe ruining your arms trying to hit a goddamn water tower? What the hell's wrong with you two?"

"We just wanted to see if we could do it, Skip," I said.

"Wonderful," said Souchock. "Those balls cost three dollars apiece. Now who's gonna climb up there and recover them?"

"I don't know," I said. "The grounds keeper?"

"No."

"The water-tower keeper?"

"No."

I was beginning to sweat. "We'll get a kid—"

"Bullshit! One of you two get your ass up there and get those balls. Right now! I'll wait."

Rich and I "choosed" to see who had to go up. He threw out two fingers and called "evens." I threw out two fingers and started climbing—three hundred feet straight up a narrow little ladder. About three-quarters of the way to the top, my eighteen years passed before my eyes and I saw the story in the papers: "Joe Pepitone, young major-league prospect, died suddenly today. He fell off a water tower."

I closed my eyes, made it to the catwalk, and threw down the balls. When I got down, Souchock wasn't finished with us. "Instead of reporting with everyone else tomorrow at ten o'clock, you guys be here in uniform at eight-thirty. You're going to do a little running."

The next morning when we got there, I knew we were dead. The only other player present was Jack DePalo, a guy from New York who loved to run and who could run all day. Even then, as a skinny kid, if I ran three laps around the field, I needed oxygen. Souchock made us run—with that maniac DePalo pacing us—150 wind sprints. "And if you quit, you start all over tomorrow," he said. "Get going."

We were still running when the other players showed up. I was dying on my feet, thought my chest would burst, and through my bleary eyes I saw DePalo up ahead, gliding along as if we'd just started. I hated the sonofabitch. The other players cheered-jeered as Rich and I staggered through the last sprint. His hands went to his knees, and he stood there gasping, the sweat streaming off him. I fell to the ground. Souchock came over and said, "Pepitone, get in the outfield and shag flies."

If I'd had the strength, I would have bit his ankle.

Rich Barry was from California, and he was wacky over fast cars. We hung out together, and every Friday we'd go to a local auto dealer, say our parents were coming down for the weekend, and ask if we could borrow a car. Certainly, they'd say, what kind would you like? Rich would say, "A Corvette," or some other sports car. We had to go to a different dealer every time, because we raced around so much we always returned the car with bald rear tires.

One Saturday we picked up a Corvette at nine in the morning and were racing all over the place before practice. All of a sudden we realized it was ten-thirty—we were thirty minutes late for the workout and ten miles from the ball park! Rich got us there in about eight minutes, and as we approached we saw that the big gate to the field was open and that everyone was working out. Rich raced straight through the gate, right onto the field, and skidded about twelve feet to a stop, leaving a cloud of dust behind us and steam shooting out of the radiator. We hopped out of the car, ran into the locker room and changed, ran back out buttoning our shirts, and all the other players were on their knees in a circle around home plate bowing to us and chanting, "Hail, the almighties are here."

Souchock fined us a hundred dollars and said, "One more trick like that and we're sending both of you home. Got it?"

"Yes, Skip."

I swore I wouldn't be late again, and I wasn't. But Rich Barry liked to have fun as much as I did, and the two of us together meant not only laughs but trouble. He had a hopped-up Chevy he liked to keep finely tuned, and we hung around a local speed shop quite a bit. We got to know the owner real well and liked to kid around with him. Then Rich came up with this brilliant idea one day. He got two masks, two toy pistols that looked like the real thing, and decided that we would pull a fake holdup of the speed shop, just for laughs. The owner would get a kick out of it.

We walked in, masks on, guns out, and said, "This is a holdup! Turn around and lean against the wall!"

The trouble started when a passerby looked in the window and flagged down a police car that happened to be driving by. Two cops ran in with drawn guns, followed within seconds by the occupants of two other squad cars. They snapped handcuffs on us, pushed us up against the wall. We yanked off our masks and said, "Wait a minute, we can explain! This is all a joke!"

The cops didn't think so—even after the shop owner identified us. We had to call Steve Souchock, who was forced to come down and verify that we were players in the Yankee organization. Otherwise we would have gone to jail. Souchock just shook his head, like he didn't know what to do with us. I guess it was a good thing that we had shown some ability on the ball field.

After that caper, Rich and I decided that it would be to our mutual benefit to keep some space between us, so I started hanging out more with Phil Linz. Several days later, Phil and I stopped at a drive-in restaurant after practice. Right behind us came these two fine-looking young chicks. We struck up a conversation and suggested that the four of us do something together. After some chatter, the girls agreed. "Great," I said, then I headed for the men's room and signaled Phil to follow me. I was still skinny Joe Pepitone at the time, and I was always getting stuck with the dingiest-looking girl in this kind of circumstance. I really dug the blond with the large hazel eyes who said her name was Barbara Kogerman. She'd said she had lived in New York until her family moved to Florida a few years before, and I figured that gave us something to talk about. I didn't have a whole lot of good lines with girls at this time.

It turned out Phil liked Barbara best, too. So we flipped a coin to see who paired off with her. I won. Then we went to a driving range to hit some golf balls. I put a ball on my tee, looked over, and saw Phil bending down by his chick's tee. Did he drop something? I wondered.

"Aren't you going to line up the balls for me, Joe?" Barbara said.

"Is something wrong with your back?" I asked her. Actually, I was embarrassed. I'd never seen anyone set out golf balls for a girl before. I didn't want to admit my ignorance. "God gave you a back like mine that bends, so bend it."

Nevertheless, we got on very well, and I was smitten by the girl, liked being with her. I dated her every chance I had until the instructional school ended. I couldn't get her off my mind when I went home to Brooklyn, either. I returned to Florida before spring training to see Barbara. I needed a girl at this time, someone to hold on to besides my mother. The bad shit was still swimming around in my head in the depths of the night, and being with Barbara seemed to help. We were not sleeping with one another, but I didn't care about getting laid as much as I did about just being with someone I could relax with, have fun with.

While I was seeing Barbara and waiting for the minor-league spring training camp to open, I asked permission of the Yankees to work out at Miller Huggins Field with the regulars. They had already started getting in shape, and Casey Stengel was the manager. I was six feet, one inch tall then and still weighed 140 pounds. I don't think the Yankees had ever before had a player as skinny as me. The uniform they gave me was so big, it flapped. But that wasn't why everyone was laughing at me. The uniform was number 69. Guys kept kidding me about it, and I'd smile back, but I didn't know what the hell they meant until someone told me.

Stengel was beautiful. He called me "Pepperone" and talked to me a mile a minute for about ten minutes one day. Then he had me sit next to him in the dugout during an intrasquad game.

"Watch this Mr. Skowron around first base, Pepperone," he said.

I had been watching him, and Skowron moved like a dump truck. "Casey, I'm an outfielder," I told him, "but I can play first better than that."

So I was watching the game, enjoying myself sitting there next to the legendary Casey Stengel in the Yankee dugout, and the next thing I knew Casey was snoring. His head slid over and leaned on my shoulder. I was afraid to move, afraid I'd wake him up and get him annoyed with me. Then my shoulder started to go to sleep, and I thought, Oh, shit. Maybe his snoring will wake him soon.

Suddenly there was a low line shot hit to first base. Skowron scooped it up on one hop, threw to second to get the lead runner, then stretched to catch the return throw for a double play. At that instant, Casey's head popped up off my shoulder and he said, "Now, did you see how Mr. Skowron did that?"

I said to myself, Holy shit, this guy *is* a genius—he sees in his sleep!

VII

"One of your goddamn ballplayers stole my elevator!"

In 1959 I was moved up to Class C ball, playing with Fargo-Moorhead in the Northern League, my first full season as a pro. I was disappointed in my batting average, .283, but I led the league in doubles with 35, had 12 triples, and 14 home runs. I was satisfied.

That fall I went back to the instructional school in St. Petersburg, only this time I stayed out of trouble with Souchock. Clete Boyer—the Yankees' regular third-baseman, who was at school to work on his hitting—Rich Barry, and I went out quite a bit and did a lot of kidding around in the locker room. I always did a lot of kidding, because I always had this tremendous need for people to like me.

But one day I did the wrong thing with Clete after he'd struck out four times in a game. As he came out of the shower, I squirted him with a Pepsi. He hit me a helluva punch in the arm. It really hurt. I got annoyed and rapped him back. And he landed a punch on my jaw that knocked me right into my dressing cubicle. I was half conscious. The next thing I knew he was pulling me up, apologizing. "It's all right, Clete, all right," I said, shaking my head and trying to focus my eyes. I had double vision for three days. I had no idea he was that strong. When we became teammates a few years later, and I'd put on about 30 or 35 pounds, I used to kid him, "Come on now, man. I haven't forgotten that shot you gave me in Florida!" I'd dance around him and he'd laugh. He was a real sweetheart, a good guy.

I spent most of my free time with Barbara, because I was in love. Or I thought I was in love. I turned nineteen on October 9, 1959, and I was finally starting to fill out a bit. I began to look a little less like a robin, but I was still very much a baby, mentally and emotionally. We were engaged to be married in December.

It seemed like the thing to do at the time, just what I needed. Until the night before the wedding, when the first doubts arose in my mind. Naturally, I didn't heed them. Barbara and I had never made it in all the time we'd been going together. No balling whatsoever. It was just a lot of hugging and kissing and getting excited and going home and playing with myself. She said she was a virgin and that we should wait, and that was cool with me.

But the night before the wedding, I was staying at the Kogerman's house, and when it got late and her parents went to bed, I snuck into Barbara's room. We started kissing and fondling and panting and—what the hell—we'd be man and wife in a few hours. I forced it, and the next thing I knew was great disillusionment.

"What about this?" I said to her. "You said you were a virgin."

"I am," she said. "I used to do a lot of horseback riding."

I didn't sleep much that night; I lay there thinking, Should I marry this girl? Then I realized how silly I was. There *were* ways to lose a hymen other than through sex, and I didn't believe Barbara would lie. I was in love with Barbara, who was so pretty, so nice. I needed her.

The next day we were married, and I felt great. But in no time at all there were problems. We lived with her parents initially, waiting for spring training to start. They had liked me when we were going together, always welcomed me, seemed to enjoy talking to me. Then we lived with them, had a few normal newlywed disagreements, and her parents turned against me. They treated me as if I weren't there.

One day we had an argument; Barbara walked out of our room, went downstairs, and told her parents. When dinner was served, nobody called me down to eat. I finally went down, walked into the dining room, and they were clearing the table. "How come you didn't call me?" I asked them. Nobody said a word. Nobody even looked at me. Shit, I was a kid, I was alone, I had a problem, and I had nobody to talk to. I went out and called my mother, my best friend, and told her what they were doing to me. She told me to be patient, everything would work out, just relax.

Relax! The next day they still weren't talking to me. But I hung around downstairs waiting for dinner. When it was served, I sat at the table, and still none of them said a word to me. The meal was spaghetti, but nobody passed it to me. I half stood, leaned over, and reached for it myself. As I was serving myself, Barbara's mother broke the silence toward me.

"Don't eat all the spaghetti," she said. "We've got to save some for the dog."

I just sat there, choking up. Then the tears started pouring down my face. I jumped to my feet, picked up the bowl of spaghetti, and dumped it over Mr. Kogerman's head. "Take your daughter and shove her up your ass!" I yelled, and ran out of the house.

I drove to a motel near the ball park, and I thought I was going to literally crack up, go out of my mind. I was shaking all over.

That night Barbara and her mother knocked on the door to my motel room. I opened the door, and Barbara hugged me and apologized. Mrs. Kogerman apologized. I said to her mother, "I don't want your apology. I just want you out of here, out of my room. And Barbara stays here with me—away from you— or I'm leaving for good."

Mrs. Kogerman left, Barbara stayed, and we got it together.

After a good spring training, I was skipped a classification to A ball in 1960 and assigned to Binghamton, New York, in the Eastern League. Barbara and I rented a nice little place there, and for the first couple of weeks I hit well. Then I got scared and couldn't hit anything—my average kept falling and falling. I'd never seen a slider before, and I'd never faced so many young fast-ball pitchers who were wild, or so many veterans who threw at you to intimidate you. They'd throw the first pitch right at your head, the second one at your belly, and scare the shit out of you. I started bailing out against left-handers, then against everyone. I thought they were trying to kill me. I spent all my time getting away from the ball. And if you don't stand in there, you can't hit. I didn't keep my eye on the ball, didn't maintain my balance, my normal stride, into the ball.

I had hit ten home runs in spring training, and the minute I saw the Binghamton park with its short fences, I said to myself, I'm gonna hit a ton of home runs this season. Then, a few weeks into the season, I was hitting nothing, and I couldn't handle it. I got so depressed, I thought I just couldn't do it, that I'd never make it as a ballplayer. Shit, I couldn't even stand in there against Class A pitching. What the fuck was it like in the major leagues?

The more depressed I got, the worse my attitude got. I began playing like I didn't give a shit—which I did, but this was a kind of defense, I guess. I stopped hustling after balls, stopped running as hard as I could on grounders I hit to the infield. It got so bad that the Yankees sent a special coach to talk to me, Bill Skiff. My average was around .220, I'd shown no power, and it looked like I wasn't even trying.

Skiff came over to me after a game and said, "What's the problem, Joe?"

"The problem is I'm all fucked up," I said, feeling the moisture swell behind my eyes. "Baseball's all fucked up, and I want to go home." My eyes filled. "Fuck the Yankees."

"Fuck the Yankees?" he said hotly. "Listen, you clown—the Yankees are the best organization in baseball, and you're damn lucky to be with them. They sent me here special just to help you out. Now stop feeling sorry for yourself and start playing baseball, goddamnit!"

The tears were running down my cheeks. I apologized and asked him to help me, told him I was scared, that I was bailing out of the batter's box on every other pitch . . . Jesus, did I need help! He told me the pitchers were not that wild, that I couldn't let them intimidate me, that I had to force myself to hang in there and watch the ball all the way into the catcher's glove.

"Bear down, concentrate," he said, "and you'll see there's nothing to fear. Another thing, when you go into a slump, you don't stop hustling, you don't give up. You bear down more, run harder on every ball. You're fast enough to steal a lot of hits if you go flat out."

He really encouraged me, picked up my spirits. And in a few more weeks, slowly but surely, I conquered much of my fear. In the second half of the season, I raised my average forty points to .260 and finished with thirteen home runs and seventy-five RBIs. I also threw out fifteen base runners from the outfield, leading the league in assists. All in all, at the end of the season I felt good.

The following spring, 1961, I hit well in Florida, around .500, and with power. I made the Amarillo ball club in the Texas League, AA ball, and even though I started slowly I didn't get down on myself. I had my confidence now—knew that if I kept taking my natural swing, the hits would start coming. They did. The quality of the pitching was tougher than it had been at Binghamton, but the control was better and I appreciated that. I'd filled out more through the chest and arms, and I was drilling the ball to all fields: line drive, line drive, line drive. I loved it.

Texas was where I started banging around a bit at night, as most players did when we were on the road. I didn't have a lot of luck picking up chicks, but the hooker scene was fun, particularly in San Antonio. Hell, just hanging around saloons in San Antonio was fun. One night after a bunch of drinks, another player named Joe Miller and I came into the hotel where the club was staying, at about 4 A.M. Sheriff Robinson was our manager, and he relied on the elevator operator at this hotel to report the late players. We hated that stool pigeon, who this night was asleep in a chair, just outside the elevator. We got down on the floor, crawled past him into the car, and closed the door. It banged shut, woke up the old stool pigeon, and he started hollering. We took the elevator up, but stopped between the third and fourth floors. I climbed up through the trap door in the ceiling and pried open the door to the fourth floor. Joe Miller climbed up behind me and we looked through the peephole in the door—all you could see was the shaft, no car. We snuck down to the third floor and checked the peephole there.

"It's perfect!" I said. "Let's go to bed."

The old stool pigeon called our manager, Sheriff Robinson, and said, "One of your goddamn ballplayers stole my elevator!"

Robinson said, "What do you mean 'stole' your elevator?

How the hell can anyone *steal* an elevator? Have you been drinking?"

"No, I been sleeping. And my elevator's gone. I checked every floor and it's gone. One of your goddamn players took it."

A little while later the phone in my room woke me up. I looked at my watch and said into the phone, "Who the fuck is this at five o'clock in the morning?"

"You know who this is—it's Skip," Robinson said very loudly. "I want you to tell me why you stole the hotel elevator. And what the hell did you do with it? Where is it?"

"Skip, what the hell are you talking about?" I said. "I've been asleep for hours. Why do you call me and blame me? It really pisses me off that I get blamed for everything."

"Don't try to talk your way out of it, Pepi. I know you stole that elevator."

"Skip, I didn't steal no elevator."

"Damn it, let me talk to Miller. Put him on this phone."

"He's asleep, Skip."

"Wake him up!" Robinson yelled.

Joe Miller had his face in a pillow to muffle his laughter, but he got control of himself and took the phone. "Hell, no, Skip. Pepi didn't steal no elevator. We been in this room since eleven o'clock." Pause. "Yes, I swear." Pause. "Okay, good night, Skip."

The hotel manager and the old stool pigeon finally opened the lobby elevator door, looked up the shaft, and saw the car. But they had a helluva time getting to it. Down with stoolies!

To this day, Sheriff Robinson doesn't know for certain that it was me who stole that elevator. For over twelve years, every time I ran into him, Sheriff would say to me, "Pepi, you stole that elevator, didn't you? Tell me. You can tell me now."

"You still believe I stole that elevator?"

"I *know* you stole that elevator, Pepi. Admit it."

"Well," I'd tell him, "I *didn't.*"

Robinson got sick during that season in Amarillo, and my old friend Steve Souchock came in to take over the team. We had an interleague arrangement with the Mexican League. The Texas League clubs each played in Mexico for about a month. When we went there, Phil Linz and I were the top hitters in the league. Phil was batting about .346, I was about .344. Souchock told us that we had to be very careful of the food and water. He warned us not to eat anything from a street vendor, that their stuff could kill you.

I thought I had a cast-iron stomach, so about two days after we were there, a bunch of us were bouncing around, and I ate a mess of *enchiladas, tacos,* and *tortillas* from street vendors. The guys had to help me back to my room. For days I thought I was dying, that I'd never see New York again, that I'd be buried down Mexico way. Guys came to see me and I'd mumble, "Remember the Alamo, you bastards." I was sick for two solid weeks, lost fifteen pounds. I got back just in time to help seven of the guys steal the team bus one night, so that we could examine the native culture a little closer. We visited a small town populated almost exclusively by prostitutes. Steve Souchock apparently got back late that night and noticed the team bus was missing. He was waiting for us when we returned at 3 A.M. We were all fined.

I was weak when I resumed playing, had no zip at all. My average fell to around .320. Phil Linz heeded Souchock's warning about the food, and left Mexico hitting over .350. He ended up leading the Texas League in hitting, with a .349 average. I finished with a .316 average, twenty-one home runs, and eighty-seven RBIs. When you also consider the fact that I led the league in stolen hotel elevators and team buses, it wasn't a bad season.

In 1962 I was asked to take spring training with the Yankees for the first time. The New York Yankees were world champions for the skatey-eighth year in a row. Joe Pepitone, from Park Slope in Brooklyn, was going to play ball with Mickey Mantle and Whitey Ford and Yogi Berra and Roger Maris, guys I'd watched and rooted for at Yankee Stadium and on TV for as long as I could remember. I was going to be dressing in the same locker room with them, playing on the same field with them—on the same *team* with them! Christ, I only wished Willie could see me now!

The Yankees had switched their training camp from St. Pete to Fort Lauderdale in Florida, and the accommodations were even nicer. What an organization—always first class. I reported to the advance camp with the pitchers and young talent. Joe

DiMaggio—the Yankee Clipper whom I'd admired for so long —had been hired as a special coach by Ralph Houk, who'd become the manager when Stengel had been fired. DiMaggio spent a lot of time working with me, giving me little step-saving outfield tips. Mainly he told me to keep doing what I was doing, because I had unusual ability. My head swelled so much, my cap almost shot off!

Til Ferdenzi, a sweet man, interviewed me at length. My mother clipped the story from the *Journal-American* and sent it. The story said that, among all the young talent in Lauderdale, I had the best chance of making the Yankees. Til quoted Joe DiMaggio on me: "Good wrists—a good-looking hitter. A nice swing and good power. And in the outfield, he's got the knack of going back for a ball. That's instinct. You can't teach a boy to take that quick look, then turn tail and run back to where the ball is dropping. That's an instinctive thing, and this boy Pepitone looks as though he might have it."

Ferdenzi also quoted Ralph Houk, "Pepitone has some pretty good qualifications. In the first place, he plays first base and he plays in the outfield. That makes him valuable to our way of doing things right there. Then, he can pinch-hit and he can be used as a pinch-runner. All these things, plus the way he played last year in Amarillo, make out a pretty good case for the boy's chances."

I'd told Til about my problems at Binghamton, how Skiff had helped me, which set up my strong season in Amarillo. "More than ever before in my life," I'd said, "I realized I had to bear down every day and produce. I feel that way more than ever now. I'm married and have a wonderful wife and a wonderful eight-month-old daughter, Eileen. And I know I can make a spot on this club if I can prove to them here that I can be useful."

Deep down I didn't believe it, though, that I could actually jump from double-A ball to the Yankees. I worked my ass off. I hit ten home runs in twenty-five exhibition games, but I watched Pete Sheehy, the clubhouse man, come up to guys and say, "Ralph wants to see you in his office." The next day those guys were gone. Week after week they disappeared, and I was still there with my Richmond (International League) contract, and every day I expected it to be my turn.

Cutdown day came, and I was still there. Then, sure enough, Pete Sheehy walked to my cubicle after the game and said, "Ralph wants to see you in his office." Oh, shit, I said to myself, here it comes. Understandably, because the Yankees were well-covered in the outfield and at first base. Bill Skowron was the first-baseman, and catcher Ellie Howard could also play there. The outfield—with Mantle, Maris, and Yogi and Hector Lopez splitting time in left—was set. What the fuck had I been dreaming about, thinking I had a shot at making this club?

I got up off my stool and walked into Houk's office with my head down, my insides trembling. As I passed through the players, they said, "You'll get it next time, Pepi." "Hang in there."

I stopped, turned to a group of the guys, and said, "But didn't I have a good spring? I mean, didn't I hit good?"

"Don't worry about it," they said. "They just want you to get a little more seasoning. No sweat."

I knocked on Houk's door. "Who is it?" he yelled gruffly.

"Pepi . . . Joe Pepitone."

"Come in." He was sitting at his desk smoking a big cigar. "What the hell do you want?" he said.

"Unh . . . Pete said you wanted to see me."

"Oh, yeah," he said, flicking his cigar. "I wanted to tell you to get your clothes packed—you're going to New York with us."

I ran out of his office yelling, "Yeaaaa! *Yeaaaaa!*" Then I noticed all the guys were smiling. They had known. "You cock-suckers!" I yelled.

The guys came over and congratulated me, shook my hand, and I was so goddamn happy I was like a little kid. I felt like my whole body had turned to liquid as those guys I'd idolized gave me skin. I was one of them, a member of the New York Yankees!

I hurried to the telephone in the locker room and made one call after another. I called my wife, I called my mother, I called my grandfather, I called my Uncle Louie—and I told them all the same thing: "I made it! I'm going to New York—I made the damn ball club!"

VIII

"Joey, you gotta make us Italians proud!"

Ralph Houk used me as a fill-in player in 1962. I pinch-hit, pinch-ran, and replaced Moose Skowron at first base late in games for defensive purposes. I covered a lot more ground, was a much better fielder than Moose. I did get to start a number of games, mostly splitting doubleheaders with Moose against tougher right-handed pitchers. I'd come off a hot-hitting spring and I stayed hot at the plate through the first month of the season. I slugged five home runs, including two in one inning to tie a major-league record.

My first at-bat in the majors taught me a lesson. The first pitch was up around my shoulders, and the umpire said, "Strike." I stepped out of the box, turned to the ump, and said, "What the fuck is this? That pitch was at my shoulders. They got better umpires in the minors!"

He stepped right over to me, his face six inches from mine. "Listen, you guinea bastard," he said, "from now on you better be swinging at *every* pitch!"

"Well, I'll tell you something, you blind bastard," I said. "I'm *gonna* be swinging at every pitch—because you are horse-shit!"

That's one reason why I never walked much in the majors, why I always went up there swinging. I swung at the second pitch that day, and hit into a double play. I went back to the dugout mumbling about the fucking umpire. Mickey Mantle came over to me and said, "Don't mess with that guy. He always tests rookies." Thanks for the early warning, Mick.

At the end of that inning, I went out to first base, a runner got on, and the next batter hit a towering pop fly between home plate and me. I had played more in the outfield than at first, and I hadn't had much practice on high pops to the infield. So I moved in for the ball, saw it was carrying deeper than I thought, and started backing up. I tripped over the bag and fell on my back, my head banging off the ground and knocking me silly. The ball bounced next to me, my right hand went out reflexively, and I caught the ball in my glove while lying on my back. Somehow, I managed to whip a throw to second and nail the runner, who had held up, expecting that I'd catch the pop.

After the game, a writer came over and asked me how I liked playing in the big league. "Well, I couldn't do much worse," I told him. "I hit into a double play and fell on my head." But I added, "At least I showed one thing. Clete Boyer is famous for throwing guys out from third base on his knees. I showed I could throw them out on my *back.*"

I was always making brash remarks like that, coming up with some kind of foolishness to make guys laugh, gain me a little attention. I needed attention, which translated to me as affection, and I desperately needed guys to like me. They called me "Pepinose" and—because of my Italian descent, my Brooklyn background, and the silky, tight-clothes way I dressed—said I was the first member of the Mafia to play for the Yankees.

"Dat's right," I'd say in a deep voice, "and you guys fuck wit me, I'll order ya a pair of cement shoes." I'd sneak a look over at Mantle, Maris, Ford, the big stars, see if they laughed. They did, and I loved it. I went along with anything they said about me, because I knew that if guys bothered to kid with you, they liked you.

I was only twenty-one years old, but I was already starting to lose my hair in front. I used to stand in front of a mirror for half an hour combing it, patting it, telling it to hang in there, fellas. I'd do this before a game and after a game. Of course, everyone would notice, make fun of me. But it was good-natured, something I came to expect . . . even look forward to. That was the way I was.

I remember one day a photographer asked Mantle, as we

stood by the batting cage, to pose as if he were talking to me. Mickey grimaced and turned his back, saying, "I can't stand to look at that face." I laughed, thought it was funny, but as the photographer shot a picture of Mantle with his back to me, I began wondering: Doesn't he like me? Was he serious about not wanting to be photographed with me? Did people in the stands see him turn his back on me? When the photographer finished, I hurried over to Mickey and started talking to him, glancing at the stands out of the corners of my eyes to make sure everyone knew we were friends, that he'd only been kidding. This was very important to me, acceptance, just as important as being with the club.

When we went to Los Angeles to play the Angels for the first time in 1962, I felt I'd really made it with Mantle. Guys had told me you had to be with the Yankees for about nine years before Mantle would ever invite you to go out with him. This night Mantle invited me to a party. The Angels were still playing in Dodger Stadium then, and the public-address announcer, who was called Tiger, seemed to know just about every good-looking chick, every starlet, in the city, as well as every party that was going on. He told Mantle about one, and when he asked me if I'd like to go along, I almost flipped.

I'd never seen anything like the scene at this party. First of all, it was at this lavish place up some canyon, and there were a dozen movie stars and starlets present. We got there late, after the ball game, and there were already people in the pool—naked. They were not swimming. And anyone who felt like joining the action, guys and girls, they simply dropped their drawers and dove in. Couples were disappearing into rooms, and when the rooms were all occupied, couples started balling right out in the open, all over the place. Incredible! The later it got, the wilder it got.

Finally, I turned to Mantle and said, "When are we going home, Mickey? We gotta play tomorrow."

"Shut your fucking mouth," he said.

I was watching the balling on the couch over here, the balling on the floor over there . . . and I began to think less and less about baseball.

I saw a girl that all kinds of guys were after. She was small, blond, gorgeous, wearing one of those short-short skirts and the high boots that were already "in" in California then. I kept watching her, she seemed so cool, rejecting in a nice way all the guys who moved on her. I was afraid to even approach her, talk to her. But she saw me staring at her and started talking to me. She said her name was Alice, that she was nineteen and trying to get into modeling. We stood there for quite a while, rapping, rapping, rapping with one another, and the next thing I knew we were upstairs balling, balling, balling.

She was the best piece of ass I'd ever had. When we finished, I just lay there staring at her, she was so good, so beautiful. Every time we went to L.A. after that, I saw Alice. I really got close to her, met her mother, the whole thing. It wasn't until three years later that I learned—when her mother called me to see if Alice was with me in New York—that Alice had been thirteen years old that first night I was with her. L.A.—what a zoo!

But that's where the partying started for me, in Los Angeles, as it did for a lot of other ballplayers. Over the years, I've heard any number of guys say they might never have gotten into banging around so much if they hadn't been exposed to that wild, wide-open scene. I know it really turned me on, and that I thought, With this going on, what the fuck am I doing being married?

That thought was strengthened by living in New York. Barbara and I took an apartment in the Bronx, which I didn't spend a whole lot of time in. I'd always thought of the Copacabana as being the greatest night spot in the city. I remembered reading as a kid that Mantle and Ford and Hank Bauer and Billy Martin, and the rest of the Yankee stars who liked a good time, all hung out at the Copa. At least until the night they got involved in a well-publicized scrap there.

One night, early in the '62 season Tommy Tresh and his wife and Barbara and I went to the Copa for dinner and a show. Sammy Davis, Jr. was on stage, and the joint was packed, full of celebrities I recognized. I kept pointing them out to Barbara: "There's Joey Bishop." "There's Phil Foster." "There's Buddy Hackett." I was thrilled.

The Copa was also liberally sprinkled with older Italians in dark, expensive suits who sent drinks over to our table and came over to meet me. Many of them spoke in very deep, hoarse voices as they wished me well with great sincerity and emotion. "You gotta make us Italians *proud,* Joey," they'd say. "We read all about ya. There aren't many Italians in the big leagues wit your kinda ability. We're countin' on ya to make us proud." Then they'd walk away with their huge diamond rings, and Carmine or one of the other maitre d's would say, "That's a very important man, Joe," and nod his head. "*Very* important." Translation: They were racket guys, some of the biggest names in the New York area.

They impressed the shit out of me. In my eyes they were more important people than Joe DiMaggio, Babe Ruth, or Mickey Mantle. I guess it was because I was born and raised in Brooklyn, had been around racket guys all my life, and had held them in awe as everyone in the neighborhood did. I remembered how I'd looked up to the small-timers who used to drive down the block selling hot merchandise off the docks, remembered the guy we'd bought the 400-dollar German hi-fi set from for 50 dollars the year before I'd signed, how I'd helped him unload it, carry it up to our apartment. I thought of Jimmy the Bug and how I used to find his numbers books under our doormat. He'd stash his record of the day's business there rather than climb the extra flight of stairs, and no one would think of touching them. Jimmy the Bug was one of my biggest heroes as a kid, and here I was receiving tributes from guys who were so far over him in their mutual business that I couldn't believe it. These were kings of the racket trade, superstars, and they all wanted to be my friend.

I started hanging out at the Copa, without Barbara, because the second time I went there, alone, the racket guys not only made me feel good but they invited me to go to one of their private after-hours places. None of them had their wives with them. They were out having a good time, and to them good times meant sex. These guys had chicks in every borough, who welcomed them and their friends with open thighs. No chatting, no courting, no nothing. This was a different type of sex than I'd ever known. I didn't have to go out and meet a girl and o through a whole big routine to get her into the sack. These girls were *there.* "Joey, I'd like you to meet this girl," a racket guy would say, "you'll like her. She got all the moves. I mean, nice. Here, take this number: Ginny. Mention my name, say I thought you two would like each other."

He'd hand me the phone number. I'd call. Terrific, she'd say at four-thirty in the morning. She'd meet me at the door in a see-through robe, or bare-ass naked, say, "Hi!" and sure enough she'd have *all* the moves . . . and then some. No talk, no bullshitting around—instant flesh on flesh, flesh in flesh, and YEAH! Screams of pleasure! At least, I thought they were, and many of them certainly were. Passion! Which translated to me as: I not only love you, Joe, but you're great, an all-star lover.

I really dug being with the racket guys. I always needed to feel that people liked me, and these people liked me. If I was Joe Schmoe, they wouldn't have bothered with me. I knew this. The fact that they made a lot of me—liked to sit around talking baseball, liked to take me different places, fix me up—convinced me that I was somebody. Hell, I wasn't even a regular with the Yankees, I was just a "scrubeenie," as Phil Linz and Johnny Blanchard and the rest of us substitutes called ourselves, and these racket guys made me feel like I was a star. These important men wanted to be with *me.* Maybe they looked at me as a young Italian who was on his way up in a legitimate business, who didn't have to worry about being sent away for ten years tomorrow, and maybe they wished they could be that way, could live like me. I don't know. But some of these older racket guys had spent twenty-five, thirty years of their lives in jail, and the way I was trying to make a living had to look better to them.

I knew they looked out for me, always protected me. Any time there was trouble, some problem coming down, one of them would brush by me right away when I'd come into the Copa and whisper, "You're not with us tonight." Or simply, "Hello, Joey, but good-bye for tonight," with a wink. I remember sitting at a Copa table one night with ten of the biggest racket people in New York. The club photographer started taking pictures. The racket guys on either side of me said, "Hey, Joey—aren't ya worried about this? You want we should get those negs?"

"What, worried? I don't care about pictures," I said. "All I know is you're nice people." There were probably six under cover detectives taking Minox pictures every night at the Copa I didn't care.

I didn't know what any of the racket guys did. I didn't want to know. That's the way it had been when I was growing up We always *heard* when anything happened, when anyone go muscled. But it was always within the families, who were vying among themselves for territory or whatever. If somebody go shot or killed, it was always another racket person, never an innocent bystander. I never personally saw or even heard of them hurting anyone I knew, anyone who wasn't in the racket business. The wise guys, as we called them, were always nice just people in a different business, doing their own thing and risking a lot of years in jail. As I look back, I really don't know if they were any worse than corporations that sell us inferior products at inflated prices and refuse to make good on the products when they don't do what they are supposed to do. Or Vice-Presidents of the United States who make illegal deals for under-the-table money, lie about it, and then don't go to jail. Or Presidents who cheat on their taxes, who cover up burglaries and invasions of privacy and lie and rip off the country, and receive a pardon.

I very seldom went to the Copa with other players. Mainly, I'd go with friends from the old neighborhood—Lemon, Patty Boy, and a few girls I'd invite. I wanted to show my old friends that I hadn't forgotten them, show them what a big man I was. I'd walk in with Lemon and Patty Boy and three good-looking chicks, get a table right up front, the maitre d' would bring over a bottle of J & B immediately, I'd pour drinks, tell everyone to order anything they wanted, and pick up the whole tab at the end of the night. I knew I was showing off, but I genuinely enjoyed giving friends a good time. And when the top racket guys would stop by my table, invite me over to theirs, take me backstage to meet the entertainers, a damn shiver would go down my spine. I met the biggest celebrities—singers, actors, actresses I had listened to or seen in the movies for years—and I really dug it. I felt so goddamn tall.

I'd be out almost every night the Yankees were in town, at

1e Copa, The Lounge, wherever the racket guys hung out. And long about four in the morning, one of them would say, "C'mon, Joey, we're all goin' to Rudy's." I remember several ights sitting with these guys in an after-hours place till 8 A.M., ist rapping, flirting with waitresses, enjoying the scene. I was wenty-two years old, hyper, liked to be going, going, going all he time, and I just didn't need much sleep. I'd go right to the •all park and be fresh, full of energy.

Staying out all night didn't help my marriage, didn't do nything positive for the vibes between Barbara and me. But I vas more concerned with who I'd meet when I was with these ;uys—with the ego-swelling feelings I'd get—than I was with naking my marriage work, being with her, taking care of her. That's where my head was then.

The racket guys really pushed me to do well. They kept aying, "You gotta make us *proud,* so when you go out there, we want you to bear down, do good. And if we can help you n any way—*any way,* Joey—you just let us know."

One night, I'll be goddamned if a couple of them didn't think they'd come up with a way to get me off the bench. We were sitting around in an after-hours place when this guy turned to me, very seriously, nodding his head.

"We're gonna help ya out with that little problem ya got wit Skowron," he said.

"What? What do you mean?"

"He's gonna have a little accident."

"No, no! I'll win the job on my own next year."

"Joey—why *wait?* We'll just get in touch wit him after a game, and the next day ya got the job. No problem. He won't play real good with cracks in his legs."

"Shit, no! Don't do that," I pleaded.

"Joey," another guy said, "he's not supposed to be playin' ahead of a Italian."

They were not kidding. I finally made them promise not to go *near* Moose Skowron. But I began to see that while being around these guys could be fun, it could also be a little frightening. Of course, I was floating so high at this time, with my whole glorious future in front of me, that I wasn't really frightened of anything.

But one day, I have to admit, I got shook up by the racket guys. One of them, whom I'll call Vince, phoned me at my apartment and said, "Joey, did ya happen to go to a party two nights ago?"

"A party? No, I stayed home that night."

"Yeah, well, that's what I figured. Look, do me a favor and come on down here—we're at The Lounge—right away. I'll be at the bar wit a bunch of the guys. You come over and say hello, just don't mention your name. Would ya do that?"

"Sure, I can be there in twenty minutes. But what's the problem? You sound angry."

"Well, some shitface here is fucking over your name, and I want to straighten this out."

When I walked into the saloon, Vince said, "Hiya, kid, come here and have a drink with us." I recognized six of the seven guys at the bar and nodded to them. Vince said to the guy I didn't know, "Say, tell the kid about the party ya were at the other night."

"Christ," the guy said, "you won't believe it. It was the worst fucking thing I ever saw. Joe Pepitone was at this party, and there was a lot of fucking going on, naked girls running all over the place. Well, right in front of everybody—Pepitone went down on seven girls."

I was speechless, because the older Italians have this thing about sex where the man never demeans himself with a woman. And to them, going down on a woman was the most demeaning act you could perform. You just didn't do it, period. At this time even I believed this, and had never gone down on a woman —didn't until a year or so later. I'd always wanted to, but I was hung up by those old beliefs that had been hammered into me.

Vince said to the guy, "You know Joe Pepitone, huh?"
"Sure."

Vince nodded. "And you saw him go down on seven girls?"
"Yeah, right in front of everyone."

Vince nodded. Then he pointed at me. "You ever seen this kid before?"

The guy stared at me. "No, I don't think I've ever seen him before."

Vince said, "This is Joe Pepitone." Then he punched the guy

n the belly—"And he don't go down on cunts!"—and chopped
im on the back of the neck. The guy went down on his face,
nd Vince kicked him in the side. "You come around here
preading lies *like that* about this kid!" he yelled, furious. Sev-
ral of the others at the bar stepped over and kicked the guy,
ursing him angrily.

Vince grabbed my wrist. "C'mon, Joey, kick this sonofabitch!"

"No, Vince, I don't want to kick him," I said.

"*Kick* him! He disgraced you!"

"Vince," I said, "I can't be bothered with a piece of shit like
him."

"He called you a *muff diver!* Kick him!"

By this time the guy was all bloody, groaning, barely conscious. "Look at him, Vince," I said. "He'll never say anything
like that again." Then I leaned over and jabbed a finger at the
battered hulk on the floor and yelled, "But watch your mouth,
bastard—or next time I *will* kick you!"

They picked him up like a corpse, carried him to the door,
and tossed him into the gutter.

Of course, when I finally did start going down on girls—if
there was any chance at all of them running into racket guys
—I'd tell them, "Don't ever mention this to anyone, honey."
I had them cross their hearts and sign their names in blood.

IX

"I'll have your job next year, Moose."

Playing as a fill-in, I never knew when I was going to get a start until the last minute, and that was a disappointment. I couldn't get tickets for members of my family who wanted to see me play when I never knew if I'd be playing. My grandfather was particularly anxious to see me in action, he was so proud of me. The first game that I got word two days in advance that I was going to start, I had my Uncle Louie bring Vincent Caiazzo to the stadium. It was a night game against the Angels, and I got them great seats, right behind the visiting dugout. I think they were the first fans in their seats.

During batting practice, I popped three balls into the right-field stands, then I trotted over to see my grandfather, who was beaming from ear to ear. "You gone do good tonight, Joe," he said. "I feel."

We chatted for a couple of minutes, and then Gene Autry, one of the Angel owners, sat down in the box right next to my grandfather. I introduced myself to him, then introduced my grandfather and my Uncle Louie. Gene Autry was very gracious, and he smiled politely when my grandfather said, "Oh, you the cowboy from the movie!"

In the game, Leon Wagner of the Angels hit two home runs and drove in three runs. I hit two home runs and drove in four runs. That was the final score, 4–3. Louie told me that after the game my grandfather tapped Gene Autry on the arm and said, "Hey, you shoulda have my grandson on your team, Gene Autry. Then you win."

I think I went something like 0-for-30 at bat after that. But didn't get upset. I realized I just couldn't stay sharp at the plate when I was sitting down four or five days between starts. knew damn well I could hit major-league pitching if I got a chance to play regularly. In fact, I kept teasing Bill Skowron: "I'll have your job next year, Moose."

When we were up at West Point for our annual exhibition game, a number of the guys boxed in the cadet ring. Hector Lopez, who displayed anything but good hands in a baseball glove, had very good hands in boxing gloves. He beat the shit out of anyone who went in with him. Ellie Howard knocked Jim Bouton out cold, and there was a lot of cheering, because Bouton already wasn't the most popular Yankee even though he was a helluva pitcher. Skowron came over to me with a little grin on his face and said, "Come on, Pepi, let's you and I get in there."

"Get lost, idiot," I said, moving away from him. "There's *no way* I'm going in that ring with you." His body had earned him the nickname Moose, and it was a very accurate description. I don't think I was a great favorite of Skowron's from the first time I was sent in to replace him for defensive purposes. As I trotted past him, I said, "Jeez, Moose, you must have the *baaad* glove."

Early in the season I roomed on road trips with Skowron, who was a conscientious player. He never missed curfews. Since I seldom observed them, we were not ideal roommates. He claimed I woke him when I came in late, but I never noticed him even stir. He also slept like a moose. He kept warning me that he was going to lock me out one night—and I'll be god-damned if he didn't.

I got in about 11 o'clock, only an hour late, and found the door to our room chained. I started banging on the door: "Moose, open up." The door was open about four inches and I could see him lying in bed. "C'mon, Moose, open up!"

"Sleep in the hall," he said. "It's after ten. Bed check's at ten."

"Moose, for Christ's sake, open this goddamn door." I started banging on it again.

"Find someplace else to sleep, and stop keeping me awake or I'll break your damn head," he said.

"Moose, open this fucking door or I'll kick it in!" I said angrily.

"Get the fuck out of here!"

I kicked the door open, ran in, and yelled, "Don't you ever fucking lock me out of my room again!"

He jumped up with his fists balled. "You sonofabitch, I'm gonna punch you right in the face!"

I stepped back in a crouch and said, "Go ahead—and I'll get my uncle after you! He's a Mafia leader and he'll chop off your hands!"

He shook his head and went to bed. I could have told him about the guys who wanted to give him an accident. But I don't think the Moose was a bad guy, even though I did get fined for missing a curfew—and the Yankees almost never held bed check.

The second time I got caught out late, it was red-handed. We were in Boston for a series in late June, and I was rooming with Phil Linz. He came in about midnight and couldn't believe it when he saw me lying on the bed watching television. "Are you sick, Joe?" he said. "You break your ankle or something?"

"No, I got a date at two-thirty. She's a hooker, but she won't be free till then. A terrific broad."

"Pepi, now that you explained it, I understand. You're crazed."

About one-thirty I shaved, put on cologne, got all dressed up, checked myself carefully in the mirror, found a few hairs out of place, combed them down. Then I went out into the hall and pressed the elevator button. A few seconds later I heard the car coming, straightened my tie, the doors opened—and standing right in front of me were Ralph Houk and general manager Roy Hamey.

A very dark cloud swept over Houk's face as they stepped out. "Where the fuck do you think you're going at two o'clock in the morning?"

I just stood there with my mouth open for about fifteen seconds. Then I said, "It's Linz, Ralph; Phil hasn't gotten in yet and I'm—I'm going out to look for him."

"Turn your ass around and get it inside your room—or you're gonna find it in Richmond."

"Okay, Ralph, okay!" I began walking toward my room. But I'm really worried about Phil, Ralph, I mean it."

"Get in that fucking room and don't *move* from it!" he said, following right behind me.

"Ralph, I'm going," I said, unbuttoning my jacket, my shirt.

"I'm *taking* you to your room."

I opened my belt in the hallway, put the key in the lock, opened the door about six inches, and tried to squeeze in quickly and close the door behind me. But Houk shoved it open —and there, asleep in bed, was Linz. "Phil," I yelled, "how the fuck did you get in the room? How the fuck did you get past me?"

Phil woke up, squinted at us. "I been in since twelve o'clock," he mumbled, rolled over and went back to sleep.

Two days later I found my ass in Richmond, Virginia.

I wasn't all that shook up about it. They'd done the same thing to Mickey Mantle during his first season with the Yankees. If they knew you liked to bend the rules, they tried to scare you right away. But at this point I had too much confidence in my ability to be scared. I missed New York, but I sure as hell didn't miss sitting on the bench. I'd never done that before, and I was far too hyper to live comfortably with that status.

Sheriff Robinson was managing the Yankee team in the International League, and the day I reported to him he called me into his office and inspired the hell out of me. "You know why you're down here?" he said.

"Yeah, well, Houk caught me out late," I said. "I guess they sent me here to teach me a lesson."

"That's part of it. But they want you to play every day at first base. They think with a little steady work, you can become the best first-baseman in the American League. I'm going to work with you, and you're going to have a helluva year."

I batted .315 in forty-six games with Richmond and really sharpened up my moves around first under Robinson's guidance. And I was a little more careful about observing curfews. I'd always had to use my name to get laid, mention the New York Yankees every other breath. But the girls in Richmond weren't all that impressed. I couldn't wait to get back to New York.

I was recalled for the last few weeks in September, when the Yankees were trying to clinch another pennant. I walked into the clubhouse amid a lot of greetings that made me feel good and went to my cubicle. It was empty. I looked around the room, checked all the cubicles, and my name wasn't on any of them, my gear wasn't in any of them.

"Hey, where the hell's my locker?" I yelled.

"It's in back, Joe," someone said.

"Yeah, way in back," Mantle said, giggling.

I figured I got it. They'd put my stuff in the trainer's room, a good gag. I smiled as Mantle came over and put his arm around my shoulders and started walking me toward the back. But he didn't take me into the trainer's room—he turned me into the john. There, on one of the stalls, was a strip of wide adhesive tape like they used over the cubicles, and neatly printed on the tape in indelible ink was: JOE PEPITONE. I swung open the door, and hanging inside were all my uniforms. On the floor were my skivvies, my sanitary socks, my spikes, and a toy telephone in honor of the fact that I had made and received so many clubhouse calls before I was sent down.

"Raise the toilet seat cover, Joe," Mantle said.

I tipped it up, and taped under the seat was a huge picture of Yogi Berra's face. I roared. Everyone roared. The Yankees were not known for this kind of foolishness, and I felt it was good for a team, helped keep everyone loose. I'd made a contribution in this area.

I also contributed on the field. Houk played me almost every day, and in the last fifteen games I drove in the winning run seven times. We won the pennant, but I was ineligible for the World Series, because I hadn't been on the roster on September 1. Yet the guys voted me a full World Series share, over $10,000.

I needed that extra money. I was paid the major-league minimum salary in '62, which was about $7,000. At the Copa alone my bill was over $3,000. I had become such a regular customer there that Jules Podell, the owner, had presented me with a gold credit card. That was lovely. All I had to do was keep signing. I didn't worry about paying. I figured I'd pay when I got the money, and that I'd get it eventually. I charged everything, ever worried about money. Just give me the bill, waiter: "Sincerely yours, Joe Pepitone."

I remember stopping by the Copa early one evening, on my way to someplace else. The day's ball game had been rained out, we'd been paid, and I wanted to cash my check. It was for about 500 dollars and I asked Carmine, the maitre d', if he'd cash it for me. "Let me take it to Jules," he said. "I don't think there'll be any problem."

A few minutes later he came back and handed me 50 dollars. "Carmine, don't fool around like that," I said. "That five hundred's all I have to live on for two weeks. Give me the other four hundred and fifty."

He shook his head. "Sorry, Joe. Jules says you've got to cut down your bill."

I didn't go near the Copa with a check after that. But I did keep signing tabs. The racket guys never let me pay for anything when I was with them. I was out all the time, though, and I enjoyed picking up checks. It made me feel good. And feeling good was the most important thing in the world for me. I tried to be happy all the time, to shove aside any worries, fears, bad feelings. Just have fun, Joe, I kept telling myself.

I know now, looking back, that I repressed a lot of things, as many of the negatives as I could. I was disappointed that the Yankees were in the World Series and I wasn't with them, wasn't a part of it. I try to recollect today what I did during that Series, and I think I saw the games, either at the stadium or on television. But I can't remember which, and I can't recall a single moment of what happened on the field.

A couple of months later, I was watching the news on television one night, lying on the couch. Suddenly, I jerked up to a sitting position. The announcer said that Bill Skowron had been traded to the Los Angeles Dodgers. "His replacement at first base"—my picture came on the screen—"will be rookie Joe Pepitone."

Goddamn! I thought. Unless I foul up, I've got the first-base job! I called Mickey Mantle in Dallas. He'd heard me kidding Skowron all the time: "I'll have your job next year, Moose." And I'd told Mickey if it happened I was going to send Skowron a telegram. "All right, Joe, now send Moose that telegram, Mantle said. I did: "DEAR MOOSE: TOLD YOU SO. JOE PEP."

Barbara and I rented an apartment in Fort Lauderdale for spring training. She was pregnant again, and my son, Joe Junior, would arrive early in the season. My daughter, Eileen, was eighteen months old now, and I got a tremendous kick out of playing with her on the beach. But I was still doing so much fooling around that my marriage was an up-and-down thing.

At Lauderdale I hung out with a guy who lived in the next apartment. One day when there was no practice, the two of us were out driving along the beach looking for girls. We picked up a couple and headed for their place. What we didn't notice was that our wives—who were out shopping together—had come back by way of the beach and were two cars behind us. We were in a convertible with the top down. Late that afternoon, we drove back home and walked into his apartment. Both our wives had very unfriendly looks on their faces.

"You do the shopping, hon?" I asked Barbara.

She didn't say a word, just walked into the kitchen. I sat on the sofa and picked up the newspaper. I glanced over at my friend who was sitting across the room and his eyes were bulging out of his head. "Joe!" he yelled. But before I could turn around, Barbara had brought a big steel frying pan crashing down on my head. My brains felt like they were going to spill out of my mouth. I pitched off the sofa onto the floor, my head spinning psychedelically. Then I saw her coming at me again, swinging that frying pan. I rolled over, managed to get to my feet, and hit her a glancing blow. She bounced off the wall and came right back at me, the frying pan raised over her head, total rage in her eyes. I ran out of the apartment, jumped in my car, and drove to a motel near the ball park, feeling a lump get bigger and bigger on top of my head.

I went back to her the next day and apologized, swore I'd never fool around like that again. Of course, that's what I always did, mess up and then apologize to her. It wasn't until years later that I realized I was following the same pattern my father had set with me, which I hated so much.

During the exhibition season I really began to feel like one of the Yankees. I was in there every day at first base, a regular, and I started putting a little flair into my play around the bag, catching throws with a downward snap of the mitt that suggested a kind of ease and confidence. I even scooped up hard-hit grounders with a flick of the mitt. Vic Power, who for years had been the best-fielding first-baseman in the American League, flicked his mitt in a similar way. While I didn't consciously copy him, I had always admired Power's style. I developed a style of my own that not only came naturally to me and got the job done efficiently, but it looked good. Obviously, I had nothing against looking good on the field. I soon heard a number of opposing players call me a hot dog, which means showoff. But once I heard that, I *knew* I looked good playing the position, that I was showing something extra. And, hell, I was covering more ground, making more plays than any other first-baseman around.

Manager Ralph Houk seemed to like my style and announced that a bit of color wouldn't hurt the Yankees. "Baseball needs new, exciting guys," Houk told a writer. "Ted Williams drew fans. So did Yogi Berra and Early Wynn and Whitey Ford. But we need a new appeal now—and I think Pepitone has everything to make it big."

Yankee general manager Roy Hamey seemed to think so, too, with perhaps a small reservation. Mickey Mantle had bad knees, and writers were always asking who would take his place when he retired. One day I heard Hamey being asked that question, and Roy said, "Joe Pepitone. If his head stays the same size." I gave Roy a big wink.

Another day, as we were taking batting practice before an exhibition game, a writer asked Mantle if he thought the Yankees would win another pennant in 1963. "Well, the only change we've made was trading Bill Skowron and putting Joe Pepitone at first base," Mickey said. "If we blow it, it's Pepitone's fault. But the more I look at him," he stared at my face, "I figure we'll win by a nose." I broke up.

It was lovely to be loved. I didn't fully realize it then, but that was the thing I was most trying to earn playing baseball. Not money. Not glory. Love.

X

"Ok, KO."

We opened the '63 season in Kansas City, and when I ran out to take infield practice I suddenly got so nervous I could hardly get my breath. I couldn't believe it. Joe Pepitone—the loose, fun-loving kid from Brooklyn who had started quite a few games for the Yankees in '62, and who now was a regular—was opening the season as a nervous wreck. I couldn't hold on to any throws during practice. Every time I stretched for the ball, it popped out of my glove. I wanted to quit, run into the dugout, and get a drink . . . do anything to get off the field.

Once the game started, the tension ended. I hit two home runs and a double. As I trotted off the field, I said to myself, Shit, I hope I can think of a way to tense up before *every* game.

As it turned out, it didn't matter. I went into a slump after the first game, but remained cool because I knew that I had a sweet stroke at the plate and that the balls would start falling in if I kept swinging. I burst out of it, started coming up with some big hits, and—shock of shocks—at midseason made the American League All-Star team. Mickey Mantle was the only other member of the Yankees who was voted by the league's players to start. I realized there was a certain amount of happenstance involved in my selection, that Vic Power of the Twins and Jim Gentile of the Orioles—the main competition for the first-base position—had started the season badly. Yet I had so much self-esteem, so much confidence in my ability to outhit and outplay everyone I'd seen in the field, that I felt I could have beaten them at their best. There just wasn't anything I couldn't do on a ball field. I was consistently making good contact at bat. Even when I struck out on three pitches, I at least took my cuts—went up there playing my game, going with my strength. When I went down swinging, I always felt, Up yours, man. Next time I'm gonna beat you, because I'm better than you—I can *do* you no matter what you throw me!

Shit, I felt like I owned New York, and I was determined to ball every chick that ran in it. I got right back into the Copa scene, and the sex took me outside myself. Now I not only had my name and my affiliation with the perennial world champions of baseball—I had the bat and the glove on the field. I was barely a second-year man and I was already an All-Star. With Mantle hurt, sidelined prior to the game, I was the only Yankee, other than manager Ralph Houk, to make the trip to Cleveland.

I went o-for-4 at bat, but I was introduced to the crowd on national television before the game, and I knew my mother and my Uncle Louie and my grandfather Caiazzo and Lemon and all my friends were watching Joe Pep, age twenty-three, the baby robin who had grown up to become the best first-baseman in the American League. In Cleveland I got to meet a lot of stars I'd been reading about for years, meeting them close up, as an equal. I also got laid three times.

It was a super trip because, while I had a ball in New York, the balling on the road usually took a certain amount of effort to arrange, and I wasn't really interested in courting, even though I was passionately interested in its end result. What I most admired were the friendly "automatics" that occasionally occurred out of town.

Like on our first trip to Minnesota in 1963. A teammate, whom I'll call Bob, and I stowed our gear in the hotel and went right downstairs and out the door to look for girls. We were standing under the marquee like in the movie *Marty:* "What're we gonna do tonight?" Then I saw this neat-looking girl—about thirty, lots of breast, sexy eyes and mouth—walking toward us.

"Hey, where are you going?" I said to her. "What are you doing out on these mean streets in Minneapolis alone? Why don't you come along with a nice couple of guys, and we'll have a drink, something to eat?"

She walked right over to us and looked at me like a dance-hall girl from an old movie, knowing but nice. "Who are you," she said, "some ballplayers?"

"Yeah, we're with the Yankees," I said. "I'm Joe Pepitone and this is Bob."

She threw back her head and laughed, in a nice, enjoying way. "Where would you like to go? You two look like fun."

I told her we'd go up to our room for a while, order from room service, relax and get to know one another, then go out. So we went to our room, and the girl walked in ahead of us, both of us eyeing her tail wiggle.

"We'd better call room service," Bob whispered. "I'll see what she wants to order. Jane," he called to her from the foyer, "would you like us to order something to drink?"

"Don't bother," she said, pulling a bottle of vodka out of the huge handbag she was carrying. "They have ice in the rooms here." She went over to the radio, turned it on loud to some rock station, and began making half-time dance moves to the sounds.

"Jesus Christ!" I whispered to Bob, "this is too easy. She must be a pro. We better get us some rubbers. We might catch some diseases or something."

"Joe, I'm not into rubbers," Bob said. "Where you gonna get 'em?"

"I'll call room service," I said. "You occupy her." Bob walked over and started dancing with her. She had opened the top two buttons of her blouse and melted right into him. I called room service. "This is Joe Pepitone of the New York Yankees," I said. "Let me speak to the bell captain." He came on. "Look," I said, "I'm in room seven fifty-six, and I need some rubbers."

"No sweat," he said. "How many you need?"

"Uh, how—" I said, not being a whole lot more familiar with them than Bob, "—are they sold? I mean, how many to a pack?"

"Three to a box."

"Bring two boxes."

He must have had them in his pocket: in 68 seconds he knocked on the door, very discreetly. I gave him ten dollars and said thanks. He made a "Ballantine ring" sign with his fingers as I closed the door. I looked around and Bob was no longer dancing. He was standing in the middle of the room with his mouth open staring at the girl. She had her blouse off and was dancing out of her skirt, her arms over her head, a smile on her face. I signaled Bob: "Pssst!" I signaled him again: *"Pssssst!"* Shit! I said to myself. "Bob," I finally said, "could I see you a moment?"

He came out of his trance, walked over to me. I looked past him at the girl, who was still dancing with that smile on her face. She was now down to her panties and bra, and her fingers were behind her back, unhooking the latter garment. "Man, we better use these rubbers, Bob," I whispered. "Here's a pack for you. I'll go into the bathroom, give you first shot."

I closed the door behind me, took off my clothes, thought about that chick getting down to her skin, that smile on her face, those sexy little dance movements . . . and felt myself come to attention. I looked at my watch: Hell, he's had twelve minutes, if he's not finished, at least I can observe.

I walked out of the bathroom, and in the middle of the bedroom floor was a crinkly unrolled rubber, lying there like a burst balloon from one of our water fights in Auburn. Three feet beyond it was another wrinkled, unrolled rubber on the floor. And standing next to the bed where the naked girl lay, was Bob with the third rubber from his pack in his hand—trying to stuff his cock into it. The girl was covering her mouth, stifling a giggle.

"How," said Bob, seeing me, "do you *work* these fucking things?"

"You roll 'em on, man," I said. "*Roll* 'em on."

He made one last stuffing effort, then threw the prophylactic on the floor and shouted, "Fuck this thing! I don't need it!"

In seconds Bob was straddling her chest getting head, and I was kneeling behind him with my thing in her thing. Bob started going, "Ow!" "Ow! Ow!" He looked over his shoulder at me with a pained expression, and I started laughing.

"Shh," I whispered, "we're gonna turn her off."

"Ow!" said Bob. "Ow! Ow!" His head tilted up in the air in pain. "Excuse me, miss," he said to the girl. "You're hurting me."

"I am?" she said. "Sorry." With that—*pop*—she pulled out

her teeth, uppers and lowers, and placed them on the bed beside her.

I started laughing so hard I fell forward against Bob's back, felt the tears running down my cheeks. "Bob," I screamed, "you finally made the ultimate! She's gonna give you a gum job! Hold on!"

She did, too. And didn't charge us a cent. I figured we must have been good.

I thought of myself as a lover, not a fighter. But, next to my start in the All-Star game, it was a fight that brought me the most national attention during the '63 season. The punches were thrown in an August series against the Indians at Yankee Stadium. I had murdered Cleveland pitching all season, with twenty-five hits in fifty-six at-bats. In this game it was obvious that the Indian pitchers were out to intimidate me—which is probably the worst thing a hitter can allow to happen.

In the third inning, starter Barry Latman bounced a fast ball off my right wrist, knocking me to the ground and sending pain shooting up to my elbow. I rubbed it away and took first, giving Latman a dirty look. But in the eighth inning, relief pitcher Gary Bell threw a fast ball *behind* me. Gary Bell never had any control trouble, and I felt anger simmer up in me as I stepped back into the batter's box. The next fast ball came right at my ribs. I leaped backward, and the ball just nicked my shirt. I jumped up and headed for the mound, mad as hell. Home-plate umpire John Stevens grabbed me, saying, "Take your base, Joe." Then he called out to Bell, "That's a fifty-dollar fine, Gary." Bell had turned his back and was rubbing up another ball nonchalantly.

You sonofabitch! I thought as I trotted toward first. You could kill a man with a fucking fast ball—or at least break a rib! By the time I reached the bag, I was furious.

"I'll get you, you prick!" I yelled at Bell.

"Come on!" he yelled back.

I took two running steps toward him, when I felt someone wrap his arms around me from behind. I struggled, thinking the guy was going to hit me in the back of the head or something. Then, holding me tightly, he wrestled me to the ground. I was six feet, two inches tall and weighed 185 pounds now, and I flipped the guy onto his back and hit him with two hard lefts to the head. The guy was Indian first-baseman Fred Whitfield, a nice fellow—but you never know what might happen when you're grabbed from behind. The next thing I knew, the players from both benches and both bullpens were on the field hugging one another, because baseball fights are almost always a series of solid hugs to the chest performed by peacemakers. Ralph Houk, a very strong, very tough man, ran out to protect me, and wrestled Woodie Held to the ground. When Ralph got up, he couldn't find his cap. Then he looked at Held dusting himself off, and saw a Yankee cap on Held's head. The entire fracas was over in about twenty-six seconds.

But it put an end to the Indian beanball tactics. I was ejected from the game and fined 250 dollars, which the club paid, and became an instant hero. The last-place Mets were outdrawing us at the gate, and one writer wrote, "In that raucous moment of Glory, Joseph Anthony Pepitone accomplished what sociologists the world over declared Couldn't Be Done. He stole the hearts of some Mets fans. In fact, he became the biggest Yankee folk hero since Billy Martin demonstrated years ago that a shot in the mouth is worth two into left field when it comes to drawing fans."

I was at my cubicle when the players trooped in after the game. Mantle came right over to me. "Anything I can get you, Joe?" he said in a mock-frightened voice. "A beer? Anything at all? Can I shine your shoes?"

Everyone kidded me for about an hour, and when I finally left the clubhouse, I passed Whitey Ford and said, "See you tomorrow."

"Ok, KO," said Whitey.

The next day someone had pasted an eighteen-inch picture of Gary Bell on my locker and signed it, "All my love, Gary Bell." The day after that, the mail started pouring in—some fifty letters, a number of which said I was a disgrace to baseball. But there were three thousand extra fans in the stands, so what the hell. Maybe, I thought, I can get a raise. Most of the letters went more like this one: "I've always been a fan of yours, but your recent sudden burst of energy convinces me that someday you'll be in the Hall of Fame." A Saint Christopher Medal fell out of the envelope, which was nice, but what I needed was a new chain for the medal I'd been wearing around my neck. In the scuffle the chain had been broken.

I overheard a writer asking Mantle about me, and Mickey said, "He's the freshest rookie I ever saw. But he's a helluva fielder and he's got a quick bat like Ted Williams had. He's going to be one of the best ballplayers we've seen in a long time."

Mickey was sitting at the picnic-style table in the center of the clubhouse filling out requests for tickets on two sheets, one for members of your family, the other for guests. I wrote in a name on the family sheet, and Mickey said, "Is that name *family?* Nobody has a name like that."

I laughed. "That's my Uncle Louie. He's a hood from Brooklyn. Don't be a snotty veteran, Mick."

Yogi Berra sat next to me and used a Mantle line, saying, "I wish I could buy you for what you're really worth, and sell you for what you think you're worth." I laughed anyway.

Pete Previte, the clubhouse man, came over and said, "Get on those balls, Joe."

"As soon as I get dressed," I told him. I hated to sign baseballs, and every day there were a dozen or so in a box on the table which all the players were supposed to sign. You had to have a specially bent hand to sign your name on a baseball, and I signed as few of them as I could. But when I got to my cubicle this day, I saw that Previte had gotten even with me. I pulled on the white sanitary socks that we wore under the blues, and I saw more skin than white. "If you don't sign the balls, he gives you sanitaries with holes all through them," I said to Linz, who was seated at his cubicle next to mine. "Pisses me off."

"Then sign the balls," he said, laughing.

Ten minutes later Previte was standing beside me. "C'mon, Joe, sign the balls."

"Just a minute, for Christ's sake. I gotta finish dressing, don't I?"

"You also gotta sign the balls."

Pee Wee Reese and Dizzy Dean, who were in to cover us on NBC's "Game of the Week," came over. Reese told me he wanted to get some closeups of me for the pregame show. "I'd better shave then," I told him.

By the time I shaved and finished putting on my uniform, it was time to get out on the field. I didn't sign a single ball, and Pete Previte cursed me as I ran out. I loved it; just as I had loved, as a kid, saying I would go to the store for my mother, not do so, and somehow manage to get away with it. Games were fun when you won them.

I continued to love New York's night life, too, and the bills kept piling up like the dog shit on Manhattan's streets. One morning I drove to Yankee Stadium for an afternoon game, parked my Corvette in the player's lot, and headed for the entrance. I was surprised to see two employees of the Copa waiting by the gate—two guys who were good friends.

"What the hell are you guys doing here at this hour?" I said. "The game's not till one-thirty."

"We're not here for the game, Joe," Bob said. "We were sent us to see you about your bill. You're gonna have to come up with some money . . . or you're gonna have a problem."

"A problem?" I said. "You mean to say you're gonna hit *me*? You gotta be kidding, man, we're friends."

He shrugged. "Joe, this wasn't our idea. We were told what to say."

"Look, I'll take care of the bill. I know it's running a little high, but I'm good for it. I'll have my World Series share in a few more weeks."

"Sure, Joe, sure. Just don't forget."

"You guys know me better than that. Shit."

I didn't pay the bill, of course, because I had too many other real living-expense bills to pay. I avoided the Copa except when I had cash on me. But nothing more ever happened. I wasn't strong-armed. I didn't really care. I wasn't worried simply because I wasn't afraid of anything in those days. I found the whole thing exciting, another game. It was a kick being able to talk your way out of anything.

I got into a bad rut at the plate in August, which I went into batting around .290. I had hit twenty home runs already, and thought how nice it would be to hit thirty in my first full season.

I started trying to pull everything down the short right-field line in Yankee Stadium, which threw off my stroke. I'd always been primarily a straightaway hitter. From August 7 until September 1, I didn't hit one home run, and my average fell below .270. I finally realized what I was doing, recalled how those close-in right-field seats had fouled up other hitters who tried to pull the ball too much. I went back to my normal swing and finished the season strongly—a .271 batting average, 27 home runs, 89 RBIs.

We faced the Los Angeles Dodgers in the World Series, and I didn't hit worth a damn against their super pitching staff. Two singles in thirteen at-bats, no runs batted in. And I became the goat of the Series, according to the press, when I dropped a throw from third-baseman Clete Boyer that let in the winning run in the fourth and final game in L.A. It was my error, but it wasn't an easy play because there was a mass of white shirts in the stands behind third. When Clete released the ball, I picked it up, then lost it in those shirts. The real problem was that the ball had been hit so hard that I never expected Boyer to get to it, and I didn't get over to the bag quick enough. Still, I really couldn't understand all the excitement over my error. Sure, I blew it. But we'd lost the first three games to the Dodgers, and there was no way we were going to win four in a row against pitchers like Sandy Koufax, Don Drysdale, and Johnny Podres.

When our plane landed in New York after that loss, there was actually a crowd at the airport to boo me. Unbelievable! A reporter pushed through the throng to interview Houk, and the first thing he asked was about Pepitone and the fact that Skowron had been traded to L.A. Houk was short with the man, telling him to look up our season's averages. "Pepitone outhit him all year," Houk said, even though Moose had hit well in the Series. The reporter said he didn't know that, and Houk exploded. "Get the hell away from me if you don't know baseball. What the hell are you asking me questions for?"

Still, the airport scene was nothing compared to that night in Brooklyn. It was late, and I stayed at my grandfather's house, where my mother lived, because it was closer to Idlewild than my apartment in the Bronx. I was exhausted and went right to sleep. A few minutes later—this was the middle of the night—I heard my grandfather yelling. I got up and saw him shouting out the window and shaking his fist.

I looked out the window, and down in the street in front of the house were over a hundred people. They had a dummy of me strung on a lamppost. They lit the dummy and pulled it up with a huge cheer.

"Go on home, you crazy bastards!" I yelled. "Get the fuck outta here!"

Then I saw—running out of the door, swinging a bat— eighty-one-year-old Vincent Caiazzo. The crowd opened, stepped away from that whirling bat. I ran out after him and started punching at everyone I got close to. Luckily for me, the police screamed up in their cruisers moments later. Brooklyn, I thought, how the fuck did I ever get through my first seventeen years in this crazy place?

All in all, though, being the World Series goat made me a lot of money in the off-season. I was in great demand on the banquet circuit, at four hundred to five hundred dollars an appearance plus expenses when I spoke out of town. I loved going out of town. Not only was the money good, the screwing was good. And I obviously had this compulsion to keep fucking outside my marriage. There were always wonderful girls on the road and at the banquets themselves. I got involved one afternoon with such a turned-on chick that I didn't even make the banquet appearance. I called in sick, which to some degree I was, even though I thought I was well. Very well.

Late in October I drove from my apartment to visit my mother in Brooklyn. She had remained close friends with Lucy, the sexy lady from the old neighborhood whom we'd all been semi in love with as kids. Lucy had moved out West some years ago. But she happened to be back visiting my mother this day. She was still very attractive, with smoky eyes that sent out moist messages. We sat around talking about old times, about baseball, joking, kidding. Then my mother left the living room to fix lunch, and Lucy moved next to me on the couch and started asking me about sex in baseball. I told her about some of the girls, how the life of a major-league player was balls and strikes off the field as well as on. She smiled and put her hand on my thigh.

The next afternoon I met her at the Golden Gate Inn in Brooklyn. We balled all day and into the evening—five times. After the last one she looked me in the eye, her arms still around my neck, her legs around my waist, and said, "You know, you're much bigger than your father was, and he came very fast."

I leaped to my feet. "Don't you *ever* talk about my father!" I yelled. "Don't ever say *anything* about him!"

The revelation shook me. I knew my father could not have done much, if any, banging around. Willie was always with his family—too much so at times. And even though I'd suspected he might have seen Lucy on the side a time or two, a suspicion is not a fact. I guess I secretly had wanted to sustain the image of him as faithful to my mother.

Yet the thought crossed my mind as I drove home to the Bronx later that night. Willie was a helluva man, but he hadn't come close to my record with chicks, and he hadn't become a major-league ballplayer, either. As I turned off the FDR Drive to the Bronx, a rock station blaring out of the radio, it struck me that it was all too fucking complicated for me. So I thought about where I'd go the next evening.

The following day, early in the afternoon, I got a call from my mother. "Joe," she said, "the most awful thing happened. Lucy, who was sitting here with us two days ago—she had a stroke last night. It paralyzed half her body."

I offered my sympathies, hung up, and immediately called Lemon. "Lemon," I said, "sit down because you won't believe this. But I want to tell you how good I am. Are you listening?" I paused. "I was with Lucy yesterday, your first real love, and we screwed five times. A few hours after I left her, she had a stroke. How many girls have you screwed so good that they had a stroke afterward?"

That's how fucked up, depraved, degenerate I was at the time. Worse, a couple of months later on a trip out West, I went to see Lucy at her place. She was paralyzed on one side, only half her body could move. I did her. She could move only one hand, one side of her mouth, but it was wildly sensuous to me. That was the bag I was headed for, the way my mind was working—the freakier the sex, the better.

IX

"Daddy, don't leave me!"

The Yankees announced some big changes following the '63 Series. CBS bought the club from Dan Topping and Del Webb, and Roy Hamey retired. Ralph Houk replaced Hamey as general manager, and Yogi Berra was named manager. Houk offered me a contract calling for a $5000 raise, the biggest I'd ever had. But it gave me a salary of only $16,000—which was a few thousand dollars less than a ballplayer with my record would have been earning if he also happened to be a firm negotiator. I was what the tough negotiators referred to as "an easy lay." I didn't give a shit. Whatever figure management wrote on the contract, I signed it. At this time—debts and all—I would have played baseball for nothing.

Barbara had delivered our second child during the season, Joseph Anthony, Junior. Barbara's water broke on the drive to Misericordia Hospital, and I saw my son in less than an hour. I was thrilled. He was brand new, pink, and shiny, and he looked just like me. He already had thick black eyebrows.

I knew that the only reason I was staying married was because of the kids, and Barbara may have felt the same way. We had absolutely nothing going together; I was making no effort to bring us together, and neither was Barbara. The bad vibes, arguments, attacks on one another were constant. But Barbara wanted a house in the suburbs, so we bought a $40,000 colonial in Riveredge, New Jersey. We thought it might change things, which was stupid. We didn't stand a chance if I didn't change my lifestyle, and I wasn't about to. I was still out screwing around all the time. Even when Barbara was with me, I was coming on with other girls right in front of her. If I really dug a girl, I'd give her my home phone number. I was compelled to fuck everything I could, compelled to keep going, night after night, in search of fun, happiness. It surely was an elusive rascal.

Reflecting on it now, it wasn't fun, it was wacky. I think I was simply trying to escape through sex the pain that was crouching deep inside my head; the guilt that went back to my father's death. Each conquest pushed aside for another night the memories I couldn't bear to think about. Of course, all the time I was accumulating more guilt over the treatment of my family, and while it was small, insignificant, in relation to those feelings about Willie, my self-destructive performance took its toll.

Soon after we moved into our house, I found that I couldn't make it with Barbara any more. That didn't help my head. For years I'd merely had to look at my dick, and it would pop up. Suddenly, I couldn't do anything with my wife, and I quickly gave up trying. Outside I was always ready, at home always limp. It wasn't just because I was tired from all the other activity. I *was* tired after screwing three other girls in one night, but I'd done that in the past and had always managed to take care of my homework. In Riveredge, with my wife I had a perpetual headache. It was sure as hell my fault, not hers.

I took to sleeping in my daughter's room to escape from the bad scenes in our bedroom. Eileen and Joseph were the only reasons I came home at all. I was particularly close to Eileen, my firstborn, who was so bright, so much fun to be with. I loved taking her around with me, to parks, shopping, anyplace. I got such a kick out of talking to her, watching her grow. Sometimes, just being with her, pushing her on a swing, I'd choke up and tears would come to my eyes. I'd feel like my heart was going to burst.

As bad as things were at home, they were nothing but good with the Yankees. The whole baseball scene was a great escape. I dug being with the guys, making them laugh, having their attention focused on me. That was something my father had always had, and I'd always admired it. Most of the guys on the team understood and seemed to enjoy my practical jokes. On one road trip in 1963, I had knocked on the doors of several of the players, and when they opened them, I tossed in lighted firecrackers. Columnist Milton Gross of the New York *Post* got word of this, and asked shortstop Tony Kubek about me.

"Joe says we keep him loose," Tony said, "but he doesn't realize he's keeping us loose. He's our Good Humor man. He talks a lot, and acts up a lot, and keeps thinking of jokes to play, but nobody's resented him. You just understand that from the beginning he was trying to get the fellows to like him."

Right on, Tony! Sometimes, of course, the butt of a practical joke would not think it was all that funny. During spring training in 1964, my roomie Phil Linz really got pissed off at me. One day I was down on the docks in Fort Lauderdale with Bud Zipfel, a young first-baseman, and we saw an enormous swordfish hanging there—and nobody around. We swiped the fish, threw it in my car, and drove to the Yankee Clipper Motel, where the club was headquartered. We carried the slimy monster into my room and put it in Phil's bed. The sheet just covered it.

Phil came in about 3 A.M. and, being a thoughtful roommate, didn't turn on the lights. He undressed and crawled right into bed. I'd been lying there for two hours waiting for him, and it was worth the wait. When he felt that cold smelly thing against his body, he leaped out of bed with a scream and peed in his pants. He put the light on, saw that fish in his bed, and almost hit me.

"You no-good sonofabitch!" he hollered.

"Phil, what are you talking about? I didn't put that thing there. I wouldn't touch a slimy thing like that."

"You put it there, all right, you prick!"

"Phil, I didn't! You gotta believe me."

He didn't talk to me for two weeks after that. Everyone else thought it was funny.

The guys definitely liked to laugh, particularly when we found ourselves in a tough pennant race in '64. We were in third place in August and had to win thirty games out of our last forty-one to edge out the White Sox by a game. The kidding around did keep the team loose, as Kubek suggested. The guys never tired of ribbing me about my nose, which I couldn't do a lot to improve, and my hair, which I was constantly rearranging because it was leaving the front of my head at an accelerated pace.

I remember a typical clubhouse scene one Sunday morning in Kansas City, because Leonard Koppett wrote about it in the *New York Times*. We were all sitting around watching the introductions for an exhibition football game. I'd won the previous night's game with a three-run homer, and everyone got on me, imagining me as a pro football player.

"After Joe caught a pass, he'd tuck his helmet under his arm and comb his hair," said Whitey Ford.

"What would you do if there was a fumble, Joe?" Mantle said. "The ball is lying there, and three guys are diving for it. You wouldn't go near it, would you? You'd say, 'Aw, come on, fellas,' and zoom off in the other direction."

"He'd be the kind of guy who likes to catch passes in the open," said Ford.

"They'd have to design an extralarge face mask to cover his nose," said Bill Stafford.

"Yeah, and when he lined up at end," Bouton said, "the referee would stop the game and yell, 'That face mask is off-side.' "

"I don't think that's so terribly funny," I said in a hurt voice. "I was one of the greatest football players you ever saw in high school."

"Bullshit!" everyone yelled, and that's what it was, but good bullshit. Good for morale.

I had a little trouble with my own personal morale in '64, because fans booed me all season long. I guess my error in the '63 Series had a lot to do with it. And where I made only eight errors in '63, I made eighteen in '64. But, hell, I was getting to more balls, covering more ground, than any other first-baseman in the league. I led the league in putouts and assists. So I finally said the hell with the boos. Mantle got booed, DiMaggio got booed. The fans paid their money, and they had a right to react any way they wanted to. When you're booed, I told myself, at least you know you're being noticed.

It wasn't a bad season. I was picked for the All-Star game—

as a reserve, but I was on the team. For the season I had twenty-eight home runs and one hundred RBIs, despite a .251 batting average, which would've been a lot higher if I hadn't been out screwing around every night. I didn't hit worth a damn in the Series, which we lost to the Cardinals in seven games. I had a grand-slam home run, but only three other hits in twenty-six at-bats: a .154 average. At least I was consistent; that's what I'd hit in the '63 Series.

The thing that pissed me off most about '64 was that Yogi Berra was fired as manager in October. The word was that Yogi didn't know how to handle the players—and I knew the player who was most often out of line. I know some of the guys made fun of Yogi when he announced the lineup, because he couldn't pronounce several names. But he made me play. I'd come to the ball park after being out all night and go to Yogi's office, blood dripping out of my eyes. "Man," I'd say, "I'm sick. I can't make it today."

"You're playing."

"But, Yogi, honest to God, I'm gonna throw up."

"You're playing."

I played 160 games, I often hit the shit out of the ball on those days, too. I'd be so bleary-eyed, I was afraid I couldn't get out of the way of a fast ball, and that would make me concentrate like crazy. Generally, in my early years, if I got two hits right away in a game, I wouldn't concentrate after that. But never on hangover days. Speed pitchers kill.

Probably the incident that most contributed to Berra's getting fired occurred in mid-August when we were in a losing streak. We'd just lost a doubleheader to the White Sox in Chicago and were on the bus headed for the airport. We were no longer in first place and everyone was quiet, kind of down. I was sitting next to Phil Linz, who suddenly pulled out a music sheet and propped it up on the back of Ellie Howard's head in front of us. Then he pulled out a harmonica. "What are you doing, Phil?" I asked.

"I'm gonna practice my harmonica," he said.

"You got to be shitting me!"

"Phil," said Mantle, sitting across from us, "you better put that away."

"We lost," Phil said, "but there's no reason to cry over it." He started playing "Mary Had a Little Lamb," and there was no question but that he needed some practice.

Most of the guys smiled, which was good, because the bus had resembled a morgue. But Yogi, sitting up front, got angry. He stood up and yelled, "Phil, shove that harmonica."

"Christ," Phil said to me, "we lost, but we don't have to act like we're dead. This is ridiculous."

"Phil," I said, "you do what you gotta do—but you might get in trouble."

He brought the harmonica back up to his mouth and started playing again. Yogi hopped up and came storming back to us, saying, "I told you to shove that harmonica up your ass."

"Why don't you do it?" Phil said. "Here." With that he tossed the harmonica to Berra who, furious, slapped at it in midair. The harmonica slammed down on my lower thigh, tearing my pants and scratching my leg. Yogi and Phil were yelling at one another now, and it was getting ugly. I jumped up shouting, "Corpsman, corpsman! I'm wounded!" I was trying to get everyone laughing, to break the tension and bad vibes.

Then dour Frank Crosetti, not one of the most popular Yankee coaches, stood up front and yelled, "Goddamnit, this is the worst thing I've ever seen in my thirty years in baseball." Everything got quiet as Yogi returned to his seat. But the bad vibes stayed in everyone's mind.

Of course, the next day the entire incident became a big joke, and everyone kidded Linz, which helped keep things loose during the stretch run. Linz was quickly signed up by a harmonica company and made about $25,000 for his trouble, which he invested in a saloon called Mr. Laff's that was successful for years. I thought of buying a base fiddle to bring on the team bus so I could pick up some extra bread. But I never seemed to have the price of a base.

Berra didn't hold anything against Linz, who filled in for the injured Tony Kubek at shortstop and made an important contribution to our winning the pennant. So in the long run, Yogi instinctively handled the guys pretty damn well. He knew everyone's moves and was very shrewd in his own way. I remember after the sixth game in St. Louis—which we won on my grand-slam home run as Jim Bouton pitched a gutty ball game without a lot of stuff—I asked Yogi if I could borrow ten dollars. By this time I'd spent all my Series meal money as well as my salary check.

"Sure," said Yogi, reaching in his pocket and pulling out a roll of bills the size of his hand. He started peeling though them, unfolding one after another: 20s, 50s, 100s. He must have had five hundred dollars on him. "Jeez, Joe, I don't have a ten-dollar bill," he said.

"Well, let me have a twenty," I said. "I'll give you the 10 dollars change later."

"No, no," he said. "You asked for 10 dollars." He shoved that roll back in his pocket.

"You cheap bastard," I said to his disappearing back.

But I loved him. I know that getting fired must have shocked the hell out of him. After we'd lost the seventh game, Yogi was supposed to join a bunch of us who were going out to dinner in St. Louis before we flew home. But as we headed out of the clubhouse, Yogi said to me, "I can't go with you guys after all, Joe. I've got to meet with the front office. I guess they want to talk about next season. Look, Joe, I want you to come down to spring training a little lighter in February. Okay?"

Obviously he had no idea he wouldn't be in spring training with us. I assume he got the word at that meeting right after the seventh game, and I think the decision to fire him had been made after the harmonica incident. It wouldn't have mattered even if we'd won the Series. When it was announced that our new manager would be Johnny Keane, who beat us in the World Series, I felt the Yankees had made a bad mistake. We were strictly a power-hitting ball club, with four or five guys who could hit between twenty and forty home runs a season. Keane had only two power hitters on the Cardinals, Bill White and Ken Boyer. He liked to hit-and-run, steal bases, play for one run at a time. We were used to going for the big inning, and I didn't know if the two styles of play could be meshed in New York.

Soon after the Series, I had to go to Youngstown, Ohio, to speak at a banquet. Since I would be gone at least overnight,

I asked Barbara where she might be reached, because I liked to call and check on the kids, and Barbara was spending some evenings at her girl friend's house. She said she would be at her friend's, wrote down a phone number and handed it to me.

After the banquet in Youngstown, I started to call her. But when I looked at the phone number she'd given me, I realized it wasn't her girlfriend's. I knew that number. I looked it up in my pocket address book, and I was right. Recently, I had wondered whether Barbara had any sex going on the side. I had no reason to suspect her, but I was a jealous guy, just like my father. I called the number she had given me.

"Barbara," I said, "what's going on, damn it? This isn't your girlfriend's number. Where the hell are you?"

"Joe, I'm right in the neighborhood," she said. "I didn't tell you, because I was afraid you'd make a scene. I knew you wouldn't understand. There's a group of people here for a little party, that's all."

"Who are you shitting?" I said angrily. "Now listen—"

She hung up the phone. I slammed down the receiver and went back into the all-but-cleared banquet hall. Blackie Gennaro, who handles all the blacktop paving around Youngstown, and who ran the banquet, saw that I was depressed. "What's wrong?" he asked.

I told him, briefly, what was going on. Earlier he had told me that he was going to Florida in the morning and he had asked me to join him. I'd told him I couldn't, that I had to get home. Now he said, "Well, shit, man, don't go home angry. Come on to Florida with me for a few days. Relax, get away from your troubles."

"I don't have any clothes with me," I told him.

"No problem."

It was almost two o'clock in the morning, but Blackie called his tailor. In fifteen minutes we met him at his store, Lord Chesterfield Clothes. Blackie gave me two suitcases and filled them with four suits, slacks, socks, shirts, underwear, shoes, about a thousand dollars' worth of apparel. By noon the next day we were in Miami.

We were supposed to stay two weeks, but we were partying every night and I think we might have stayed forever. About a month later, two private detectives knocked on the door of my room. "Your wife's looking for you, Mr. Pepitone. If you don't get home today, you're going to be hauled in and charged with desertion."

Throughout the trip home, my head was all messed up. What am I gonna say to the kids, being gone a month in the off season? I knew it was time to end the marriage, but how could I give up my kids? How could I leave my little girl and my son?

The big thing in my mind was, No matter what happens when you get there, don't let anything hurt you. You've got to push aside any pain and say fuck it. So I went home with a head that was scrambled, not knowing what to expect, what I would do—except that I was determined not to let anything hurt *me.*

I drove up to our house in Riveredge, and sitting on the front porch were six suitcases full of my clothes. The suitcases were open to the weather, lying flat. I bent down and looked at the clothes, which were mildewed, moldy, as if they'd been out there for weeks. Will you look at this shit! I thought. I tried the front door and it was locked. My key wouldn't open it. Barbara had changed the lock. I kicked in the door and walked into the living room.

Barbara came running in from the kitchen carrying Joseph in her arms.

"What the fuck is the matter with you?" I asked.

"I want a divorce!" she yelled.

"Why?" I said. It occurred to me that wasn't a very clever question, but I didn't dwell on it. Barbara started screaming about my behavior, all my fucking around.

"What the hell are you talking about?" I yelled.

"I want you out of this goddamn house right now!" she screamed. "For good!"

"Where's Eileen?" I asked, because losing my little girl was the main thing on my mind, and I could feel the pain rising in my head.

"She's next door, playing."

I wouldn't go see her until after I'd packed, I decided, walking out to the open suitcases on the porch. I began rummaging through the mildewed clothes, and remembering the day Eileen was born. I was playing in Amarillo, Texas, and Barbara had stayed in Florida with her parents to have our child. Barbara, who had gained sixty pounds, wanted to be with her family doctor. We were off on a road trip the day the baby was due, traveling in a sleeper bus, and I had the driver pull over every half hour or so when we saw a place with a phone. I kept calling, calling. Finally, at a blistered-paint Mexican restaurant, I got the word on the telephone. A nurse told me I was the father of a little girl. I let out a yell, and everyone in the place looked at me like I was crazy. I bought a big box of cigars, ran onto the bus and passed them out. I'll never forget, when we returned from the road trip, waiting at the airport and seeing Barbara walk down the ramp with my child. When I held Eileen in my arms for the first time, she smiled, and I went out of my mind.

I salvaged the clothes that weren't damaged, closed the suitcases, and tossed them in the trunk of my car. I had just slammed the lid when Eileen came running toward me from next door, her arms outstretched and tears in her eyes.

"Daddy, don't leave," she said, hugging my leg. "Daddy, don't leave me. I'll never see you any more." She was crying.

I knelt, hugged her to my chest, swallowing the choke in my throat. "I'll be back, sweetheart," I told her. "I just have to go away for now. . . . But I'll be back to see you. I love you. Don't cry, sweetheart. . . ."

She was only two and a half, but she knew. She knew. I cried all the way home to my mother's in Brooklyn.

I called Barbara six or seven times in the next couple of weeks, but there was no answer. I was getting ready to drive over there to see what was going on when Barbara called. She sounded hysterical, and I heard screaming in the background. She mentioned the name of a man who lived in the area and said, "He's here, in this house, Joe, and he's making Eileen cry. He won't leave. Joe, I'm afraid he's going to hurt our daughter!"

I got so upset, I started trembling. I jumped in the Corvette and stood on the gas—90, 100 miles an hour. I made it from Brooklyn to Riveredge, New Jersey, in about twenty-five minutes. I screeched up to the house, ran to the door, and didn't even try the knob. I kicked it in. Standing in the living room was a man in his forties. He was arguing with Barbara as I burst in, and my daughter was bawling, trying to knuckle away the huge tears rolling down her cheeks.

I grabbed the guy by the front of his shirt, and for a split second I thought I would kill him. I threw him away from me in disgust, and he fell down the four or five steps to the playroom. I stood at the head of the stairs, fists clenched, enraged, my mind swirling, and then the guy got up off the floor, crying.

"I love her," he said. "I thought she loved me, that she was going to marry me." He was crying so hard, he couldn't talk for a moment. "But she says she doesn't want to have anything to do with me," he sobbed.

I turned to Barbara and said, "I'm taking Eileen out of here."

I packed some of her clothes and drove her to my mother's place. The next day the police came and took Eileen back. A few days later, I called Barbara and got no answer. I kept calling for over a week. Nothing. Finally I drove to Riveredge to see my daughter, but when I pulled up to the house, I knew they were gone. There was a For Sale sign in the front yard. I went to a neighbor's. Barbara had taken the children and moved to her sister's in Oakland, California. Jesus Christ, I thought, I'll never see Eileen!

I stayed with my mother for a week or so, but I couldn't stand it. All I could do was think about Eileen, how far away she was. I'd lost my daughter.

I had to distract my head, get some shit going so I wouldn't have time to think. I moved in with a friend of mine, I'll call Mike Jackson, who owned a motel in the Bronx, where he also lived. Mike was a good guy, but he was about as careful about his finances as I was. He also had a wife and two kids to support, in Jersey, and liked to party. We piled up the bills between us. I couldn't wait for spring training to start, knowing my basic living expenses would be taken care of, and figuring playing ball would help get my head off my loss. I was partying night and day, yet I still had too much time to think.

XII

"Please get over here right away. . . . I'm coming apart."

For me, the 1965 baseball season was one long angonized scream. I tried to muffle it with endless partying and rebelling against authority, and before the season was over I was in Lenox Hill Hospital feeling my mind might snap, crack, pop at any minute.

When the season started I knew my head was in a lot of trouble, but I thought I could arrange enough fun to submerge the loss of my kids and the constant harassment by my creditors. I went to Houk and got permission to room alone on the road. I had to pay the difference between the double rate—the Yankees paid that—and a single. I didn't care. I was already something like forty-thousand dollars in debt. I told the guys that Mantle and Ford had single rooms, and I was a star, too.

Actually, I just didn't want to be bothered with a roommate in those bad times. Linz and I were friends, but we were two very different people, and eventually we'd gotten on each other's nerves. I was a slob and left my dirty clothes piled on the floor until I sent them all out to the cleaner at once. It bugged Phil. It also bugged him when I'd walk into a room with a piece of ass and interrupt his hypnotizing sessions. In '64 he'd bought an album on how to be successful at anything by hypnotizing yourself. I came in one morning around two o'clock and Phil was sitting on his bed staring into the mirror with the record going, repeating its words to himself. I laughed and Phil said, "Jesus, Joe, you broke my concentration." He really got into hypnotism after he tried it and got two hits the next day. He'd psych himself every night, then go 0-for-12 and break his album on hypnotism. Three days later he'd buy another one and start psyching himself again. So while Phil and I were friends, had some terrific laughs together—the few times we jointly partied with girls ended in us laughing ourselves sick— we weren't meant to be roommates. I was a very difficult guy to room with if you were a person who happened to need a normal amount of sleep.

I think what really tore it for Phil and me was an incident at the Concord Hotel after the '64 season. A number of Yankee players who lived around New York were going to this resort in the Catskill Mountains because it was a nice place and there were always a lot of girls there. I happened to be at the Concord once when Phil was there, and I saw him spending a lot of time with one very pretty girl. A few weeks later I was back at the hotel, and so was the girl. We got together and she was sensational. I ran into Phil when I got back and said, "Hey, that girl I saw you with at the Concord, man, she was some piece of ass. Wow! We balled for a whole weekend. . . ." Blah, blah, blah; I went on and on.

What I didn't know was that Phil had been truly smitten by the girl, that he was thinking about her seriously. I kept bumping into him around town after that and he barely spoke to me. Then I found out how he felt, that he had broken off with the girl, and I felt like shit.

Rooming alone didn't help my wallet in 1965. I was so short of cash that I'd order all my meals in my room and sign for them. Then I'd have the daily meal money, which was nine or ten dollars, to spend. Of course, hotel room meals ran twenty to thirty dollars a crack. I also had parties and signed for everything. When we got back from the road trip, instead of getting a check for, say two thousand dollars, I'd get one for two hundred dollars. "What's going on?" I'd ask. "Incidentals on the road, Joe. You're a pretty big spender." When we returned from one road trip, I got a paycheck for—I didn't believe it but it was printed right on it—fifteen dollars. That was when I asked for a roommate again.

I was lucky to be able to move in with Tom Tresh, because I was really beginning to come apart by this time. I'd played with Tom at Binghamton in 1960 and made the Yankees with him in 1962, and I'd always liked him. But it wasn't until I started rooming with him that I found out what a special kind of person he was. He didn't bitch about my dirty clothes piled on the floor of our room. I'd come in and find them hung up. Tommy never said a word to me. I'd say to myself, Jesus Christ, this guy didn't call me a slob, didn't say anything; he just hung up my clothes for me.

Tom Tresh became like a big brother to me. He never *told* me what to do. But he was concerned about me, he advised me, made *suggestions* about my behavior that I knew were heartfelt, and in my interest. I was out every night, fucking around all the time, and going badly on the field. There was no way anyone could do well on the field keeping my hours. Tommy would suggest it wasn't the best thing for *me,* that it might be hurting *me.* I'd never had anyone talk to me like he did—a father, a mother, an uncle, a brother who sat down with me and calmly, quietly, suggested a way to act that might be better for me, without *telling* me this was what I *had* to do.

Tommy would point out that we had a doubleheader the following afternoon, that I wasn't hitting well and that it might be better if I didn't stay out until four or five in the morning, that I might be stronger, fresher, quicker with the bat. I would listen and nod, say yeah, yeah, that makes sense. Then, of course, I would talk to my cock and see how it felt about going out. If it would say, "We're going to get a piece of ass," I would go. When you're into escapes, when you're running from pain, you run no matter what else you hear. But I didn't know what I was actually doing until I talked to a psychiatrist years later. All I knew was that I was distracting my mind—and that was desperately necessary.

I'd say, "Thanks, Tommy, you're right. But I gotta go out."

"Okay," he'd say, understanding. I think back on all those nights now and marvel at the guy, at how well he knew the human condition, how he could stay cool when he cared for me, when he offered up some simple truths yet saw me continually going off on my self-destructive course. He never got angry with me. That, it seemed to me, was the greatest kind of affection.

I'd come in at five o'clock in the morning, or not at all, and I wouldn't see Tommy until the next day at the ball park. I'd look like death, having done what he knew I would do, and he'd say with genuine concern, "How are you, roomie?" That was all.

Where I'd been wacked out in other years, had to pursue chicks almost every night, now I not only had to pursue them every night, one conquest per evening was not enough. I'd see a girl, get off with her, say good night, then go out in search of another one. There were some nights when we were on the road, where I wouldn't score, of if I did I wouldn't have a chick to bring back to the room with me. I'd come in at four, five, six in the morning, whatever, go to bed and lie there, tossing and turning, get up to get a drink of water and stand with it at the window, staring out. And the debts would enter my mind, all the bill collectors who were after me. And Eileen, my daughter, who was so far away in California, and whom *I* had lost, whom *I* had deserted, had left with a mother I didn't respect who, in my deranged mind, would foul up the child, unintentionally not do the right thing by my little girl, just as my father, unintentionally, had not done the right thing by me. I knew in my heart that I was not prepared to fully and consistently give Eileen and Joseph what they needed. But, God, how I wanted to be able to. And the beat went on.

I'd be back in the room empty-handed, no warmth in my bed, and I'd get up, get dressed, and go back down into the streets, the bars now closed, no place to go, and I'd look for a chick. I'd stand on the corner and look for a prostitute, an old lady —any woman who happened to come by. Sometimes they would. Women with warts on their faces and age on their bodies, the dregs of the street, still out at 5 A.M., looking for a trick, a hapless soul like me. I'd take their hands, lead them up to my bed, telling myself, "Fuck Bo Belinsky and the guys who hang out with stars, with nothing but beauties all the time. Somebody's got to fuck the ugly broads."

Tommy Tresh loved his wife, had a good thing going at home, and we hung out a lot, but he'd peel off after dinner and a few drinks and go back to our room. I'd go out in search of girls. I don't think getting laid was as important as the pursuit. I remember Vic Ziegel, a writer for the New York *Post,* telling me that he'd admired my coolness one day in Kansas City. I didn't know what he was talking about. It seemed that the day we'd checked into the Muehlebach Hotel he'd been standing by the desk when I walked up and asked for my room key.

"You're Joe Pepitone!" the girl at the desk had said.

"That's right," I'd said.

"I *know,*" she'd said. "I'm coming in my pants."

I'd taken my key and walked away, according to Ziegel. The point is that I don't even remember what she'd said. "Was she nice, Vic?"

"Joe, you know the girl," he told me. "She's a knockout."

I don't remember.

I do remember many nights sitting in the lobby of the Muehlebach Hotel in Kansas City between eleven and one, because that was where the airline stewardesses checked in. Two fine-looking girls would come in, I'd casually follow them to the desk, overhear their names and room numbers, go to my room and call them.

"Hey, Michele, you don't know how lucky you are," I'd say. "The New York Yankees are staying here tonight, and there's a party in room 704. Can you make it? Beautiful, see you in fifteen minutes." They'd knock, I'd open the door standing there in my shorts, with Tommy sitting in the room behind me. They'd laugh and come in, or suggest what I might do to myself. If they walked away, I'd get dressed and go back to the lobby. I don't think it ever took more than two tries to acquire company. The girls who flew into the Muehlebach were fun, and Tommy was very understanding.

The worse my head got, the more bizarre my escapes became. I'd bring a girl into our room at 3 A.M. and Tommy would be asleep until the bedsprings woke him. Then, very coolly, he'd sleepily raise his hand in front of his face and peek through his fingers at us. He was a fantastic actor. I'd be really into it, glance at him, and see him make a little signal: *Move over this way a mite so I can see better.* I'd be laughing and balling at the same time.

I loved to party with groups, to direct the action with another couple or two. "Pardon me, would you move your tongue down a little lower? Fine. Thank you." If it was a good show, I'd applaud. If it was a bad show, I'd boo. It was fun while it was happening, I didn't think of anything else during the performances. A great escape.

Mike Jackson and I rented an apartment together in Phil Linz's building on the East Side during the season. Mike still owned the motel in the Bronx, but he was also managing the Pussy Cat bar in the city, scrambling to make a buck. About 75 percent of the tenants in our building were airline stewardesses, which was very pleasant, and it simplified party arrangements. There were girls in our place twenty-four hours a day. They'd stop by in shifts. We were fucking so much and showering so often that at times we'd run out of towels. We had to dry ourselves with bed sheets.

We had only one bedroom, and one guy had to sleep on the couch that opened up in the living room. Mike and I had a deal. Whoever got there first with a chick for the night got to use the bedroom. The guy in the room would leave a bat outside the door as a signal that he was in with a girl. No one would be disturbed. It worked fine until the night I had the room and rushed off the next morning on a road trip. I forgot to move the bat, and the girl I was with must have closed the door behind us. I was away for five days. When I got back, I walked in carrying my luggage and found Mike asleep in the living room. He sat up rubbing sleep out of his eyes.

"What the hell are you doing?" he asked.

"What am I doing? Coming back from a road trip."

"You've been on a road trip? When did you leave?"

"Five days ago. What the fuck are you doing sleeping out here?" Then I saw the closed bedroom door and the bat outside it. I roared. Mike never got in till early in the morning, he was working all the time, and hadn't realized the Yankees had gone out of town for a quick trip. He had abided by the bat.

We had some wild times because of our mutual financial problems. We'd run up bills at the local grocery stores, couldn't pay them, and get cut off. I'd met Rocky Lee, who owned a restaurant and bar in the area, through Julius LaRosa and Jerry Vale, so Mike and I started running up a tab there. We'd stop by and pick up takeout orders, or call and have them deliver food to our apartment. When the bill totaled a thousand dollars, we couldn't even go there any more. It was becoming harder and harder to eat in New York City.

I always had a little money, but I couldn't afford to pay my bills and still be able to go out at night. When I got paid, some nights I'd spend five hundred, six hundred dollars, bounce all over the city and pick up every check. I'd be with guys worth $200,000, $300,000, and I'd pay the bill in the restaurant, act like a big man. Berserk! And I kept buying toys. I had a beautiful, brand-new Pontiac and I was driving down the street and saw the newest Corvette. Wow! I drove right to the nearest dealer, traded the Pontiac—at a huge loss —and tooled away in a new Corvette. It was repossessed two months later, of course. A guy from the finance company showed up at the stadium.

"You're going to have to make a payment, Mr. Pepitone," he said, "or I'm going to have to take the car."

"Well, this little problem is easily solved, sir; it's no problem at all," I said, reaching for my wallet and looking inside. "You're gonna have to take the car." I walked away. "The ashtrays are full, anyway."

My creditors were getting somewhat impatient. I was receiving daily letters, phone calls. So were the Yankees, and my mother. My mother was very cool: "Joe Pepitone? No, I don't have a son named Joe. My sons are named Jimmy and Billy and they are New York City policemen."

But the collection men were out after me in force. I had to be the first guy at the ball park and the last one to leave in order to avoid them. Once, when we flew in from a road trip, I got off the plane at LaGuardia and a guy came up to me and said, "Excuse me, Joe. Can I get your autograph?" He handed me two pieces of paper, one on top of the other.

I signed my name and the guy walked away. "Hey, here's the autograph," I said.

"Who the fuck wants *your* autograph?" he said. "Look underneath."

I looked at the bottom sheet of paper. It was a subpoena to appear in court about a long-overdue bill. I started checking out every piece of paper before I accepted it from an autograph-seeker. I got so many subpoenas I became paranoid. I'd see a guy with a piece of paper the size of a baseball card and wonder, Do they make subpoenas that small? The other players would look out for me: "Joe, that guy's a process server." I'd duck, hustle away. When I'd get a summons to appear in court, I'd give it to my attorney and he'd go. A $600 bill from three years ago was now $875, and my lawyer would have to make a settlement. "All my client can pay you is two hundred thirty. He's flat broke. You can take that or you can take nothing and get on line to collect. You'll be number three hundred eight-four on line." The guy would take the money and run. Not even a thank you.

It was a bitch trying to play baseball with all the worries about bill collectors. I thought any day one of them would run on the field and serve me in front of twenty thousand people. I'd go up to bat, the pitcher would release the ball, and I'd see a bill flying up to the plate.

When I wasn't thinking about debts, I was thinking about Eileen, which was worse, much worse. I would be sitting in the dugout during a game, and all of a sudden I wouldn't know what was happening on the field. My daughter's words on the day I left would flash into my mind: "Daddy, don't leave me." Tears would come to my eyes and I'd bow my head so no one could see me wipe them away. I didn't want to let anyone know what I was going through, to show any weakness. But I couldn't keep those words from shooting into my head—in the clubhouse, in the on-deck circle, at bat, in the field—"Daddy don't leave me." I realized that I wouldn't be seeing Eileen any more—the Yankees didn't even visit Oakland then—that I had lost her forever, and no matter what escapes I engaged in, I couldn't permanently escape that fact. Lord, I tried. I couldn't bear to be alone. I had to be around people all the time, had to have a lot of things happening, anything that might keep me from thinking.

It didn't always work, though, no matter how much I went out, how much I partied. I'd be with a chick, really getting it on, balling away, and *wham*—"Daddy, don't leave me". Then I'd instantly slip out, be left with nothing but wrinkled skin and the feeling that my head was about to explode. I look back on it now and I am sure I never would have gotten through this period if I hadn't been so young, if I hadn't been able to trick myself into *not* thinking. If I'd been older, more mature, if I had *known* anything, I would have been forced to think—and they would have had to haul me away.

But all of this didn't do a lot for me as a ballplayer. With the boozing and lack of sleep, I was never in shape. It wasn't that I drank that much, but most of my time in bed I spent fucking or trying to fuck. Small wonder I loafed on the field. When you're hitting well, it doesn't matter what you do at night. You never hear from the guys. I heard from a number of the guys this season: "Joe, you didn't run out that ground ball. You're making us all look bad, as if you don't care."

"Fuck you," I'd say.

Ralph Houk called me into the front office to see him. He'd observed my half-assed play, and he knew about my debts and that I had split with my family. "Is the divorce bothering you?" he asked.

"No, shit no," I told him, refusing to admit there was anything wrong other than the financial problems.

"Well, what's on your mind?" he asked. "What's bugging you?"

"I don't know," I said. "The whole team's going bad. It's depressing."

The whole team *was* going bad. We were in sixth place all season. Roger Maris, Elston Howard, Tony Kubek, and Mantle were all injured. Mickey drove in forty-six runs in '65. Bouton won exactly four games. I batted .247, hit eighteen home runs, and drove in all of sixty-two runs, and nobody looked as bad on the field as I did at times. Even Mantle got annoyed one day.

I think I lost about three inches of hair off the front of my head this season, and after a game it would take me twenty minutes to get the remaining hair to cover the bare spot. I combed and combed to get it just right after one game in which I hadn't hustled on a play in the outfield. Mantle was sitting next to me rubbing ointment on his aching knees and watching me. When I finally finished and gave my hair a last pat, Mantle stood and mussed it with his ointment-smeared hand. "Damn it," he said, "that's what you deserve." He was right, but if it had been anybody except Mickey, I would've smashed him in the face.

There was a moment in '65 when I came close to punching manager Johnny Keane. The guy who'd beaten us in the '64 Series with the Cardinals had become Yogi Berra's replacement, and Keane and I didn't hit it off from the beginning. Keane reportedly got upset in spring training when he heard I was after his daughter. I didn't understand why he was upset. Shit, I was after everyone's daughter. He must have fined me nine or ten times during the season. Once, though, he was absolutely wrong and I got furious. Hell, there were certainly enough legitimate reasons to fine me. On this day there were several bad accidents on the Belt Parkway. I was coming from a visit to my mother, and I sat in traffic, not moving an inch, for ninety minutes. I got to the park only thirty minutes before game time, and explained to Keane what had happened.

"At least you could think of an *original* excuse," he said. "That'll cost you two-hundred and fifty dollars."

"That's not an excuse—it's the damn truth!" I yelled angrily.

"The fine stands," he said. "Now get your uniform on in a hurry and get on the field."

"How the hell much money do you think I'm making?" I asked him. "Every time I turn around you're fining me. Two-fifty, huh? Why don't you make it a thousand? And take it out of next year's pay. You already got this year's!"

"Get on the field," he said. He stormed out of the clubhouse, slamming the door behind him.

Which was a lucky thing for both of us, because I'd had enough. My uniform shirt was half buttoned and I ripped it off my back and threw a wooden stool across the dressing room. The game was starting by the time I got to the dugout.

As if I didn't have enough shit coming down on me, Mike Jackson and I had some bad vibes and I had to find another place to live. One day I went to the cleaner to pick up my

clothes. Most of the stuff I owned was there. But the clerk came
out with a helluva lot more clothes than I owned. I looked
through them and saw that about half the stuff belonged to
Mike. He'd put all his cleaning on my bill. I really got pissed
off. He was heavily in debt, but he wasn't in my league. I went
back to the apartment, threw him against the wall, smacked
him a couple of times, and cursed him out.

A few days later I arranged to move into Roger Maris's
apartment in Kew Gardens, Queens. Relief pitcher Hal Reniff,
who had been sharing the place with Roger, had recently married a girl in the building. Then I went to a furniture buyer and
sold all the furnishings in my apartment. Barbara had left a lot
of our stuff in the house, and everything in the apartment Mike
and I shared belonged to me. He really wasn't a bad guy, but
I was still so angry with him I didn't tell him I'd sold the
furniture. Two days later four men walked into the apartment
when Mike was sleeping and cleared out everything in the place
until they got to the bed. Then they woke him up.

"Would you mind getting up, mister? That bed belongs to
us."

I picked up my money, then went by the apartment to tell
Mike I was moving, though I suspected he had a clue. He was
sitting on the carpet in the living room, smoking a cigarette and
flicking the ashes into an empty soup can.

"Couldn't you at least let me know in advance what you're
doing, man?"

"Sure," I said. "But you're an asshole. Sleep on the floor."

It wasn't a nice thing to do, and Mike and I weren't friends
again until about a year later. But that's where my head was
then. On a countdown to derangement.

By the end of the regular-season schedule, I was literally
disassembling before my very eyes. We had four games left to
play in Boston, and I couldn't face them. I could barely face
myself in the mirror, and I didn't know what I was going to do.
But I felt it was something self-destructive, something crazed.
It wouldn't do any good to go out; I couldn't see any even
momentary escape in partying. The party was over. I needed
help.

My family posing after a family wedding, left to right: me at age seven, my tough father Willie, my beautiful mother Ann holding baby Billy and my brother Jimmy, age five. Love the tuxedos—and Willie's socks.

My amazing grandfather, Vincent Caiazzo, on his sixty-ninth birthday, holding my cousin Clair. Jimmy, at right, is six, and I am eight, minus one tooth. Vincent is now ninety-two and still looks the same.

Rockaway's Playl
1957: My brother Jin
fourteen, and me, six
at a shooting gall
Jimmy's been a good
ever since. In fact, not
ago, as a New York
detective, he got shot i
head. Didn't hurt him

After my first workout in Florida, I sent this photo to my
mother and wrote: "Don't mind
the looks, it's not the looks that
make a ballplayer. The man with
me has the world's biggest collection of autographed baseballs."

Clinching the pennant in my first full season with the Yankees, 1963. I hit a home run and got rid of the dry look as Johnny Blanchard, who also homered, and Jim Bouton, who pitched the 2-0 shutout against the Twins, poured champagne on my head. (UPI)

alph Houk became gen-
al manager after the 1963
ason and quickly signed
e to a new contract. I
rdly looked at the salary
gure. In those days I
ould have played for
othing. (WIDE WORLD)

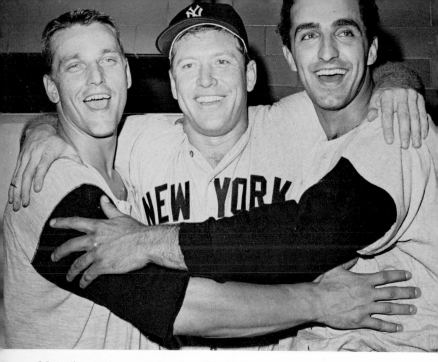

My only great game at bat in a World Series. I hit a grand-slam home-run and Roger Maris, at left, and Mickey Mantle hit solo homers, as we evened the 1964 series against the Cardinals. (UPI)

My batting average was a miserable .154 in that 1964 series, but I was proud of my fielding. Here Lou Brock tried to bunt past me, and I touched his sole. Out. (UPI)

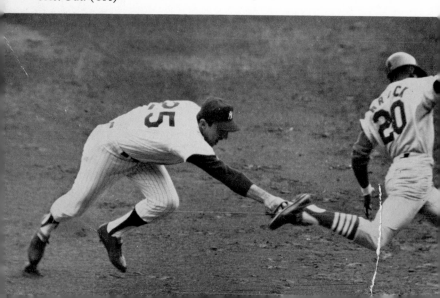

Classic home-run hitting form in 1966—when I had thirty-one. (UPI)

In 1967 I hit exactly thirteen home runs, then made a comeback in 1968, above—hitting fifteen. Nobody's perfect. (UPI)

Posing in 1969 with my idol, Joe DiMaggio. When I had a long hitting streak, writers asked me if I was going for Joe D's record of hitting in 56 consecutive games. "No way I'd want to break his record," I said—lying. (WIDE WORLD).

Midway through the 1970 season, I went to work for Leo Durocher and the Chicago Cubs. I already knew Leo was my kind of manager. Hadn't he introduced me to Frank Sinatra? (WIDE WORLD)

At an off-season show at Chicago's Mill Run Playhouse in 1970, I sang into a microphone held by Milton Berle. He smiled. (WIDE WORLD)

the Cubs' Arizona ng-training camp with hanie Deeker, who be- e Stephanie Pepitone, favorite person. Incred- pretty, incredibly pa- t, *incredible*.

At "Joe Pepitone's Thing," the lounge I owned in Chicago that was so successful but didn't last. What else is new?

I called my two best friends from the neighborhood, Lemon and Fat John. And I called my Uncle Louie. People I could trust, could count on, was safe with. I told them all the same thing.

"I'm in my apartment in Queens. I'm coming apart. Please . . . please come over here right away, or you're not gonna see me again. I need . . . I need someone with me. Right away."

They all came, my friends, within the hour, and I sucked it in, got myself semi-together. The club went to Boston without me that day, and Houk called.

"Ralph, I'm sorry," I said, "I just couldn't make another trip with that man [Johnny Keane]. I'm coming apart. I'm going out of my fucking mind."

"All right, Joe, take it easy," he said, seeming to understand. "I'll call you right back."

In two minutes he did. "Joe, listen to me," he said. "You've got to do me a favor. You owe me a favor, right?"

"Right."

"Just to protect the club, let me put you in the hospital for the last four days of the season."

"No, Ralph, I'm not going in any fucking hospital." I didn't want people picking at my head. I just wanted to get through these last nights of the season, to get away from the hopeless goddamn season I'd gone through, and I figured I could work out the personal shit myself. People who don't know anything always think that.

But Ralph kept talking to me, talking to me, telling me he'd appreciate the favor, telling me I could rest up, that I would feel better, that I had to be near exhaustion after the hours I'd been keeping for so many months. He finally talked me into going to Lenox Hill Hospital, and I went that night. I'm sure now, in retrospect, that his "protect the club" line was a ruse to get me to some shrinks, to try and help me. I had so much ability, and the Yankees needed me straightened out, if that was possible to achieve. I guess Houk wanted to know if it was, too.

It was great in the hospital. Four days of total rest, and the psychiatrists came right away, a man and a woman. My mind was engaged with fooling them for the entire stay. They questioned me every day, and I really didn't tell them anything—

about Willie, about Eileen, about any of the guilt that was smothering me. I didn't even tell them about all the debts. I put the whole thing on Johnny Keane and baseball, that it was fucking me up, that I couldn't stand the regimentation, the authority telling me how to dress, how long to wear my hair, telling me everything I had to do like I was a child. I'm not a child, I told them. I'm twenty-five years old and I'm a good professional baseball player if people would just leave me alone and let me play baseball and not lay a lot of bullshit on me that has nothing to do with baseball. I yelled, ranted, raved, got a lot of shit off my chest.

But none of the real shit. I didn't talk about any of the heavy stuff that was happening inside me. I'm not sure I understood even half of it then, but I knew damn well I didn't want anyone to know about what I had done to my father and my own first-born child, my little daughter. I wanted them to think that, except for a few superficial things, this guy is okay. Both of the psychiatrists kept walking out shaking their heads, as if to say, this guy is crazy, but not really. Just momentarily disturbed.

It was a hell of an act. It always was. People always thought of me as the happiest, wackiest guy in the world. Shit, I'd worked hard enough to conjure that image and sustain it. I didn't want to show the pain underneath, that I had any weakness, anything that was beyond my control, that was eating at my head. Who wanted to be around a man who was living in agony? Who, I wondered subconsciously, could possibly love such a man?

XIII

"Get your clothes on and get out of here."

There was one bit of light in that horror-show season of '65. I met a tough, sharp, beautiful girl, the girl I would marry early in 1966. She was an actress named Diane Sandre, who had appeared on Broadway with Alan Arkin in *Enter Laughing*. She was working as a cocktail waitress at the Pussy Cat, and one day I gave Mike Jackson two tickets to a game and he showed up at the stadium with her. I saw them sit down just before the game started, and she knocked me over. I've got to meet her, I said to myself.

It so happened that the first time up that day I hit a home run. The seats I'd gotten for Mike were right behind and on the first-base end of the Yankee dugout. After rounding the bases, instead of running into the home-plate end of the dugout—the normal point of entry—I trotted up to where Diane was sitting and gave her a shit-eating smile, like, Not bad, huh? When I ducked into the dugout, Mike later told me, Diane said to him, "Did you see that clown?"

I didn't know this, of course. When I hit another home run in the fifth inning, I again entered the far end of the dugout, only this time I gave Diane a big wink and ticked the bill of my cap to her. "What a silly sonofabitch!" she said to Mike. "Your friend has to be the world's biggest jerk. Let's get out of here."

"Wait till the end of the game," Mike said. "He got me the tickets."

"Screw him," she said.

121

I ran out on the field after the inning and looked over to give the chick a nod—and I saw the seats were empty, that she and Mike were gone. What the hell happened? I wondered. Maybe they're gonna meet me after the game.

They didn't. I went to the Pussy Cat that night, was introduced to Diane, and came right on with some bullshit like, "How would you like to go out with a *star* later?" It was not effective with Diane. I went in there every night we were home after that and tried to get a date with her. Two months later I was still trying. So late one Friday night, with the place jammed body on body, I was in there and she was waiting for an order at the service bar. I elbowed my way over, dropped down on my knees in front of her, and yelled at the top of my lungs: *"What the fuck do I have to do to get a date with you? How long do I have to stay on my knees to get you to go out with me?"*

"Shh, you crazy bastard," she said in a half-whispered plea. "Get up off your knees."

I didn't move.

"I'll meet you when I get off—*just get up off your kneees!*"

I embarrassed her into going out with me. We stopped for one drink, then went right to her apartment and I smoked a joint. (I'd smoked marijuana occasionly ever since I was seventeen.) Diane was just an all-time super chick. Very deep, very sharp—much sharper, more mature than I was. I dug the shit out of her.

I got her into bed and got right to it. As I finished, Diane looked up into my eyes and said, "Get your clothes on and get out of here. You are *terrible.*"

That destroyed my ego, and I got mad as hell, throwing on my clothes as fast as I could and cursing her. As I walked out the door I heard her say, "What a mistake."

I had to go right back out on the street and find another girl to fuck—prove to myself I'm *good.* Actually, that wasn't the first bedroom complaint I'd heard. I was generally a maniac in bed: open your legs, let me put it in, bang, bang, ooooh, off. That's the way I was. I'd ball a girl and I wouldn't want to be with her again. Thanks for the memory. I wanted a different girl every night, one after another, after another, after another. And every conceivable type: blacks, whites, Puerto Ricans, Chinese, Indians, Serbo-Croations . . . you name it, I'd surely love to try it.

I can't relate to this behavior today, don't know what drove me to act this way, except that it did something for my ego. I kept at it after that night with Diane, didn't go back to the Pussy Cat because she had cut me too deeply. But I couldn't get her out of my mind, and a few weeks later I ran into her one night in another bar. She was pleasant, a damn nice, intriguing girl. We sat around talking, and the next thing I knew three hours had gone by. I had never been able to sit around with anyone just rapping for hours, and I was particularly hyper at this time, I had to keep bouncing around, doing something. But I actually enjoyed talking to Diane, relaxed with her. She was so intelligent, so hip, made so much sense to me. She was different from any girl I'd ever met. I made an *effort* to get to know her, to listen to her, which was a unique experience for me. Soon after the season ended, we started dating.

Diane introduced me to her friends, who were entirely different from the racket guys I'd been hanging around with. Like Diane, her friends were all hip, relaxed, nice. They'd sit around and just rap all evening. This was at a time when a large percentage of people in this country were rising up against the Vietnam War, when the kids were burning their draft cards, marching in protest: "Ho, Ho, we won't go!" I wasn't into politics. These people made a lot of sense, and I'd sit around and listen and nod because they did make sense. After a while, though, I wanted Diane and me to get going so that we could get laid. But she was digging the conversation, contributing to it. And I'd start recalling the Korean War, when I was a young kid, and all the guys in my neighborhood were saying, "Man, that's what I want to do. My uncle, he's a Marine, and that's what I want to be, go over there and kill gooks." I wouldn't say anything, because everyone had the same point of view, until they'd ask me, "What about you, Joe, wouldn't you like to get over to Korea and kill some of those gooks?" I'd have to say, "No, man, that's not me. That's bullshit. Those gooks aren't fucking with me. I don't want to be a hero. I don't want to get dead." "Man, they'd say, you're chicken. You don't want to fight for your country." "Right," I'd say. "I don't want to fight anyone. You guys know me. I just want to go my own way."

I would offer up those conversations in the rap sessions with Diane and her friends, because that's the way I really felt. I wasn't hip, I wasn't political, but from way back I was very much into doing my own thing. And I always thought that fighting was ridiculous, that only crazy people went out looking to fight. Now people were going off to fight and die just because some politician told them to, and it was pure bullshit. This was something I felt and dug talking about. If a kid refused to go to war, didn't want to fight—fuck it, don't fight. At that time, a kid who refused to go to war knew he'd have to hide for the rest of his life, which was something I couldn't do, which took a lot of guts. But if that was what he had to do, right on.

Diane and her friends opened my mind on this subject, and I enjoyed being with them. They were into a lot of what seemed to me heavy subjects. And they never talked to me about baseball. They asked me about what I was into. They asked me about *me.* For the first time since I'd been playing ball professionally in New York, I felt bigger than my Yankee label, that my identity wasn't totally locked into a baseball uniform. I didn't have to come on with bullshit with them—I did to some degree, me still being me, but not as much, because I was relaxed enough to feel like a whole, regular person for hours at a time.

My debts had been battering me all season, and now I didn't even have that lump of World Series money to ease any of the pressure. I not only wasn't making payments to support my children in California, I couldn't even pay the rent on my Queens apartment. It was suggested that I find other quarters. The girl who was sharing Diane's apartment moved out, and Diane took care of me. She was earning four to five hundred dollars a week as a waitress. Just about every cent I earned had to go to creditors to keep me out of jail. My head would have survived about nine and a half seconds in jail.

In February 1966, Diane and I got married. The Yankees found a financial adviser and attorney, Bill Sherr, to handle my money problems. My debts now amounted to something like

$70,000, and the Yankees were paying me about $23,000. All my checks went to Sherr; he gave me fifty dollars a week to live on and used the rest to make settlements with my creditors. It took me two and a half years to get out of debt. The first year I got fifty dollars a week. The second year Sherr gave me a tremendous raise to sixty dollars, and nothing extra. He was very strict.

I remember going to him just before Diane and I were celebrating our first anniversary. "Bill," I said, "I just can't make it. We've got to have more money to celebrate our anniversary. Let me have a hundred dollars." I'd been to him many times and begged for more money, and he'd never given in. Even for emergencies. Diane had become pregnant, and we'd moved out of the city and taken an apartment in Fort Lee, New Jersey, and we needed a second car. It was a necessity. He'd said all I could afford was a used car, and he looked around until he found one. So now, when I went to plead with him for a lousy hundred dollars for our anniversary, I got down on my knees in front of his desk and said, "Bill, please, just this once—just a hundred dollars."

He reached over his desk and handed me thirty dollars.

Ralph Houk called me into the Yankee offices on Fifth Avenue and talked to me that fall. He told me I had to change my ways or I wasn't going to be a Yankee much longer.

"Are you going to trade me?" I asked him.

"I couldn't get much for you right now," he said. "If I could get a decent player for you, I might do it. But all they offer are some mediocre guys who are four or five years older than you. I'd rather keep you, but you've got to change."

"I want to stay with the Yankees," I said.

"Then show me," Houk said. "It makes me sick the way you're throwing your life away. My God, what a future you have. You could almost be a Joe DiMaggio. You can do it all —run, throw, hit all kinds of pitching. There's no telling how far you can go. You should drive in a hundred runs every year."

"I know," I said. "I had a lot of trouble this year, Ralph . . . the debts, the family split . . ."

"I know about your troubles, Joe. I'm sorry. But that's all

behind you now. You can't destroy your life. You have to think of yourself. You've got to start thinking about baseball as a business. You should be making forty thousand by now, on the basis of what other players are being paid."

"I know, Ralph. And I'm going to change. I am."

"It's not just for yourself, either," he said. "It's for your teammates. You owe them an honest effort. You're not playing up to your ability. You have great potential. You have more than potential, because you've proved what you can do."

Then he told me to get a haircut, and I promised I would. I meant to, until I read about our conversation in Dick Young's column in the New York *Daily News*. I don't know how Young got his information, but he always seemed to know exactly what was going on in baseball. I know he always had me right, everything he wrote about me. But I was embarrassed. I didn't like to see all that shit in the newspaper. I went to spring training with my hair growing down my back. I started hitting the ball like I did in 1963, and nobody mentioned that my hair was a good deal longer than the basball "style." Long hair was "in" throughout the rest of the world, but baseball managers tended to think you hit with a crew cut. When my batting average dropped fifty points at the end of spring training, I got a trim to keep the bullshit from raining down on me. Just a little off the back, please.

In the opening game of the season, I hit a home run and a single off Mickey Lolich of the Tigers, a tough left-hander, and I felt I was going to have a good season. I did. My batting average was only .255, but I led the club in doubles with 21, in RBIs with 83, and in home runs with 31. I'd always been a streak hitter—get 20 hits in 25 at-bats, then go 0-for-20. The '66 season was no exception. In a single month, July, I hit 10 home runs, which gave me 22 at that point. I would have had 40 for the season if I hadn't jammed my right wrist late in August on a slide into second base. Being a wrist hitter, I didn't stroke a home run through the entire month of September. Forty homers would've made for a helluva comeback. I couldn't complain, though. I had to play over forty games in the outfield in '66, as I had in '65, yet I still played enough at first base to win the Gold Glove award as the outstanding fielder in the league at that position for the second year in a row.

The team itself was horseshit. Tony Kubek's bad back forced him to retire before the season even started, Whitey Ford's circulatory problems in his left arm allowed him to win all of two games, and there were all kinds of injuries and aging troubles that struck the Yankees that year. We finished tenth in a ten-team league. After we'd won only four of our first twenty games, Johnny Keane was pushed out as manager and Ralph Houk returned to the dugout. At least I played better for Houk. I liked him because he would never embarrass you in front of the rest of the guys. In private, of course, he could scare the shit out of you.

I remember early in the season I hit a line drive up the alley between left field and center. I thought I'd really nailed that ball and that the left fielder would cut it off and hold me to a single, so I didn't run hard. Well, the ball died, and if I had run hard I could easily have had a double. Ralph had one of the coaches mention it to me. I apologized. Then, in another game, I didn't run out a grounder to the infield. Sure enough, the sonofabitch at shortstop bobbled the ball, but still had time to throw me out. I would have beaten it if I'd run flat out. Ralph got me aside after that, and I promised him I wouldn't dog it any more.

A couple of weeks later I hit a high fly to the outfield, an easy out. I trotted to first. Just as I got there, the outfielder dropped the ball. I should have been on second. Mantle singled behind me, which would have scored me if I'd been on second. The next batter struck out, and we lost a run. We also lost the game by one run.

Afterward, everyone was undressing in the locker room. I was taking off my shirt at my cubicle when I saw Ralph Houk come out of his office—which was right across from me—with a cigar between his teeth and a little smile on his face.

"Pepi," he said, "could I see you for a minute?" He waved me over, still smiling.

I dropped my shirt and walked into his office. I went over to the chair by his desk and sat down. He closed the door behind him and locked it, snapped the bolt. He took the cigar out of his mouth as he turned around, and he was no longer smiling. His eyes were slits and there was a mean look on his face, a kind of controlled anger seething just under the skin. He was a big man and he had a ferocious temper, and I knew there was no way anything good was going to come to me in that room.

He took off his shirt, tossed it in the corner, and said, "Stand up, you prick. I'm gonna knock you on your ass."

"Ralph, what do you mean?" I said. "What the hell's wrong with you?"

"You crossed me," he said, shaking his finger at me. "I told you to run out the goddamn balls, and you loafed again. You are making me look bad, you are making yourself look bad, and you are making the team look bad. Get on your feet, you prick."

"Ralph, I swear to God—I thought he'd catch that pop up, I—"

"Shit on what you *thought!* You crossed me!" He took two steps toward me, his fists balled up.

"Ralph, I swear to God I won't do that again!"

"Don't give me that shit, you always tell me that. Then you go out there and cross me."

He took another step, and I thought he was going to throw a punch. I ducked my head and said, "Ralph, I swear on my *mother*—I'll never do it again. Never!"

I would have signed something, for Christ's sake, anything to show that I wouldn't dog it again. I couldn't win in that situation. There's no way you can hit your manager back. There's no way you want to when your manager's as tough as Ralph Houk. He didn't hit me. He had these little discussions with me periodically, and I think he came very close to rapping me a couple of times. The thing was, after these scenes, I'd hustle like crazy for a few weeks, a month. Then I'd revert to my old pattern, just playing according to my instincts, moods. Fuck the book.

There was no question but that being married to Diane was an important factor in my solid season in 1966. She was a solid woman, younger than me but much more mature, much more together. She'd been through a lot of crap and was very sharp, street-smart. I was somewhat in awe of her.

Diane convinced me to go to a psychiatrist for help. He took me on for nothing, because I only paid him for the first few visits, and he kept seeing me for two years. He helped me with that guilt about Willie, made me realize that I wasn't responsible for his death, showed me that my father had done some things that warped my head a bit. These sessions were both enlightening and depressing. They both took some weight off my mind, and laid some on. But I liked the shrink. I went to see him or called him whenever I really got down, any time at all.

Meanwhile, emotionally I was still about nine years old when it came to being married. I had hardly mumbled my vows when I started fucking around again. It was the same old routine, this hyper need to be out bouncing all the time, scoring with a lot of chicks to massage my ego. When the ball club was home, I wouldn't stay out all night, but I continued to flaunt my activities in front of my wife. Diane and I went out together all the time, and I'd come on with her girl friends. A lot of her very best friends, girls she counted on, were star-struck by a baseball player. They wanted to fuck me, and they'd let me know that, under the table, at a booth in which Diane was sitting with us. I wasn't exactly discreet.

Not surprisingly, I suspected Diane of doing all kinds of fucking around, too. She didn't, she was a good girl, but that's where my head was. I'd been around, she'd been around. I was out screwing, so she had to be. I'd come home from a three-week road trip—during which I'd been to bed with some chick every single night—and I'd immediately start questioning her: "What'd you do the past three weeks?" Then interrogating: "Who was at that party?" "Who brought you home?" "Did you dance with so-and-so?" Blah, blah, blah.

No matter what she said, she was suspect. I was consistently lying very coolly, so I figured she was, even though there were no facts on which I could base my suspicions. It is very difficult to catch someone fooling around when they are not fooling around. But I kept trying.

And I kept fooling around until she caught me. "I'm sorry, Diane," I told her. "It didn't mean anything."

I swore to her that I would not do anything like that again. Then I called my girl friend, whom Diane knew, and told her it was over. It was. Two days later I found another girl friend.

I got caught again, apologized again. It really hurt Diane, cut the shit out of her that I was doing that to her. I felt bad, witnessing her hurt. I felt even worse when I would think about my father, realize that I was following his pattern of hurting someone, and immediately apologizing for it. I kept telling myself, You've got to stop doing that shit, hurting people, then apologizing for it. You know how that hurt you. But I couldn't stop.

I thought I was in love with Diane. She did everything for me, everything she could to help me. She had four thousand dollars saved when we got married, and she gave it to me. I had nothing coming in except the fifty dollars a week spending money. Diane worked till she was a few months pregnant, then I made her quit. When our daughter Lisa was born after the '66 season, Diane went back to work to keep us going. We would never have been able to go out, to have any fun at all, if she hadn't worked as a cocktail waitress. But I was such a jealous bastard I even made her quit that. I'd go to the place she worked and see her get hassled and I'd get pissed off. I couldn't stand to see guys coming up and hugging her, grabbing her leg, bullshit like that. She could handle it, get rid of the guys in a nice way, without causing any bad vibes. I'd see that shit and challenge the guy, want to break his head . . . just like my father.

Diane got angry. We needed the money. I knew it. But I just couldn't tell her how I felt, seeing her at work and guys flirting with her. She'd kid them along, and I'd want her to tell them to go fuck themselves. When she didn't, I took it as a personal putdown, a guy flirting with my wife with me in the place. I felt the guy was saying to himself, "Hey, Joe Pepitone's old lady wants to fuck me." That's what I'd sit there and think, watching the action. And I could never explain it to Diane, never admit how I felt, that my ego was so sensitive, that I bruised so easily. I couldn't tell her that I saw this as a putdown, guys coming on with her, and that I couldn't stand to have anyone put me down, that that was the kind of ego trip I was on. I felt if I told her, I'd be admitting a kind of weakness . . . which was an ultimate putdown.

At the time, it was all very confusing in my head. I didn't even tell the shrink about it. I didn't tell him everything, all my flaws, weaknesses, confusions. I felt if I revealed everything, he'd think I was a total, full-house sicky. So I covered up, kept stumbling along as best I could. It was not best.

Diane had been a good actress and she decided to get back into the profession after I had her quit waitressing. She started going into the city a lot in search of work. I'd call her at her agent's, where she was supposed to be, and she'd be gone. I'd get pissed off, thinking she was fooling around someplace. When she'd come home, we'd have a big brawl because of my jealousy. She'd been out trying to get a job to make some money for us, and I'd start a fight, then go out and screw around. That would make me feel bad and I'd call the shrink, he'd talk to me, relieve the guilt of the moment, I'd feel better, and the beat would go on.

After I'd been talking to the psychiatrist for about two years, one day he suddenly announced to me, "Joe, I should be with you all the time. You've got a lot of problems and I should travel around with you and the ball club. I'm sure there are a number of players on the Yankees I could see as well as you."

I went berserk. "Will you look at what you're doing? I'm coming to you for help, you seem to really like me, you're helping me get some things straightened out in my head—and here I see you're just trying to use me. You've been helping me just to use me. You're a phoney, man." I never spoke to him again. I went off, alone again, on my merry way.

XIV

"I think I'm old enough to handle it now."

When my daughter Lisa was born in November 1966, I again got off on the parent trip. She was as beautiful as her mother. But I just couldn't handle marriage. I cared about Diane, but I cared about myself so much more that we never had a chance. All I really thought about was keeping my fun-ball rolling. I don't know why I married her, knowing full well that I wasn't about to settle down, work at a one-to-one relationship. All I knew was that I felt the need to have somebody there, somebody I could count on to love me. I guess I also had a need to constantly test that love.

I was even more crazed the second year of our marriage. We had some great times together, really nice, just the two of us. It was a new experience sitting home and enjoying being with a wife. There was often a third party present, though: pot. We didn't have that many good vibes when I was straight, because I couldn't sit still, could seldom relax. But when I was smoking dope, I'd relax and really listen to what Diane had to say, groove on her words, on being with her. And, of course, pot was the greatest thing in the world for balling, intensified the pleasure of every texture. I was such a child that I always felt guilty if I didn't feel like balling. There were times when I was just too tired, when the night had run on too long. But I felt I *had* to fuck, that I had to prove myself to Diane. That's where my head was. I was into so much bullshit at this time that I look back now and marvel at the fact that I didn't completely disintegrate.

132

The Yankees gave me a $15,000 raise after my thirty-one home runs in '66. I was making $38,000 a year and living on $50 a week. Although Diane was Jewish, she turned out to be a fantastic Italian cook, and I went to spring training weighing 218 pounds. It took me weeks to get into shape, which didn't help my quickness in the outfield. I had been switched to center field so that Mickey Mantle could move to first base and save his aching legs. I got a kick out of working around the bag with my idol, giving him tips on the footwork you have to employ at first. Mickey was a natural.

I was loose, enjoying the training season. "This is going to be my year," I told the sportswriters. "I have the best contract I've ever had, my mind is free, and everything looks great. I won the Gold Glove the past two years at first base, now my goal is to win it as an outfielder. I don't think anyone's ever won the Gold Glove at two positions."

One of the writers asked me if I would showboat it as much in the outfield, and I told him, "Sure, I'm a bit of a showboat. If I'm feeling free and easy and can showboat a little, then I hit better, play better, and enjoy baseball more. I've always hit better as an outfielder, perhaps because I don't have to worry about fielding as much there.

"I like to hear the fans' reaction, so I'm looking forward to playing center field. If you make a good play at first base, there's polite applause. But if you make a sensational catch or a good throw in the outfield, they come right up out of their seats. That's what I like."

It was true. I loved to have the fans react to me. That's why I'd always been something of a hot dog on the field. Why not give fans something to turn them on? Baseball is essentially a dull game with a lot of dead time between plays. I always believed that the players who gave the fans something extra to yell about were doing the game a service. They booed me more than they cheered me, on balance, but I loved all the noise I drew.

I gave everyone ample reason to boo in 1967. I was back on the old nightly partying treadmill, staying up till all hours of the morning. And at age twenty-six, I just couldn't bounce back as quickly any more. Not being in shape also made me susceptible to injuries. I missed thirty games with injuries that season, and there were a lot of others I played in hurting. I had to play, because it seemed half the team was in Lenox Hill Hospital that season. Only their injuries weren't the result of screwing around at night. I kept getting hit on my right elbow at bat, which sapped my power. On a couple of those fast balls, I think I was just too tired to get out of the way. On the season I hit exactly thirteen home runs, drove in sixty-four runs, and batted .251. Those 64 RBIs led the team. No wonder we finished next to last.

Diane had managed to hold up through a season of bad times. She was hanging in, struggling along, trying to keep us going. But the key to our ultimate split went into the lock on the season's final day.

I had the names and phone numbers of about 150 girls I'd been balling written on slips of paper in my cubicle at the stadium. We had to clean out our lockers for the incoming football Giants, and I put all those slips of paper in a suitcase, along with some other things I wouldn't be needing over the winter. I told Pete Sheehy, the clubhouse man, to store that bag for me at the stadium. I had to go off to a banquet right after the game. A limousine was picking me up, and a friend was dropping off my wife to drive my car home. I had another suitcase of clothes that I did want for the winter, and I told Pete to put that in the trunk of my car.

"Fine, Joe," he said. "No sweat."

No sweat, shit. He put the wrong suitcase in my car. I did the banquet out on the Island and got home late that night. I opened our apartment door, and Diane was sitting on the couch with a drink in her hand, looking like she'd been crying all evening. Her eyes were red, puffy . . . and full of pain.

Laid out on the carpeting like a mad mosaic were those 150 slips of paper with a girl's name and telephone number on each of them. And among the batch were names of Diane's closest girl friends I'd balled. For one of the few times in my life, I couldn't think of anything to say. I just stood there, staring at all that bloody evidence, and feeling the pain on my wife's face creep into my stomach.

Diane finally got up off the couch. "Sit down, Joe," was all she said. Then she turned, walked into the bedroom, and closed the door.

I walked through that sea of paper with the names scrawled

on them, and every time I saw the name of one of her girl friends, I felt a jab in my gut. I lay down on the couch, but I didn't sleep that night.

In the morning I apologized, I was sincerely sorry—I always was, every time I hurt her—because I felt shitty myself. Diane still didn't say anything, didn't berate me, didn't tell me to get out, as she had every right to. I swore to her that I would stop the shit, and this time I meant it. Or thought I did. I didn't go out for two months, stayed home every night with Diane trying to make up for the agony I had laid on her. It was the only thing I could do.

We tried to make love, and I failed. I couldn't get it up. I tried and tried. Suddenly I wanted her so badly. We waited a few days, and it worked. It was good, very good. Then nothing again. Just sweat and strain and anguished breathing. The next night the good feelings would be back, I'd get excited, we'd jump right into bed, start making it, and—*wham*—the feeling was gone, the guilt was back. And I'd roll away, limply, throw my arm up over my closed eyes, and just lie there with the pounding in my head. "Joe," Diane said, "it's all right." It wasn't all right, nothing was right.

After two solid months of this, I couldn't stand it any more. Diane went out shopping one day, and I just sat there thinking. It was crazy. I couldn't make this work. Even if we got through this, I couldn't change my basic pattern. That lifestyle was the only thing that was getting *me* through the nights. It was bizarre, berserk, but I was making it through to each new dawn, and I didn't see how I would otherwise.

I called our baby-sitter in the building to come stay with Lisa, packed up all my clothes, and left Diane a note: "Nothing's happening, and I don't think anything's going to happen," it said. "We'll see. Joe."

I drove to my mother's house in Brooklyn and waited for Diane to call. I waited and waited, for days. Then I realized: she's not going to call. I sat in my mother's apartment, looking at the old family photographs displayed around the room, and I said to myself, fuck it, it's no good, so forget it. I loved her, but I couldn't live with her. I thought about the night before Diane and I were married. We were driving someplace in the city and we got into a fierce argument. Funny, I couldn't remember what it was about. All I remembered was that I slowed the car as we yelled at one another, slowed to about fifteen miles an hour, and suddenly Diane opened the car door and dove out into the street. I looked out and saw her rolling on the asphalt behind me. I jammed on the brakes and ran to her, held her. That was one way to put an end to an argument.

After five days of sitting around my mother's, I couldn't stand it there, either. I moved in with a friend in Brooklyn. Within two weeks I knew that everyone concerned was better off. I went back to visit Diane and Lisa every so often, stayed overnight. I still couldn't make it with Diane in bed. I tried. Christ, I tried everything I could. I wanted to make it with her, and Diane wanted to make it. Like our marriage, because of me it was just no good.

Then on visits we just began talking, trying to sort things out, ease the pain a bit. Even that was no good. It just brought out all the bad vibes in her, all the shit I'd put her through. I asked her to talk about some of the good times, too, to remember some of the great feelings we'd shared, the nice moments. She'd been hurt too much.

She wanted me to change, to come back. I wish I had been able to change. I wanted to, but I just wasn't ready. I still had to be out, party, be with people. I couldn't stand to be with myself alone.

I had to have a lot of shit going all the time, because I'd get instantly bored, have to move on in minutes. I'd go out with a real dynamite-looking chick—show-off-able pretty, lovely breasts, perfect legs. One night, and it would be over for me. I had to go elsewhere. As soon as I balled a girl, case closed. It was the same with a hard-to-get chick. I'd stay after her for days, weeks. Till I balled her. Then the challenge was over and I wouldn't see her again. I didn't want to get involved with anyone. I'd been involved twice too many times.

At first I worried about how I'd feel being away from Lisa. I remembered when I drove to my house to see Eileen that day and saw the For Sale sign on it. It was like someone had hit me in the back of the neck with a baseball bat. Eileen was gone forever. But it wasn't like that with Lisa. She was right across the river in New Jersey. I could see her any time. I didn't feel as if I'd lost her.

Living alone, I really began to feel better. I'd been lying, cheating, deceiving for so many years, it was a relief not to have to do that shit any more. I thought about how, when something went wrong between Diane and me—or Barbara and me—I'd run away. Find me, wife, I'm in one of fifty saloons in the city. I was running so hard, even my conscience couldn't keep up to me. Here I was still running, but on my own, with no one to fuck over except myself.

The Yankees didn't cut my salary after my awful season. At the press conference to announce my signing for 1968, Lee MacPhail, the general manager, said, "Joe never uttered a word of complaint, but moving to the outfield the way he did just for Mantle's sake after being the best defensive first-baseman in the league—that was a difficult thing to do."

I told everyone, "It was a bad year, and I just have to take it as it came, without excuses. But now the biggest thing in my life is the season coming up. I'm determined to prove I can do well. This year means everything to me, to the ball club, to my family—and to my lawyer."

Someone pointed out that I had a lot of injuries, saying you can't play well when you're hurt. "But you get injuries when you're not in top shape," I said. "Maybe I didn't come out to the ball park quite as early as I should have and get properly loosened up. That's the kind of thing I'm going to change. I also started last year overweight. I came in at two-eighteen."

I heard one of the writers up front say to the guy next to him: "Does he mean two-eighteen A.M.?" I smiled, thinking, Man, at 2:18 A.M., I was just shifting my act into *gear*.

I was sincere about wanting to get in shape for the '68 season. I even went down to spring training early and began working out. When the season opened, I was probably in the best condition I'd been in since 1963. I was down to 201 pounds, my muscles were loose, toned. I felt great.

But in the season's third game I suffered a freak accident. We were playing the Twins at the stadium and Ted Uhlaender lined a shot to right center. I raced over and cut off the ball, stabbed it before it went through to the wall. I whirled and threw off balance to second. It was a good play, holding Uhlaender to a single, but it wasn't worth it. I threw so hard that a bone in back of my left elbow cracked. It hurt like hell. I thought it was a pinched nerve, because I'd had those before. I tried one practice throw and the pain jerked my head down to my chest. X-rays revealed the fracture.

The thing that pissed me off was the fans. They booed the shit out of me when I left the game. I didn't stay mad. After my picture appeared in the papers the next day showing the cast on my arm, I got a lot of nice letters.

I was sidelined for over a month, but I didn't allow myself to put on weight or get too much out of shape. I ran regularly, and when I returned to the lineup I went on one of my streaks at bat. I drove in nineteen runs during my first twenty games back, including five home runs, and batted .295. The problem was I didn't do much the rest of the year. I hit fifteen home runs all told, drove in fifty-six runs, and batted .245 for the season. I had some other injuries, including a torn muscle in my side that I sustained swinging a bat, and missed almost sixty games altogether.

But the main reason I hit so badly was that I simply lost all interest in baseball in 1968. Hell, I was twenty-seven years old now, and I was sick and tired of being told everything I had to do—how to dress, how to wear my hair, the exact time I had to be someplace or they'd take money out of my salary, how I should perform on a baseball field how I should *think,* for Christ's sake, the same shit I'd been hearing for a goddamn decade of my life.

We had these outfits we were supposed to wear when we traveled as a team. A blue blazer with a Yankee emblem on it, a blue tie, gray slacks. We looked like we were all about to make our first Holy Communion. What bullshit. Everyone would board the airplane dressed like that, and I'd get on wearing blue jeans and a sweater.

Houk would say, "Come on, Joe, where's your blazer and slacks?"

"They're dirty. I didn't have a chance to get them cleaned."

"Well, next time you wear them," he said.

The next trip I got on the plane wearing the filthiest, most wrinkled blue blazer and gray slacks anyone had ever seen. I'd tied the jacket and pants in knots to set the wrinkles in them, then soiled them on the floor.

When we went on the road again, I wore one of my own outfits and Houk just shook his head. Some of the other players had things to say. "Shit, he dresses like that, why can't I?" Two reasons: they didn't have the guts to butt heads with the establishment, and they couldn't have gotten away with it because they weren't very good ballplayers. I knew what they were thinking, even though they never said anything to my face. Fuck them, I said to myself. I never bugged them, told them what they had to do. It was none of my business what they did, and it was none of their business what I did. The veterans who were still around, Mantle, Tresh, they didn't care how I dressed. They were comfortable in their own skins.

I also found in 1968 that I hated the outfield. You run in, run out, sit down, stand around and pray for a ball to be hit your way, give you something to do besides talk to the monuments in center field. I just had too much time out there to think about everything except baseball. Too much time to think about old guilts that tracked me like collection agencies. Too much time to think about my father's death, about blown marriages, about lost children, about debts.

Early in this season I went to Bill Sherr's office to beg for an increase in my allowance. He stood up behind his desk with a smile on his face and stuck out his hand. "Congratulations, Joe," he said.

"For what?"

"You're all through living on an allowance," he said. "Your debt's wiped out."

"No shit?" I said. "You mean I'm clear?"

"All clear."

"Wow!" What a relief! I almost did a cartwheel. I was *free!*

"If you like, Joe," Bill Sherr said, "I'll go on handling your checks so you won't have to worry about getting in trouble again."

"Mr. Sherr," I said, "I think I've learned my lesson. I'll never *ever* let myself get in a situation like that again. I just can't believe it—I've finally got everything paid off."

"Right, but you've got to watch your spending, Joe. You've got to keep up your payments to Barbara, and you've got to take care of Diane and Lisa now. You're making a good salary, but you've got to meet your obligations or you'll be right back in a hole in no time."

"I think I'm old enough to handle it now. I don't ever want to go through that scene again."

I left Sherr's office, and before I was outside I was already thinking about things I wanted to buy, about spending—about *living* again! I went right out and bought a new car, a whole mess of new clothes, anything that caught my eye. Yours truly, Joe Pepitone, New York Yankee star. I could sign fucking tabs again, take people out, *enjoy!*

Within two months, I owed over twenty thousand dollars out on the street again. Once more the line of creditors started forming behind me, started knocking on my door, ringing my phone, bugging me.

In a game on September 3 of that season, against Baltimore, with left-hander Pete Richert pitching, Houk sent up Rocky Colavito to pinch-hit for me. It was the first time in the majors I'd ever been replaced by a pinch-hitter. Writers reported that I was shocked. I was a little embarrassed, but not shocked. I hadn't hit left-handers all season. In my good years, I'd hit them better than I'd hit righties, because I'd concentrated more against the lefties. But I wasn't doing the job, and even though the Yankees as a team had a .214 batting average, we had tremendous pitching from Mel Stottlemyre, Stan Bahnsen, and Fritz Peterson and had a chance to finish in the first division, in the money. As it turned out, we finished fifth. Houk platooned me—I batted only against right-handers—from September 3 on.

If the truth be told, I didn't give a shit. I didn't mind a little rest. I had had a very strenuous season at night.

XV

"Cheer up, Slick."

The 1968 season wasn't all bad. At one point when I was in between apartments in Brooklyn, I moved in with Mickey Mantle at the St. Moritz Hotel in Manhattan. Mickey lived in a suite there during the season. I loved the guy. We'd had a lot of laughs together over the years, we'd been close, and I was sure this would be his final season with the Yankees. He played in too much pain to continue, even though he could have used the money, because his "investment counselors" over the years had put his bread into some very steep holes in the ground.

The night before our annual exhibition game at West Point, Mickey and I went out to celebrate St. Cadet's Eve. The day at the U.S. Military Academy was always a lot of fun, and we didn't have to worry about what time we got in that morning. I never worried, but Mickey was much more concerned about his health. It was at this time that I began wondering how well I would have done with the Yankees if I'd ever been just a little bit concerned about my hours. Mickey Mantle and Whitey Ford had always enjoyed having a drink now and then, now and then, now and then. But they were careful. They knew when to stop and come home. They were going to make the Baseball Hall of Fame. I would make the Hall of Fame only if they introduced a new category: Most Times Fined for Lateness. I never drank that much, but early on someone sure as hell busted my watch.

Since we could sleep on the bus ride up to the Point, we didn't devote a lot of energy to checking any clocks the night before.

141

I think we got back to the St. Moritz about 5 A.M. It was just an exhibition game, and neither of us figured to play more than an inning or two. And it didn't matter whether we hit the ball or not. So we hit a bunch of saloons, then I took Mickey to one of my favorite after-hours places, and a rollicking good time was had by all.

The only problem occurred about ten-thirty the next morning when I awoke. We were supposed to have met the team bus at nine-thirty. I woke up Mickey: "Didn't you leave a call?"

"No. I thought *you* left a call."

"Mick, I thought *you* left a call."

"Shit," he said, "what're we gonna do?"

"I don't know," I said, "I guess we'll have to call a limousine. I don't know any other way to get all the way up to West Point. My car was repossessed again."

Mantle picked up the telephone and called a limousine service. Then he said he wanted to speak to the driver, the guy who would chauffeur us. What the hell's going on? I wondered.

"Here's what I want you to do," he said to the guy. "Stop someplace and buy us a gallon picnic jug, and fill it half full with ice. That's right. Then we want you to pick up three quarts of vodka and three quarts of orange juice. Right, quarts of both. And get us some plastic cups. Thank you."

About forty minutes later we got a call from the desk that our driver was there. He was driving a twenty-five-foot Cadillac full of our provisions. We climbed in, each carrying our uniforms in a bag, and instantly set about mixing breakfast. In a few moments we were toasting the morning. All that lovely vitamin C. We would not get scurvy on this trip.

By the time we passed Yankee Stadium on the Major Deegan Expressway, we no longer needed the driver or the limousine. We could have floated to West Point.

By the time we reached West Point, we were fully, totally, completely bombed out of our trees. As we turned into the academy, we began pulling on our uniforms, it being approximately game time. Amidst a great deal of laughter—I fell off the seat twice trying to get all those stockings over my feet and up to my knees—we finally managed to arrange our uniforms over our bodies as we approached the ball park. We could see people in the stands and our teammates just finishing up infield practice.

Mickey sat up straight and said to the driver: "Pull ri' up on the field."

"On the field? Are you sure, Mr. Mantle?"

"Ri' up on the fieeeld."

"Yessir."

He drove through the gate and onto the ball field. I leaned out the window and started waving my hat to everyone. I could hear the laughter, and I started laughing.

The driver stopped the car by the base line, and Mickey yelled, "Let me out—we're gonna play some baseballll."

The driver hopped out and opened his door. Mickey stuck one foot out the door, heaved the rest of his body—and fell right on his face. I staggered around from the other side. Everyone was breaking up. I saw Ralph Houk was trying to hold in his laughter, but not doing a very good job of it.

Mickey got up off the ground with a silly grin on his face, and the players gave him a tremendous hand and a few words: "Way to stand, Mick."

Ralph Houk came over and said, "Very funny—but you're both playing."

In the first inning Mickey got up and took three swings that looked like they'd been grafted onto his body by some Little Leaguer, then sat down. Houk took him out of the game after one inning. Good old Ralph made me play seven innings.

We still had over half the vodka and orange juice for the ride home, and we finished it just as we pulled up to the St. Moritz. We had planned to change out of our uniforms and back into our clothes, but somehow we forgot. So we made a determined —if not altogether convincing—effort to pull ourselves together as we walked into the St. Moritz lobby. A little old lady who passed us coming out said, "My what nice costumes."

"Sank you, mam," I said, strolling inside.

It was great fun until we got upstairs and Mickey happened to count the money in his pocket after he'd paid the driver. Instead of giving the guy his fifty-dollar fee plus a fifty-dollar tip, as he'd intended to, Mickey discovered he'd actually handed the chauffeur two hundred-dollar bills. Mickey didn't get too upset, though.

"Screw it," he said. "He was a good driver."

He was beautiful, my idol from the day I joined the Yankees. But one day, during one of my extracrazed, extrabad years, I really fucked up with Mantle. If a right-hander was pitching, I usually batted fourth, right behind Mickey. If a lefty was going against us, Ellie Howard batted fourth. On this day we were playing in Minnesota, and the Twins were starting a right-hander, so I was hitting behind Mantle in pregame batting practice. At times Mickey would be late getting out on the field because it took so long to tape up his bad legs. Any time he came down with a new problem, the taping took even longer.

We had all taken our first ten swings in batting practice, and I hadn't noticed that Mickey wasn't there. There was a lot of kidding by the cage that day. The second time in the batting cage, we only had time for five swings apiece. So Mickey was in the cage, and when he took his fifth swing, I jumped right in there. But he just stood at the plate.

"Five swings, Slick," I said.

"I just got here, man," he said, annoyed. He gave me one of those looks that said, Don't you ever run in the cage when I'm in here. When I get out, then you come in.

I stood there, staring at him. I was embarrassed because all the guys were around the cage, and there was absolute silence, nobody saying a word. I got annoyed, feeling he was making me look like an asshole in front of everyone.

"Why don't you get out here on time," I said, "like the rest of the fucking guys?"

He turned full around to me, his eyes squinted in anger. "What did you say?" he said.

"You heard what the fuck I said." This was the strongest guy on the Yankees, but I was in too deep to back off now. "It wouldn't hurt you to get here a little early to get your fucking legs taped, then you could get on the field with the rest of us."

He was furious. "What the fuck are you gonna do about it?" he said.

"What the fuck are *you* gonna do about it?" I said. I thought he was going to kill me, punch me out right there in the batting cage. There were only about three feet separating us.

Mickey, who had been holding his bat by the knob, slammed it to the ground and walked out of the cage. He walked right to the dugout, went down the steps, and up the ramp into the clubhouse, his eyes straight ahead. He looked like a kid in a schoolyard, which was appropriate because the whole scene had been childish, two kids arguing about bruised feelings.

Then I really felt bad, like the asshole I hadn't wanted Mickey to make me seem. I walked out of the batting cage and threw my bat at the netting. I followed him into the clubhouse. He was lying on his stomach on the trainer's table getting his legs rubbed down. His head, resting on the backs of his hands, was turned to one side.

I went over and crouched down by his face. "Slick, look, I'm sorry, man," I said. "I got out of line out there. I'm sorry. I mean it."

He stared right through me. Then he turned his head to the other side.

I stood up. "Man, I'm apologizing. I fucked up. Let's not hold any grudges, all right?"

He just lay there with the back of his head to me, not saying a word.

Mantle didn't speak to me for three weeks, and it really got heavy for me in the clubhouse. I loved the guy, and I needed his attention, his acceptance. He wouldn't give an inch. We'd come to the clubhouse in the morning and he'd turn away from me without even a nod. It went on like this, day after day. I said to myself, Shit, is this going to go on all season?

Then I started wondering, What's going to happen if he hits a home run and I'm batting behind him? Is he going to embarrass me in front of the crowd the way Lou Gehrig embarrassed Babe Ruth? I remembered reading about a World Series game in which Gehrig got pissed off at Ruth, and when Lou homered and trotted to the plate, he ran right past Ruth's outstretched hand, left him standing there holding air. Is Mickey going to do that, not shake my hand as he goes by?

He went into a slump after that scene in Minnesota, though I don't think that was any kind of factor. The whole team was going bad this season, nobody hitting much, driving in runs. Mantle was probably more depressed than the rest of us, because he always felt it was up to him to pick things up when the team fell off.

Three weeks later we were behind in a game, 3–2, in the ninth inning. We had a man on first when Mickey came up. He hit the second pitch deep into the stands to win the game. I was standing at the plate, waiting, tense as hell. Here he comes, I said to myself, and stuck out my hand. He grabbed it and dragged me toward the dugout.

"Man," he said, "I'm sorry, too."

I was also in a slump, but after that I didn't give a shit if it lasted another month. I felt good again.

Later that season, Mickey went like 0-for-25 at one point, and we were in next-to-last place. Before a game in Washington, I saw Mickey sitting in the corner of the dugout with his head down, looking very depressed. I went over and sat next to him.

"Cheer up, Slick," I said. "We'll bounce back."

He just kept staring down at his feet. His arms were on his thighs and he was leaning forward, motionless, expressionless, just staring down. "I ain't helping the club, Joe," he said quietly. "I just can't do it any more."

"Cut the shit, man," I said.

He jumped up, ran past me, and turned down the stairs. I went after him, thinking he'd headed for the clubhouse. But when I went down the stairs, I heard him in the bathroom on the left. Bang, bang, bang! I ran in and saw him punching the door on one of the stalls, pounding his fists into the metal. He was crying like a baby.

I grabbed him around the chest from behind, pinning his arms. "Slick, knock it off, for God's sake!"

"I can't hit the fucking ball. . . . I haven't got it any more. . . . I'm just letting them use me. . . ." He broke away from me and punched the door again.

I ran up to the clubhouse and went into Houk's office. "Ralph, Mickey's going wild down in the bathroom . . . crying, punching a door."

"Leave him alone," Ralph said. "He's done it before. He'll come out of it."

I hurried back to the bathroom. Mantle was gone. I walked into the dugout. Mickey was sitting on the steps with a couple of the guys, listening to some anecdote. The knuckles on both of his hands were pink, but he was sitting there enjoying whatever was being said.

It was very hard for Mickey in his last few years with the Yankees. He'd always played with outstanding ball clubs, was used to winning. He was a fierce competitor and wanted so much to keep on winning, to end his fantastic career at the top. But suddenly the Yankees were at the bottom. The team got old, and Mickey's body abruptly deserted him. During the last year or so, he could barely pivot on his right knee batting left-handed. He never knew when it might buckle under him. But the front office pressed him to keep playing, he needed the money, and he did his best, never stopped trying.

They were real down times, and Mickey seldom came out of his room. On road trips, he'd play a game, then come back to his hotel room, order dinner and drinks sent up, and just stay in all evening. Whitey Ford would stop by and have a couple of drinks with him, and that would be it. Mickey was tired of the traveling after all those years, tired of all the hassles every time he went out for dinner. So he stopped going out.

He couldn't go any place without being recognized, bugged. In New York, he'd order his meals from room service at the St. Moritz and relax by himself. It bothered the hell out of me when I was staying with him. He was a thirty-six-year-old man, finishing up one of the greatest careers in baseball history, and he couldn't leave his room to get a decent meal because people wouldn't leave him alone in restaurants, wouldn't let him eat in peace. I saw this and said to myself, Fuck that kind of recognition. It ain't worth it, being a prisoner of fame.

I got Mickey out to a few restaurants that last year. Little places with good food that were out of the way. I called the owners in advance to tell them I was coming with Mickey Mantle, that we wanted a table off in a corner, and that nobody was to bother Mickey while he was eating. "Sure, Joe," they'd say. "I guarantee no one will come near Mr. Mantle." Then we'd go there, and the owner himself or the maitre d' would come over and want to talk while we were eating. It was difficult; Mickey was such a star that people couldn't help themselves when he was around.

I remember in one restaurant we were having a great meal, really digging it. Mickey commented on how good it was, and he had a forkful of food by his mouth when a kid came up behind him and grabbed his elbow, asking for an autograph. Mickey instantly tensed up as the food spilled off his fork. But he didn't show he was upset.

"If you'll come back when we finish eating, son," he said politely, "I'll sign for you."

The kid went back to his table and the next thing we knew his father was standing over us. "Who the hell do you think you are, Mantle," he said, "sending a kid away without signing his autograph book? That kid and thousands more like him pay your salary, Mr. Star. And don't you forget it."

I started to tell the guy off, which is not the smart thing to do in a public restaurant, but I was mad as hell. Fortunately, he turned and walked away. Mickey just shook his head and ordered another bottle of wine.

In another restaurant one night we were sitting in a corner and Mickey had his back to the crowd. Nobody recognized him. Some kid spotted me, because I was facing the other tables. He came over with an autograph book in his hand, and when he was about five feet from us I said, "Would you mind coming back after we've eaten, son?" His face fell as he turned away. Then I said, "Aw, come on back here. I was only kidding." I seldom refused autograph-seekers, unless they were old enough to look like collection agents. I guess I needed the attention too much.

When I stayed with him, Mickey picked up so many checks that it got embarrassing. He wasn't in really great financial shape, either, but he wouldn't allow me to pay for anything. I remember one evening Mickey was in the shower when the guy from room service came to the door.

"I have Mr. Mantle's order," the guy said.

"Oh, bring it right in," I said. "I'll pay for it." I figured I finally had my chance to grab a check. I looked in my wallet and I had forty dollars. That would cover dinner.

The guy carried in a tray of food. He carried in a second tray of food. He carried in a third tray of food. Then he rolled in a cart that was loaded with booze, ice, mixers. He handed me the check. The total was $332.75.

"He's in the shower," I said to the guy, handing back the check. "You can catch him later. Thank you."

Mickey walked out of the shower a moment later with a towel tied around his waist and another one rubbing at his hair. "Oh, the stuff's here," he said. "Good. Did I tell you I'm having a little party tonight, Joe?"

Mickey and I were sitting around the St. Moritz one afternoon, and I was cleaning a new batch of grass I'd just gotten. Mickey never smoked marijuana, refused to even try it, saying Scotch whisky was plenty good enough for him. I'd been after him to just take a toke or two, told him it wasn't as harmful to your body as booze, and that it made you feel a lot better. The guy who'd gotten me this batch had told me it was super-good. I kept after Mickey, told him he really ought to give grass a shot, but he declined.

I finished cleaning the grass, rolled a joint, and lit up. "Wow!" I said. It tasted different from anything I'd ever smoked before. In seconds I was *up,* and a second toke delivered me to the following Tuesday. "This is sensational, Mick," I said. I was beaming, couldn't stop smiling.

"Shit, let me have that thing," he said. "I just hold the smoke in?"

"Just draw it into your lungs and lean back," I said, feeling like my lips were spread so wide they were going to split. Very pleasantly.

He took a toke, sat back, waited a minute, and a smile came to his face. He took another. "Kinda nice, Joe."

This was over three hours before game time, and I knew the stuff would wear off way before we had to play. It always wore off within a couple of hours. We finished the joint and drove to the stadium, giggling all the way. But instead of wearing off, this dope seemed to get stronger. I found out later that it was Colombian, which I had never used before. Two tokes of it will keep you aloft for hours.

Mickey went to bat in the bottom of the first inning. I watched him swing from my seat in the dugout, and I had to hold back the laughter. His swing was perfectly level, but it was so relaxed it looked like he was swinging under water. Mickey, of course, was notorious, after he struck out, for slamming his bat into the ground, throwing his batting helmet in anger. This day when he took his third slow-motion swing, he turned around, very carefully placed his bat on the ground, and carried his batting helmet back to the dugout tenderly. I had to cover my mouth with my hand. Everyone was looking at him strangely as he walked back with the tiniest little grin on his face.

He struck out twice in that game, and I struck out three times. The dope still seemed to be getting stronger. I finally took myself out of the game in the eight inning. I was afraid I would get killed by a fly ball. I don't know how, but Mickey played perfectly at first base. If I'd had to handle the throws there, I think I would have taken myself out in the fifth. Incredibly, Mickey came up in the ninth with a man on second, and singled in the winning run.

He still had that little smile on his face when he walked into the clubhouse. But he came right over to me and whispered, "Don't ever give me any of that shit again."

"I didn't know it was *that* strong, Mick."

The next time I rolled a joint at his place, Mickey got up and left the room. I never smoked before another baseball game. Ever.

Toward the end of his final season, Mantle's next home run would be the 535th of his career. He would pass Jimmie Foxx on the all-time list. Only Babe Ruth, Henry Aaron, and Willie Mays had hit more home runs in the majors than Mickey.

We were playing in Detroit, and Denny McLain was pitching for the Tigers. McLain had already won thirty games in 1968, and he had something like an 8–0 lead against us in the late innings. Mantle came up for his last time in the game, and on the first pitch I almost collapsed in the on-deck circle where I was kneeling. McLain just lobbed the ball in, right down the middle. Mickey was so startled, he froze, just watched the ball float past him.

He looked out at McLain, who had a shocked expression on his face, like, *What was wrong with that?* Mickey understood. He made a little gesture with his bat: *A bit lower, Denny.* I didn't believe it. McLain smiled.

The next pitch floated in right where Mickey had called for it, and Mickey fouled it off. Bill Freehan, the Tiger catcher, chuckled. McLain grimaced: *What do you want?* Mickey nodded: *Just one more.* McLain lobbed it up and Mickey drove it into the upper deck in right field at Tiger Stadium. The fans gave him a tremendous hand as he rounded the bases.

I stepped up next and, figuring McLain was in a good mood, signaled with my bat where I'd like a pitch. McLain smiled, went into his windup, and fired a fast ball that hopped about a foot over the inside corner of the plate—a pitch *nobody* could hit. The players on both benches roared.

Mickey and I became very close in that month I bunked with him, and one night we got into some really heavy shit. It was late, and we'd had a pile of booze. He told me something that I'd always heard be believed, but I'd never heard it from him before. Mickey's father had died at age thirty-nine, and he talked about that, and about the fact that there was a history in his family of males dying young. Mickey said he was convinced that he would die before he was forty, that he'd had that feeling for years, and now there weren't too many left on his calendar.

I couldn't do much to comfort him. I told him that I felt the same way. My father had died at thirty-nine, his father had died at about forty-two, and a number of other men on the Pepitone side of my family had got dead early.

Mickey leaned his head on my shoulder and started weeping, saying, "It's too young." I put my arm around him and hugged him. "Take it easy, Mick," I said. "Take it easy."

He couldn't stop crying.

"What the fuck difference does it make?" I said. "It's been fun. There's been some real shitty shit, too. Fuck it."

Then I told him about a time when I was eight or nine years old. My father and I were out crabbing early one morning on the Cross Bay Bridge. I remembered how still the air was, and how the bright-bright sun was hitting the water at such an angle that it looked like a vast mirror on one side of the bridge, and on the other side the water was bumpy, and it looked like you could reach out and touch the bumps, smooth them, even though the water was way beneath us. It was kind of other-worldly, nice. I looked up at my father and said, "Dad, I feel like I'm never gonna die. Like I'm gonna live forever and ever." He gave me one of those smiles that warmed my whole body.

But after Willie died like he did, and I went through that bad year, it suddenly came to me: I'm also going to die young. I'll never make forty, either. That's how it's going to be. That's how it is. I'd talked to the shrink about it, and he couldn't convince me otherwise. I told Mickey that that was why I partied so much, why I tried to stuff in so much living when I could. Then I laughed, but there was no mirth in it. Underneath that laugh, I was thinking about my father, wishing he were sitting with us right then, with Mickey Mantle and me. Things wouldn't have seemed so bleak.

XVI

"Okay, Frank, if you're God like they say you are— let's see you make that shot."

I was still very much a celebrity freak. I still loved to be around big-name racket guys, big-name show business stars. Acceptance by these people continued to do something large for my ego. This fact had caused trouble between Diane and me. She thought my liking to hang out with celebrities was bullshit and said so. She was right, as she was right about so many things, but I couldn't see it. All I could see was that being around these people made me feel good. Or seemed to. And anything that made me feel good was the only thing that mattered to me.

When I went to Florida in the fall of 1964, I met Frank Sinatra and went to a party with him. That experience really blew my mind. Frank Sinatra was like a God to me—all that talent, all that power, the way he lived exactly as he pleased, having to answer to no one for what he did. Who the hell, I asked myself, had more control of his life than Frank Sinatra?

Leo Durocher introduced me to Frank. I was going into the nightclub at the Eden Roc Hotel to see the show when I ran into Leo in the lobby. I think he was a coach with the Dodgers then. Anyway, we'd bumped into one another several times at night and had shared some laughs. So we chatted there in the lobby for a couple of minutes, then Leo asked if I'd like to sit at Sinatra's table. Frank had a big table down front for his friends, and Leo said there were several empty seats. Lead the way, Leo.

He took me inside and introduced me to Jilly Rizzo, who was probably Sinatra's closest friend and unofficial bodyguard; the actor Harry Guardino; comedian Pat Henry, who was just going backstage because he led off shows for Frank; and about six beautiful girls. Sinatra did a great show, and afterward we all went backstage to congratulate him. Leo said, "Frank, I want you to meet Joe Pepitone of the Yankees."

"Hey, paisan!" Frank said, jumping up and hugging me. I stood there, paralyzed, with a stupid little smile on my face. "I know he's with the fucking Yankees, Leo," Frank said. "Hits left-handed, plays first base better than anyone the Yankees ever had, and makes the All-Star team every year when he's brand new." He hugged me again. "Good to see you, Joe."

Jilly had his houseboat—a huge, fantastic showpiece—docked right across from the Eden Roc, and afterward we went over there and partied all night. When the sun came up I was still sitting there, just staring at Frank, the same thing I'd been doing all evening. Joe Pep from Brooklyn, hanging out with God.

After the '68 season I started dating a girl I liked. I actually saw her three or four times. One day I went out to her place on Long Island, and she told me a friend of mine lived right down the street. Pat Henry, the comedian. So I took a walk down there and rang Pat's bell.

"Hey, Joe, how are you?" he said. "Come on in. I'm just getting ready to pack. I've got to go see Frank in Palm Springs." I followed him to his bedroom. "Say, why don't you come with me, Joe?"

"To Sinatra's? I don't know if he'd go for that. What's going on out there? I mean, what're you going to be doing?"

"Not a helluva lot. Just screwing around, mainly. Why don't you come? There are going to be a bunch of people there. Frank's got all these cabanas behind his house for guests to stay in. He'd love to see you. Come on along. We'll have some laughs."

I walked out the door, and as soon as I got outside I started running to my car. The girl came out of her house. "I've got to go see Frank Sinatra," I yelled to her. "Give you a call when

I get back." I raced to my apartment in Brooklyn, threw my best clothes into a suitcase, and met Pat Henry at Kennedy Airport about ten minutes before our flight took off.

As Pat had said, there were a bunch of people at Frank's, including Harry Guardino, and Jilly Rizzo, who owns a club in New York but has a house near Sinatra's in Palm Springs, California. That evening we all went into Frank's audiovisual room, which was about the size of a small theater, except there were couches to sit on. Someone said there was over fifty thousand dollars' worth of sound equipment set in the walls. There was a control console with all kinds of switches and dials and buttons and rheostats by the couch where Sinatra sat. All of a sudden I heard a whirl, a panel opened in the ceiling at the end of the room, and a screen descended. Then a projector popped out of the wall behind Frank.

"When this comes on, Joe, start snoring," said Jilly, who was sitting beside me.

"Yeah, snore loud," said Pat, laughing. He was sitting on the other side of me. "This'll kill you."

An old reject grade C gangster movie came on the screen, starring people no one had ever heard of. The film was so bad it was funny as hell. But it hadn't been on more than a minute when Jilly, Pat, everyone started snoring as loud as they could. When I was sure everyone was participating, I snored, too. The snores got louder and louder. Frank had all kinds of trays sitting around the room full of packs of cigarettes. When the snores reached a peak, suddenly one of those trays full of cigarette packs caromed off Pat Henry's head. He let out a yell, and I slid down next to him, so that my head was lower than the back of the couch.

"For Christ's sake, Frank!" Pat said. Everyone except Pat laughed.

After the movie, we sat around talking and drinking for a couple of hours, and Jilly said to me at one point, "Joe, you don't know Frank that well yet, so I think you should know that he loves opera music. And sometime in the evening, he's gonna play some opera music on the stereo. Don't say anything when it comes on. Be absolutely quiet, because Frank is very serious about this. He loves opera music and he likes to conduct when he plays it."

Sinatra? I thought. Opera music? Frank Sinatra likes to *conduct* opera music?

Jilly was not kidding. Some drinks later into the evening, Frank stood up and shouted, "Quiet! Music time. Time for you clowns to absorb a little culture."

Harry Guardino, who was sitting on a couch in front of us, hated opera music. He was making that clear to the person sitting beside him: "We gotta go through this bullshit again."

"Harry," said Frank, "shut the fuck up."

Harry shut up, the lights went out, and the music came on —reverberated off the walls, made the whole room vibrate with sound. I sat there with my hands folded, breathing as softly as I could, because there was a very heavy air of intimidation in that room. Frank always had a couple of heavyweights around like Jilly Rizzo, and I didn't want to do *anything* that would upset Frank. I really admired him, respected him as a great entertainer, as a music genius. And I really dug the fact that anything he wanted he could get, because that's the way I wanted to be at the time. The first time I met Frank I saw him drinking Jack Daniel's, so I started drinking Jack Daniel's. But now I sat there liking this scene and hating it. I was enjoying it because I admired the man so much, but then I thought, Do I want to hang out with a guy under these fucking terms? Be *afraid* of somebody—which I have never been, even around some of the toughest racket guys in the world?

So I sat there for almost an hour, fearfully listening to opera. I peeked over my shoulder and saw Sinatra, his head going up and down and his arms waving in front of him, conducting with an imaginary baton the music that was swelling and crashing around us.

Abruptly, I saw Harry Guardino's head disappear on the couch in front of me. Then I saw Harry was on the floor, crawling on his hands and knees toward the back of the room in the dark. I peeked over my shoulder again. Frank was still conducting. I peeked over my other shoulder and saw Harry was by the door. His hand reached up, turned the knob, and he opened the door a crack.

The instant that slice of light burst into the room, the ceiling lights came on, the music went off, and Frank Sinatra was standing over Harry holding a .45 automatic.

"Where the fuck do you think you're going, Guardino?" Frank said. "Get back to your fucking seat."

Harry did not hesitate.

After holding my breath for almost an hour, when the opera music finally was over, I was so tense I could still hardly breathe. Fortunately, Frank came over and started talking to me about baseball, about Leo, about life in New York City. He was very loose, warm, fun. He laughed at my stories, put his arm around me and loosened me up. I relaxed and started enjoying myself again.

A while later, Frank said, "All right, everyone, let's shoot some pool."

We went to this beautiful room that had huge fireplaces on either side of it, and a pool table that looked like it had been hand-crafted. The game, Frank said, would be pill pool. We each took a pill from a leather bottle, not letting anyone else see it. The number on that pill was your ball. If you sunk your ball, you won fifty dollars from everyone else in the game. If you sunk anyone else's ball, you won from that player. I only had about two hundred dollars in my pocket, but I was fairly confident. I'd played enough pool as a kid to become a pretty good shooter.

In the first game I drew the "1" pill. Harry broke, nothing went in, and I was up next. And the "1" ball was hanging on the edge of the corner pocket. From where the cue ball lay, I had a clear shot. There were seven other guys in the game, and I was already counting the 350 dollars that was coming to me.

I stepped up to the table, tossed my pill on the cloth, and said, "The game's over." I leaned down to line up the shot, and just as I hit the cue ball—*crash*—a wooden gambling block bounced on the table and knocked my ball away from the pocket. The cue ball I'd stroked hit the wooden block, which Sinatra had thrown.

"All right, Frank," I said, "that was my '1' ball. I won the money."

He was leaning on his cue stick, grinning. "Joe, this is my game, this is my table, this is my house—and we are playing *my* rules. What we happen to be playing tonight is called Dirty Pool."

"I can't believe this," I said, turning to the others. "Will you look at this shit!"

Pat shot next and missed the "2" ball, but he left a simple shot for the man after him—Sinatra. He smiled, chalking up his cue stick. He leaned over the table, lining up the shot into the side pocket. I picked up a twenty-pound log off the hearth of the near fireplace. As Frank stroked the cue ball, I threw the log onto the table in front of the "2" ball. It ripped the cloth. I was scared to death, but I blustered right ahead.

"Okay, Frank," I said, "if you're God like they say you are —let's see you make that fucking shot."

His stick fell out of his hand, and he fell forward on the table roaring. He looked over at Jilly and said, "Where the fuck did we pick up this crazy bastard? He's beautiful." He kept laughing.

I let out a sigh of relief. It was about five in the morning by this time, and Frank said, "That ends the pool shooting for tonight. Let's eat." He'd had his cook stay over and he told him to fix us a huge pile of pastafazool, which is peas and macaroni, one of Frank's favorite dishes. So as the first light of dawn shone on the windows, we were sitting there eating pastafazool and drinking wine. I was thinking, This is one very peculiar god.

Everyone was up the next morning a little after nine, I guess because Frank was. Two girls came to the door, and Frank told them to come in. They were wearing big badges on their chests and collecting for some Palm Springs charity. It was apparently a big annual charity; anyone who didn't contribute got put in jail for a day, as I recall.

We were all in the living room, and Frank turned to Jilly Rizzo and said, "Give me a thousand dollars." He turned to Harry Guardino, "Give me a thousand dollars." To Pat Henry, "Give me a thousand dollars." He was going around the room, and everyone was reaching for his wallet, pulling out cash.

Holy shit, I thought, thinking about the two hundred dollars I had on me, he's going to ask me to throw in a grand and I'm going to have to say, "I can't. I haven't got the money." I'll be embarrassed to death.

I edged over toward the door to the patio. Frank saw me: "Hey, where are you—?"

I ran outside and dove into the pool, fully clothed. I held my breath on the bottom as long as I could. When I came up, Frank was crouched on the edge of the pool with his hand out and a smile on his face. "You crazy bastard, give me twenty-five dollars." I peeled off twenty-five damp dollars and handed them up to him.

That afternoon, four or five girls came over to Sinatra's, and we all sat around talking and having a good time. There was one really striking girl, a tall redhead with great big eyes and a husky, sexy way of talking. She turned me on, and I was rapping away with her, really digging her. I noticed Harry Guardino eyeing the girl from across the room. I kept talking away, telling the girl a story, laughing. Then I saw Harry was slowly creeping toward us. I told the girl about a great painting that was hanging in the dining room, and took her to see it. We went in there, admired the painting, and I kept her there, talking by ourselves. For about two minutes. Harry appeared in the doorway, staring at the girl. I maneuvered her around so her back was to Harry.

In a moment, Harry came over and tapped me on the arm. "Excuse me," he said. "Joe, could I speak to you for a second?" He grabbed my arm and led me away from the girl. He stopped about ten feet from her and whispered, "I just want to tell you something, man. Give it your *best* shot—because I'm cutting in on you with that chick."

I looked at him. He was serious. "All right," I said. "Go ahead and take it over if you can—if you can handle it. If I lose, I lose. But I don't think you can take this chick away from me. We got a nice thing going here."

So we both marched back over to the girl and started doing our things, turning on all the charm, using all the moves, doing every number we could think of. He'd say something to her, and I'd top him. I'd come on with something to make her laugh; Harry would come back with a story that made her laugh harder. We wandered back inside and continued to play Can You Top This? Harry and I were really laying it on, and the girl was obviously digging it. Abruptly Harry laughed and walked away, as if he'd been kidding.

Then a bedroom door off the living room opened, and

Frank stepped out and stood there observing us. For about five minutes he stood there, listening to one of my anecdotes. "Honey," he finally said. The girl, who was standing in profile to him, didn't hear Frank. "Honey," he said a little louder. He had his index finger crooked and, when she turned her head toward him, he wiggled it. Two rapid bends of the finger, no words.

The girl's face lit up. "Excuse me," she said to us. Frank leaned his mouth close to her ear, slipped an arm around her waist, and ushered her into the bedroom. The door closed behind them.

I stood there with my mouth open, staring at the door. It opened in a few moments and the girl came out carrying a small portable color television set.

"Look what Frank gave me," she said to me. "Isn't he sweet?" She went around the room and showed that television set to each of the other girls. She was beaming as if he'd awarded her the chairmanship of the board of RCA. When she'd finished her tour, she carried the television set back into the room. Once again the door closed. This time it stayed closed.

I walked over and started talking to Harry Guardino.

That evening we all went out to dinner at Frank's favorite restaurant in Palm Springs, the Ruby Dunes. On the way we passed an enormous house with ten or fifteen cars parked in the driveway. "He must be having a helluva party," I said.

"No," Frank said, "that's Red Skelton's house. Red owns all those cars. But he doesn't drive the Buicks, the Oldsmobiles, the Pontiacs—only the Rolls and the Mercedes you see at the back of the line. He keeps all those cars there because he's convinced burglars will think there's a crowd in the house."

I laughed. The used-car lot in Red Skelton's driveway was actually his home-protection service.

There were about a dozen of us who went into the Ruby Dunes, and the maitre d' arranged a big table for our party. I had observed that Pat Henry had this thing about wanting to be close to Frank all the time. It was as if he felt that if he wasn't right at Frank's elbow every moment, he'd fall out of favor. Pat is a good comedian, a funny man. But for years an awful lot of his work had come from kicking off Sinatra's shows. Frank had Pat precede him, warm up the audience before every show, and I'm not sure this did a lot for Pat's confidence in himself.

Anyway, when we sat at the table, I happened to be next to Frank. Pat came hustling over and said to me, "Hey, Joe, let me sit there." No reason, no explanation, but he said it in such a way that I would have felt bad if I hadn't given him the seat. I shrugged and moved.

Frank ordered several bottles of wine and we were having a good time. I was diagonally across from Frank, sitting between a girl and Jilly, and there was some funny conversation. But Pat Henry wasn't hearing much of it. His contribution was to say every few minutes, "Frank, you want some more wine?" "Frank, you like some bread?" "Frank, you need cigarettes?"

He was driving me crazy. I got disgusted. I was also getting pretty high on the wine, which made Pat's performance bug me more. I pushed my chair back and stood up, wanting to get away from the scene for a couple of minutes.

"Where are you going?" Frank said.

"I'm going to the bathroom," I said. "You think I should tell you every time I go to piss?"

He chuckled. "Go on, you crazy bastard."

Hanging on the wall outside the bathroom was this big blowup picture of a bare-assed baby lying on a fur rug. There was a metal plate on the bottom of the frame that said the baby was Frank Sinatra. I was standing there looking at it, and weaving slightly from the wine and Pat Henry, when Frank walked up beside me.

"Joe, you know who that is?" he said.

"Sure," I said. "There's a clue on the plate."

"Well, why the fuck are you standing here looking at it like that?"

"I'm trying to decide whether I should kiss your ass like some of the other people at the table out there."

He laughed, but I didn't think it was all that funny.

Frank loves Harry Guardino and thinks he's one of the finest actors in the business, but every time Harry was subjected to that late-evening opera music he'd go berserk. He couldn't stand it. Several times Harry had made such a scene, he told me, that Frank had actually thrown him out of the house. "He's nuts, playing that shit," Harry told me, "punishing his friends. *Conducting,* for Christ's sake!"

The second evening Harry had made it through the opera music with merely a number of initial god-awful sounds spewing from his throat. On the third night, though, when the music came on, Harry jumped up off the couch he was sitting on.

"Fuck you, Frank, and fuck your operas," he shouted. "This time I ain't gonna give you a chance to throw me out of here." He walked out and went home.

It was really something to see Frank Sinatra conducting that opera music, to watch him get into it, leave the rest of us in that room and slide right inside that orchestra that was producing all those sounds, become a part of it, the conductor of every instrument. He was such a musical perfectionist and had such an ear that you could see he was hearing things none of the rest of us heard. It was thrilling to watch. It would have been more enjoyable for me if I could have shaken off that heavy feeling of intimidation that ran through me during the performance. But I couldn't shake it, and that was the first time I ever wondered whether hanging out with celebrities was all that great.

XVII

"Everybody likes to give his mother something, and I can't give mine anything except trouble."

The Yankees did not call a press conference to announce my contract signing for the '69 season. I'm sure they tried to trade me, but found they couldn't get much for me after two dismal seasons in a row. Another factor was that the Yankee management wasn't at all sure that Mantle was coming back. He didn't. But he also didn't announce his retirement until after the Baseball Players' Association had won better pension concessions from the owners in April. Mickey's support of the demands helped the rest of us, which showed class.

Houk told the press during the winter, "I would say that Pepitone will have to earn whatever job he winds up with in the spring. He didn't hit left-handers much last year, so I'd have to figure him as a part-time performer. I'll have an open mind when training starts. All I want is the best team we can field. This will be the first time Joe has really had much competition for a job, so maybe it will be good for him."

I wasn't worried. I knew what I could do if I wanted to. I wouldn't find out if I wanted to play until I reported to spring training. I arrived at 10:30 P.M. because heavy rains delayed all the flights out of Palm Springs, California. I knocked on the door of coach Harry Craft's room at the Yankee Clipper Motel

163

in Fort Lauderdale and said, "Is Ralph mad at me for being so late?" Harry did a double take. I was wearing a yellow big-apple cap, oversized pink-tinted shades and carrying a shoulder bag and a clothes bag. Harry finally recognized me and said, "No, Joe, a lot of the guys are late because of the Players' Association strike."

I knew this was probably my last chance to show I wanted to stay with the Yankees. That appealed to me, as did returning to first base full time. I felt good in the spring and worked my ass off—as well as my waist, getting it down from thirty-six inches to thirty-three. It made me more agile. I felt good, hit well.

I told the late Milton Gross of the New York *Post,* "New York needs a star, and if I can do it I can own the town. I can make a load of money. I can live. But I've got to have fun. I've got to be happy in anything I do, and I have to be left alone. I don't put on an act for anybody. I'm me."

The writers spent a lot of time trying to figure out who, with Mantle gone, would be the Yankee leader. Some reporters even asked *me,* but I couldn't quite see myself in that role. Social director, perhaps, if they were pressed for such a man. A radio interviewer asked Vic Ziegel of the *Post,* "Can Joe Pepitone be the Yankees' spiritual leader?"

"He has enough hair to be the spiritual leader," said Vic. "But he lacks the beard."

I was now missing so much hair in front that even using a hair dryer-blower to tease it into a bouffant wouldn't cover the skin in front. I had begun wearing a partial hairpiece in front, but I hadn't told anyone. Now after games I would put a handkerchief on my hair before taking a shower, and I wouldn't stick my head under the water. Better still, I bought a yellow rubber rain hat to shower in. Afterward I'd comb, blow, and arrange my hair, then spray it to hold it.

Dick Howser, a former teammate who had become a coach, would say, "Joe, you don't need a batting helmet. All we have to do when you get up is paint *NY* on your forehead."

It was all fun. I remember a doubleheader early in the season against Washington in which I hit a tenth-inning home run to win the first game. A writer asked me what kind of pitch I hit, and I said a fast ball. Bobby Murcer, who was dressing nearby, said, "I was near second base when Dennis Higgins threw it, and it was a slider."

"Bobby's hitting five hundred," I said. "If he said it was a slider, it was a slider." I never cared all that much once the ball was in the stands. But Higgins, a relief pitcher, was also in the second game when I came to bat. I told Ziegel afterward, "I was thinking, Maybe this guy is gonna throw at me because of the homer. The one thing I didn't want was to get hit in the head the last time at bat. It might mess up my hair."

When I set myself in the batter's box, I heard Washington catcher Paul Casanova say, "Joe, good luck. And hang loose."

I thought, Uh-oh, that's it, he's throwing at me. If they want to drill you, they can drill you. There's no way he can miss me.

The first pitch came in and I was ready to dive out—only the ball was low and outside, four feet away from me. I stepped out of the box and glared at Casanova.

"What is this 'good luck' stuff?" I asked him. "What's this crap about 'hang loose'? You trying to scare me?"

"No, Joe," Casanova said. "All I meant was good luck for the season."

I had a pretty good season statistically, all things considered. I won another Gold Glove award at first base, led the team in home runs with twenty-seven, and drove in seventy runs, even though my batting average was only .242. But I was still going as hard as I could at night. I remember getting up so many mornings, crawling to the window and looking out at the sky, craning my neck in search of black clouds. "Rain, damn it," I'd say. "Rain!" When I first joined the Yankees I'd get up in the morning, see there wasn't a cloud in the sky, and cheer: I'd feel great. It's going to be a beautiful day for baseball. Now I prayed for rain, hailstorms, a plague of locusts upon us . . . anything that would allow me not to report to the stadium.

Going out wasn't always all that swell, either. For the last few seasons I had been hearing more and more bullshit in saloons. Everyone knew who I was because I was always in the papers; my whole life had been on newsprint. I was colorful, I was news, and I always talked to writers.

So I'd be in a joint sitting across from a guy who had a few drinks in him, and he'd say—purposely loud enough for me to hear—"There's Joe Pepitone, the asshole." Or, because of the fact that I dressed mod and because of the way I wore my hair, "There's Joe Pepitone, the faggot." Or I'd walk into a place and a girl at a table would squeal, "Oh, that's Joe Pepitone! I want his autograph." And the guy sitting with her would say, "What do you want *his* autograph for? He's a queer."

I don't know how many times I heard that kind of shit. The words would vibrate through my head, make me furious. I wasn't brought up to sit still behind bullshit, not by Willie, not by the neighborhood I came up in. I had to learn to control myself, learn to bite my tongue or leave the place. I'd say to myself, Fuck it, they're envious of you, don't let it bother you. This may be one of those hard-ons who gets off trying to push ballplayers, who wants to provoke you into slugging him just so he can sue you. There are a lot of those around.

I'd often meet a guy in a club and we'd exchange two sentences, then the guy would say, "I always thought you were a prick, but you're a nice guy." Again I'd have to bite my tongue. Sometimes I'd get disgusted and say, "Well, fuck you, buddy. You thought I was a prick? Well, I am a prick. Shove it up your ass, if you don't like it." Then I'd walk away, because I just didn't need that shit. Why should anyone think that way about a person if they don't even know them? And if they did think it, why—when they find out different—do they say it?

This was one of the reasons why Mickey Mantle became so reclusive in his last years with the Yankees, because he got tired of the crap he heard spoken about him whenever he went out in public. There's only so much a man can walk away from, can ignore.

For some reason, I heard more crap during the 1969 season than ever before. It was like all the bad-ass freaks were out en masse. I remember dropping into a friend's bar one night in Chicago. I'd met this guy, whom I'll call Ralphie here, on my first trip to Chicago in 1962. He was in the rackets and had just taken over the bar. Over the years we'd become good friends. He was about my age, and we sort of grew up together.

So I stopped in to say hello to Ralphie and ordered a drink

at the bar. A guy walked right up to me and said, "You're Joe Pepitone. Mr. Cocky. You're a real fucking smart-ass hotshot on a ball field."

"Man, what the fuck are you talking about?" I said. I knew right away this was a racket guy, a junior wise guy; tough, out to prove something to himself. I'd never seen a top racket guy ever come on with anyone like that. A top racket guy would tell anyone he had trouble with to move on, or he'd *move* him. No bullshitting around.

"Come on with me, Mr. Cocky," the guy said.

"Come on where? You don't even know me."

"I know you, smart-ass. Come on outside."

"What the fuck did I ever do to you?"

"I don't like your act. I don't like the way you play ball. I don't like the things you say in the paper. You think you're such a great player, such a great lover. Shit. Come on outside."

"You call those reasons for fighting?" I was scared. I read the guy as mean, and I didn't know what he had on him. But I didn't think he'd pull out anything in the bar. "If you're gonna start something," I said, "you better do it right here. Take your shot. I'll fight ya."

"Outside, you smart-ass punk!" he yelled.

Just then Ralphie, whom I hadn't seen on the other side of the room, heard the loud voices and picked up on what was happening. The next thing I knew, the guy was flying against the wall. "What the fuck do you think you're doing?" Ralphie said angrily. "This kid's been a friend of mine for seven years."

"What seven years? He's a fucking smart-ass and I'm gonna straighten him out."

Ralphie grabbed the guy by the shirt and smacked him in the face. "This kid's a friend of mine, and you ever lay a hand on him you're gonna find your ass in the fucking lake."

Then the wise guy started apologizing to me. "Get away from me, asshole," I told him. But I was goddamn happy Ralphie had been around to look out for me. There are a lot of crazy-mean wise guys around like that nut. And I never wanted to find out what any of them were carrying, or what in fact they might do outside in the dark.

I also had a problem that year in a bar in Detroit. Mel

Stottlemyre and I went in for a drink after a game. Earl Wilson, the Tiger pitcher, was sitting at the bar. I met a girl from the Playboy Club and started dancing with her. I was wearing trim-fitting pants, which I always wore, and a shirt that was open in front to show my hairy chest. I heard some big bastard at the bar yell something, but I couldn't make it out over the music. When we danced a bit closer to the bar, I heard him say, "Look at that faggot dancing with that pretty girl."

I just laughed and said to the girl, "Don't pay any attention to that clown."

But Mel turned to the guy and said, "Keep your mouth shut."

The guy ignored him. "Look at the faggot," he said loudly.

"Listen," said Mel, "that guy is a friend of mine, and he's no faggot. Now keep your mouth *shut.*"

When I heard this, I had to say something or Mel was going to get into a thing with the fat-mouth. "And if you don't keep your mouth shut," I said to the guy, "*I'm* gonna shut it."

"You ain't gonna do nothing, faggot," the guy said.

I leaped over the low railing between the dance floor and the bar, I grabbed the guy around the throat, and my momentum drove his head down on the bar. I started banging it as hard as I could. He broke my grip, flopped to his feet, and picked up a chair. He threw it and I ducked. Then I stepped in and punched him. As I started to hit him again, two arms wrapped around me from behind. The guy spun me around and said he was a detective. He snapped handcuffs on my wrists, saying, "You're under arrest."

"What the hell are you arresting *me* for?" I said. "That guy started the whole thing."

"I saw what you did. You attacked him."

Mel confirmed my story. I glanced at Earl Wilson, who was still at the bar and whom I'd known for years. With a second witness, I'd be freed in a moment. But Earl Wilson wouldn't even look at me!

Mel and I had to sit down with the detective and explain the whole incident in detail before he took the handcuffs off me. Then I had to go to the station house and press charges against the other guy to protect myself, in case he pressed charges against me.

When I returned from spring training in 1969, I lived in a building on the East Side of Manhattan called the Carriage House. But creditors were still pressing me, particularly Barbara's attorney. So I moved in with a friend I'll call George who lived with his family in Brooklyn. I'd met George through a very close friend, Dominic Morello, who owned the Diplomat Club in Brooklyn. I was looking to get into some business that would make a lot of money and allow me to pay my debts and give me a hedge against the future. I was only twenty-nine, but I was already wondering how long I could make myself keep playing baseball. I thought about opening a lounge, a restaurant, something to capitalize on my name which was always in the papers. Then it occurred to me that men's hairstyling was about to become a big thing. Everyone was wearing long hair now, and it had to be styled regularly by professionals to look nice. Your average barber just didn't know what to do with long hair, and many of them weren't interested in learning. All they did was cut in the old-fashioned way and bitch because they were losing business.

George, who owned a small business, and Dominic, who wasn't doing much of anything since he'd left the Diplomat, also wanted to get a business going. They liked the hairstyling salon idea. We were going to have a big place with twenty chairs in it, as well as a men's apparel and jewelry boutique. We found a perfect location in Brooklyn, then went to some people who underwrote new businesses. They liked the idea, but wanted more information. We put together all kinds of figures on how much business we could expect. It took us two months to convince the underwriters to put up the money. Meanwhile, throughout that period, I was getting publicity about my hair, my hair dryer, my hair spray, my entire hair act. One day I hit a home run to win a game and I told everyone in the locker room afterward that I was so happy I felt like yanking my hair out. With that I pulled the partial hairpiece off the front of my head, and everyone laughed.

Until that time, I'd been too embarrassed to admit I was

wearing a hairpiece. A year or so before I had done a hair spray commercial on television, and later I had been offered five thousand dollars to do a hairpiece commercial, which I had turned down in embarrassment. It had taken me a while to realize that the fact that a man wore a hairpiece was nothing to be embarrassed about. Hell, guys wear hats on their heads to make them look better. If a hair hat made you look better —and feel better—why not?

The underwriters agreed to invest $100,000 in "Joe Pepitone's My Place," and we were all excited about the shop. It was going to be a beautiful place. We got twenty of the very best hair stylists in New York to take care of our customers. We made them an offer they couldn't refuse. We rented them the chairs for a flat fee, and they in turn paid us five percent of their profit and kept everything else they made. George and Dominic and I were there every day supervising the construction. We could hardly wait for My Place to open.

Then we had a serious problem among ourselves. Dominic and George had a heavy disagreement that ended up in a fight. Dominic is a sweet man and a very funny guy. But he's husky, can handle himself physically, and he comes on a little like a racket guy, talking in a raspy, full-bore Brooklyn voice. George had a tendency to put him down regularly. One night George accused Dominic of being dishonest. Dominic dove over a desk and busted open George's face. George threatened to get even with him. And I'll be goddamned if a few nights later I didn't run into two guys I knew and they were out looking for Dominic. They said they were going to work him over good.

"Dominic's a close friend of mine," I told them. "What if I'm with him when you come around? You mean to tell me you're going to give him a beating in front of me?"

"Joe, that's the way it is. We got the job."

"Well, fuck that," I said. "If I'm there, there's no way I'm gonna stand around while my friend catches a beating. You guys wouldn't think shit of me if I did that, and you know it. I'm not gonna just stand there. That's how it is with me."

I walked away from them, called Dominic immediately, and told him to stay off the street until I straightened things out. If that was possible and if George would listen to reason.

But I just couldn't believe any of it. Every single thing I touched turned to horseshit. Even when I made an effort, tried my damndest, nothing ever fucking worked out right.

All my past failures were also bombarding my head without letup. In the blackest, quietest moments of the night, I was still hung up on Diane, on the fact that I'd destroyed a marriage to a fine woman. I couldn't live with her, couldn't make it with her, but I couldn't get her out of my mind, either. I visited her and Lisa less and less frequently, even though Diane and I were still married, were not even legally separated. I *was* separated by some three thousand miles from Eileen and my son, and that fact continued to fester in the back of my mind like a tumor.

As if I didn't have enough shit coming down on me, I was now such a popular target for subpoena servers that even friends were nailing me. I'd bought a hairpiece from a friend for three hundred dollars early in the season. He had asked me for the money several times, and I'd told him that I would take care of the bill as soon as I got the cash. One night he was in a box seat at the stadium, and he called me over before the game. "Joe, come here. I want you to meet someone."

I walked over at the end of batting practice, and he introduced me to the girl with him. Then he said, "I'm sorry," and handed me a subpoena. I saw fans all around looking at us.

"Thanks a lot, you prick," I said. "I really appreciate your doing this in front of all these people."

Everything was depressing me, particularly the Yankee situation that I had to live with every day. Although we had been going bad for the last four years, we had always had a number of veteran stars, former super players whom I kept telling myself would get over their injuries, recapture the magic, do it all again in time. Time, of course, was what had taken them. Tom Tresh was traded early in 1968, Mickey Mantle was retired, and the rest were all gone: Bobby Richardson, Tony Kubek, Clete Boyer, Roger Maris, Elston Howard, Yogi Berra, Johnny Blanchard, Hector Lopez, Phil Linz. Of the players who were with the Yankees in my first season in New York, only pitcher Al Downing and I were left. I had always been a follower, and in the early, winning years I had fought to keep up with the stars. Now there was no one to keep up with. Now *I* was the guy who should have been carrying the club, coming up with the big hit. I wasn't doing it. Even when I did drive in the big run late in a game, the run that should have given us the win, we somehow seemed to find a way to lose. We were fifth in a six-team division on merit.

There were moments when guilt and regret overwhelmed me. I thought about what I could have had, what I could have been, if I had had an attitude like Tom Tresh. I had all the talent. Only two months earlier Ted Williams had said, "With his talent, Joe Pepitone should have been a hundred-thousand-dollar ballplayer." With just a little more concentration, a little more conditioning, a little more sleep, I could have been the leader on the field the Yankees needed. Shit, I could do it right now.

But all I kept thinking about was the chick in the stands I was going out with after the game. Please, I'd say to myself at first base, don't let it go into extra innings, don't keep me here any longer than I have to be. Let me go party and try to shove the shit aside. Even though the parties are brief and the nights are long, during those brief moments at least I can breathe.

It took several days of steady talking to George to straighten out things between him and Dominic. I pointed out that if he didn't knock off the vengeance bullshit, he was going to blow the whole hairstyling business. The three of us had started the thing together, and I said we were going to finish it together or not at all. He finally came around, and then the three of us spent a lot of time telling each other how well we were going to do, what a tremendous success "Joe Pepitone's My Place" was going to be. But, based on my own corroded history, I wasn't really that certain, not in my heart.

One afternoon the three of us were goofing around the Deauville Beach Club in Coney Island. When it came time for me to leave for the ball park, I lent Dominic my car because he was coming to the game that night, and I took a cab to the stadium. But during the ride toward the Bronx, all the shit in my head suddenly surfaced at once, hit me like a punch from my father, and I began thinking, *It's not going to work . . . nothing's going to work right for me, no matter how good it looks going in.*

I became so depressed, I thought I would choke. I told the

cab driver to turn around and take me to a boatyard at Sheeps-head Bay. I had the keys to a friend's boat that was docked there. I went aboard, smoked a joint or two, and escaped into good thoughts, convinced myself that "Joe Pepitone's My Place" would be my thing, would make me independent, would allow me to once and for all be free of the bullshit I was dragging around like a 1940s wedding car.

Dominic was sitting down front in a box before the game that night. Elston Howard, now a coach, went over and asked him, "Where's Joe? He's not here yet and the game starts in thirty minutes."

"Not here?" said Dominic. "I was with him this afternoon when he left for the ball park. He's gotta be here."

Ralph Houk walked over and told Dominic to hop the railing and come into the clubhouse. "Get on the goddamn phone and call everyone you know who might have some idea where Pepitone is."

"I don't understand it, Ralph," said Dominic. "He was fine this afternoon. Look," he held out a paper bag, "I brought him peppers-and-egg sandwiches."

There was no way he could have called Freddy's boat, even if it occurred to him that that was where I was. Dominic found me by accident the next day. I was having lunch in the Barge Restaurant in Sheepshead Bay when he walked in, followed minutes later by my brother Billy and a friend of my mother. They talked me into calling Houk. I apologized, said I knew I was hurting the team, but my head was messed up and I needed another day away from baseball to straighten out. Ralph gave it to me.

I got it back together enough to play for a couple of weeks. Then I hurt my neck and shoulder overswinging (someone asked, "On the field, or off?" I didn't say, but the answer was, "Both") and sat out a game. I couldn't stand sitting in the dugout through an interminable baseball game, so I left the stadium without permission. I couldn't play the next night, either, and Ralph warned me not to leave until the game was over. I sat through four innings, almost went berserk sitting there thinking about all the debris in my head, then left. *Ran.*

Ralph got me on the telephone the next day and screamed at me. He told me that if I didn't show up that night, I'd be suspended. No problem, Ralph. I didn't show that Friday night. I became the first Yankee ballplayer to be suspended since Buddy Rosar in 1942, which was a disappointment. I had thought the last one was Babe Ruth, a nice league to be in. Who the hell was Buddy Rosar?

On Sunday morning I realized I was being stupid, that I wasn't doing myself any good at all running from baseball. I was a baseball player. The hairstyling business was for the future, but I wasn't helping it by not playing ball. We could use all the publicity I could get us in uniform. I wasn't going that bad at the plate; I had twenty-four home runs, which gave me a good shot at thirty for the season if I could regain some feeling for the game and concentrate. I couldn't do that by running away.

I called Ralph and told him I wanted to come back. He asked me about my neck and shoulder. I told him they were still sore, that I wouldn't be able to play the doubleheader that afternoon, but that I should be all right by Monday. He said I was being fined five hundred dollars. It could have been a lot more. Both Ralph and Michael Burke, the president of the Yankees, were very understanding with me.

The Yankees called a press conference for me to make my explanations in public on Monday morning. I met with Houk for forty-five minutes and approved the release the club would issue which said I "was not psychologically prepared to rejoin the team." Then I met the press for twenty-five minutes and tried to be honest in general terms about my emotional problems, my depression, without specifying the depths. My mother was very much on my mind, all the sorrow I'd brought her, and at one point I said, "Everybody likes to give his mother something, and I can't give mine anything except trouble. I gave her grandchildren, and they're gone." I hadn't meant to say that much, it just slipped out, and I was happy when no one pressed me on these words.

I spotted Howard Cosell with his television crew edging close to me, and I gave him a big smile and said, "I'll be with you in a minute, sweetheart." Everyone got a kick out of that. I had nudged them away from follow-ups on the kids, and my mother, who knew how I felt, what I was going through. Her heart went out to me so much, and that only made me feel worse.

One of the magazine writers started pushing me on my debts, and I got defensive. "I only owe out forty-eight hundred dollars," I lied. "Who doesn't owe forty-eight hundred dollars?"

"He's confused," I heard Michael Burke tell Bob Lipsyte of the *New York Times,* "but I think most of the problem is money. We'll see what we can work out together. Maybe you're always more lenient with the sheep that strays."

When I went back and finished the season, some of the writers reported that my teammates had had it with me. Certainly I'd given them plenty of reasons to be annoyed. But I didn't hear anything personally. I think Jim Ogle, writing in *The Sporting News,* conveyed the feelings of most of the Yankees toward me:

" 'I'm glad we have him,' said one teammate. 'People forget he is a great defensive first-baseman, and he's the most dangerous hitter we have. He is a lot more of an asset than he is a liability, so we take him as he is. Sure he does some crazy things and makes you mad at times, but he also produces.'

" 'Pepi is Pepi,' said another teammate. 'He makes you mad, but he also makes you happy. The infielders love him because he saves them a lot of throwing errors with great catches.' "

I just wished I could live on infielders' love.

XVIII

"The last and most controversial of the old imperial New York Yankees was traded today."

"Joe Pepitone's My Place" opened to sensational reviews. All kinds of men were getting into long hair, mod clothes, and jewelry, and we happened to have some of each. The money poured in. George, Dominic, and I were suddenly entrepreneurs. We started making plans to franchise the shops in cities around the country and in Puerto Rico. The underwriters were also excited and talked about the corporation going public, issuing stock. That would really make us tycoons.

The corporation owned an enormous six-room apartment over the shop. I had the use of it (as well as a corporation car) and lived there some of the time, and at the Carriage House in the city the rest of the time. Dominic and I decorated the apartment, which was a small mistake. We opened a gallon of red paint to do the large, raised dining area. While we stirred it, I smoked a joint, and it felt so nice I had another one as we started applying the enamel. By the time we finished the three walls, I decided the white ceiling wouldn't do. It needed something arty to set off the area. We awoke the next morning and found the ceiling covered with childlike renderings of red cows, chickens, and horsies.

Soon after we opened My Place, I took Dominic, George and

his daughter, and a few other people from the salon to the Copa one night. Tom Jones was opening there, and the club was packed. Joe Namath came in with a party and couldn't get seated. I'd called Carmine in advance and he gave us a front-row setup. When we walked in, my eyes bugged out of my head. In all the years I'd been going to Copa, I had never seen so many racket guys in there at once. It looked like Appalachin. There must have been more than fifty wise guys at tables.

As we walked to our table, I heard about twenty-five "Hey, Joey's," which made me feel good. I also heard a few remarks I didn't need: "Joey, wha' happened? You coulda made us proud. You coulda made us all proud of ya." I had the feeling right then it was going to be a weird evening. It was.

Tom Jones hadn't been performing more than two minutes when several beautiful girls at tables down front took off their panties and threw them at him. The racket guys didn't think a whole lot of this. They started yelling wisecracks at Tom Jones. When the panties continued to fly up at Tom Jones, a racket guy I knew named Larry, a nice man who has since passed away, went into the bathroom. He came out carrying his shorts in his hand. His shorts were white, and covered with bright red hearts. He walked down to the stage, threw the shorts, and they hit Tom Jones in the head. He was a great performer, very cool, and simply laughed it off as if the whole bit was part of his act.

Then some of the racket guys who were sitting around us started saying in their deep, husky voices, "Joey, get up there. You can outsing him." They'd heard me sing a number of times in clubs late at night over the years, but there was no way I could even compare with a professional. I wasn't about to leave my seat, make a fool out of myself.

Then they started saying, louder, "Joey, get up there. You can outdance him." They started chanting it. Jules Podell, the owner of the Copa, was going crazy in back. He sent his manager down front to call for quiet, ask everyone to let the man do his show. A racket guy rose about three inches off his seat and said, "You—get outta here." The manager spun some rubber and withdrew. And the shouts at me grew louder.

"Joey, get up and dance."

"No, no. I can't do that," I said.

"Joey, get up and dance!"

"No. C'mon, you guys."

"JOEY, GET UP AND DANCE!"

There was no way of getting out of it. I looked up at Tom Jones, who had stopped singing and was just dancing around, smiling. I guess he figured the only way to shut them up was for me to get up there with him. He gave me a wink.

I stood and climbed on stage to a tremendous hand, a lot of cheers. Carmine came running down, saying, "Joe, you gotta get off the stage." One of the racket guys stood and, amidst a barrage of shouts, leaned his lips next to the maitre d's ear. Carmine vanished. *Pooff.*

Then they all started shouting at me. "Dance, Joey! Joey, Dance! Do it! Do it! Show him how!" It sounded like there were two hundred voices, and I felt as if I were having bullets shot at my feet. I danced. Tom Jones danced. Everyone in the place went berserk. It was a wild, weird, embarrassing, fun moment. When I sat down, Tom Jones was able to finish his performance without having to dodge any more shouts or snotty remarks.

Afterward, about a dozen racket guys—who regarded the whole thing as great fun—took me and my party backstage to see Tom Jones. I apologized to him, and he said, sotto voce, "It wasn't you. No big thing."

Singer Paul Anka was on the other side of the dressing room, and one of the racket guys led me over and introduced me to him. He proved once again that a millionaire can have the mind of a four-year-old. "Oh, you," he said. "You're the guy who got up on stage and started dancing in the middle of Tom's act. You're not supposed to treat a performer like that. It's juvenile."

I got angry. He had been in the audience and should have understood what had taken place. "Hey, man," I said. "It's none of your fucking business."

When Anka mouthed off, the racket guy who had introduced us stiffened, his entire face stoning up. He pointed a finger at Anka and said, with about a second's space between each word, "You keep your mouth shut." Paul Anka got very quiet.

But he had made me realize what an uncalled-for scene I had

been forced to engage in. That was the first time I had experienced, personally, a heavy, heavy time around racket guys. I had to admit to myself that *I* had felt fear out there, and that wasn't pleasant. All kinds of things that I had once admired were dying away. That was the last time I ever went to the Copacabana, or to any of the other places where I knew racket guys hung out.

In the December 4, 1969, edition of the *New York Times,* Joe Durso wrote: "Joe Pepitone, the last and most controversial of the old imperial New York Yankees, was traded to the Houston Astros today for Curt Blefary. The straight interleague exchange ended Pepitone's eight-year career as the long-haired, long-talking Peck's Bad Boy of Yankee Stadium. His exit had long been rumored but never quite attained, though the Yankees began to make strenuous efforts to trade him after he disappeared twice last August. . . .

" 'In a sense, I feel relieved of a problem,' acknowledged Lee MacPhail, the general manager of the team. 'But it'll be hard to imagine the Yankee club without him. He's been a real good player, but not as good as everyone hoped he'd be. He was colorful and he had the spirit of youth, and some of the problems that go with it.' "

All of the problems, Lee, I thought, plus maybe a few I invented. I can't say I was overjoyed at the prospect of playing in Houston, Texas, even if I could have left all my problems in New York. Astro manager Harry Walker was widely rumored to have a rare talent for driving players crazy with his unbending rules and his unclosable mouth. I told my partners I wasn't going to report, that I was going to spend all my time overseeing the hairstyling business. But within a week they had convinced me I had to keep playing. As an active ballplayer I could get publicity for the place; as a former ballplayer, that would soon end.

Late in January I flew to Puerto Rico on a vacation-business trip. Orlando Cepeda had an eleven-story building under construction in Puerto Rico and we planned to put one of our salons on the ground floor of it. Then I stopped in Houston on the way home and got my first look at the Astrodome, which

I labeled "the world's largest hair dryer." I told the writers, "I'm looking forward to a new start, a new league, new pitchers, new everything. I expect to raise my batting average playing on the artificial turf half the season. I hit a lot of hard ground balls, and I should get a lot more through the infield here."

I met the Astros' general manager, Spec Richardson, and he gave me a nice raise to $45,000 a year for 1970. I told him the only other thing I wanted was to room alone on the road, that I had done so with the Yankees last season, and that it was definitely best for me and the ball club. "As long as you're willing to pay the difference between a single room and a double, that won't be any problem, Joe," Richardson said.

Even manager Harry "The Hat" Walker seemed okay on first meeting. I was afraid he might say something about the length of my hair in back. "I don't care if you grow it down to your ass," he said, "as long as you hustle on the field."

I looked forward to playing for Houston (we figured on putting a hair salon and boutique in there) until I got to spring training. The Astros trained way outside the city of Cocoa, Florida, and all of the single players had to live in barracks. The doors to the barracks were locked at midnight. If you came in after midnight, you were automatically fined $250. That was one of about twenty fines Astro players were subject to if they failed to follow the rules and regulations that were posted all over the training camp. I most admired the one that said, "No girls are permitted in a player's room." Another said you could not talk to a girl in a hotel lobby when the team was traveling. One of the guys told me, "You *can* talk to your sister—as long as she's not pretty."

It didn't take very long for the concentration-camp atmosphere to get to me. Shortly after twelve o'clock every night, one of the unmarried coaches who lived in the barracks with us would walk into your room shining a flashlight to make sure you were in bed. I was breaking my ass during the day to get into shape, working as hard as I could, because I had a feeling I could really have a big year in the Astrodome. And just to make sure we were getting in enough exercise, every day after the three-hour workout in the blazing sun, Harry Walker had us run a mile. You had to do it in under six minutes or you started over. So I was literally pooped at night. The first time a coach came into my room after midnight, I had the light out and had been in bed for an hour.

"You asleep, Joe?" he asked.

"I was until you shined that fucking flashlight in my eyes," I told him.

A few nights later he woke me again. I jumped out of bed and yelled, "The next time you come in my room like that, I'm gonna blow your fucking legs off."

"You have a gun in here?"

"I room alone and I always carry protection because I have a lot of valuables with me," I said. "And the next time you burst into my room, I'm gonna treat you like any other burglar. I'm gonna shoot you and ask questions later."

"You're going to get yourself in trouble talking like that," he said. "I've got a job and I've got to do it."

"You do it in this room again, you're going to end up with a hole in you. Fuck the rules, fuck your job, fuck the manager, and fuck the owner of this concentration camp. I'm not ten years old, and I'm sick of being not only locked up but fucking checked on every night. This is the last time."

He never entered my room again, bless his heart.

Of course, after a few weeks of unrelieved training and detention, I came in after midnight. The barracks were locked. I beat on the door, kicked it, and yelled that I was going to knock it down if someone didn't open up in thirty seconds. A coach came and said, "You're a little late, Joe," then went back to his room. The next morning I got a note that began, "Dear Joe," and announced that I had been fined $250. I didn't get too upset. The chick I'd been with had been worth the price.

The following day I told Harry Walker that my wife was joining me tomorrow for the rest of the training period. I went out and rented a room for myself and the girl friend who flew in. What a relief! We could never go any place with the other players and their wives, but that was no problem until all the wives got together and organized a party. "My wife," I told them, "is not feeling well."

The Astro players were all good guys, particularly Jimmy Wynn, and I was always laughing at Doug Rader, who was flat-out crazy. When the season opened Doug sent me a cake. It was wrapped in tin foil on the table in the locker room when I walked in. I peeled off the foil, and on top of the cake, blending in perfectly with the color of the icing, was a circular pile of shit. I complimented Doug on his rare talent.

From the start, I loved National League pitching. Nine out of every ten pitches are fast balls or sliders, and I was a fast-ball hitter. In the American League, five out of every ten pitches are breaking balls and change-ups, which were not my thing. I batted from a crouch and was therefore primarily a low-ball hitter. The American League strike zone was from the top of the letters to the top of the knees. The National League umpires called strikes from just below the letters to just below the knees. Overall, the National League played a much more aggressive, faster, better brand of baseball. Every team had two or three superstars, and there was a lot more base-stealing—with guys sliding into bases with their spikes consistently high—more hit-and-run, more hustling for the extra base.

The first few months of the season I hit well, though Walker wasn't happy with my RBI production. He moved me out of the cleanup spot and once even had me leading off, which was stupid I felt. But then I felt almost everything Harry Walker did was stupid. In June I had to take a couple of days off to fly to New York for an appearance in alimony court, where my child support payments were reduced from two hundred dollars a week to one hundred. When I returned, Harry kept my fill-in, Bob Watson, at first base and sent me to the outfield.

I didn't mind. What I minded were the picky fines Harry had hit me with. Like the fifty dollars for running three laps instead of five before a game. He yelled at everyone during clubhouse meetings, but Jimmy Wynn and I were primary targets. I quickly had enough of that demeaning bullshit.

One day he yelled at me about breaking his rules, and I said, "Don't yell at me; talk to me like a man."

"I don't have to talk to you like a man," he said. "You have a reputation."

"Why bring that up?" I yelled. "That's supposed to be forgotten here. Talk about my performance here, for Christ's sake!"

"Don't raise your voice to me," he yelled.

"You're always yelling at everyone, Harry, and everyone is breaking his ass for you. There's no reason to yell at grown men constantly. It's ridiculous."

He got so angry I thought he was going to have a heart attack. But it didn't make any sense to put down players in front of everyone. It didn't help the guys, it didn't help the team.

One day during a clubhouse meeting Harry started yelling at Wynn, and Jimmy yelled right back. Harry was referring to Jimmy—who is black—as "boy." Every sentence was "boy" this and "boy" that. It pissed me off, and not just because Jimmy was a friend and Harry was a fool. I had heard the word "wop" too many times to go along with that kind of talk.

I finally said, "Harry, what is this 'boy' shit? Can't you call a man by his name?"

Walker got angry, but said he didn't mean anything by the word "boy," that it was just his way of speaking. Probably he was being truthful, but his use of the word didn't improve the players' feelings about him.

I bought a .357 Magnum rifle one morning and brought it to the clubhouse in the Astrodome that afternoon. The bolt action was stiff, and I was sitting at my locker working it with a live shell. I had the rifle on safety, but someone called me at one point and I just stood the rifle in my cubicle and walked away. A few minutes later I turned around and saw that Jimmy Wynn had the rifle up to his shoulder and was aiming it at the doorway to Harry Walker's office. Then I remembered that I'd left a cartridge in the chamber!

I leaped over to Wynn in one bound, yelling, "Jimmy!" I pushed the barrel up toward the ceiling and said, "It's loaded."

Jimmy, who was thoroughly pissed off at Harry Walker, handed me the rifle and said, "I'd like to blow that bastard's head off."

"If he'd walked out that door, you sure could have," I said, wiping sweat off my forehead.

"Don't sweat it, Joe," Jimmy said. "I saw it was on safety."

On July 9 I was hit on the elbow by a fast ball from Pete Mikkelsen of the Dodgers. For two weeks after that, I could bend the elbow but I couldn't swing a bat, as the Astro team doctor, Dr. Harry Brelsford, confirmed. During the All-Star game break, I went to New York, and when I returned to Houston I found that I had been fined $250 for missing a team workout. That was silly. How could I work out when I couldn't swing a bat? Spec Richardson suspected me of malingering and implied I was lying about my injury despite his own doctor's testimony. Richardson told me, "If you can't play, maybe you should go into a hospital until you're well." I told him I wasn't going to spend a week or more in a hospital with a sore elbow. Who ever heard of such a thing?

A Texas magazine had taken some pictures of me lounging around the pool at the singles' apartment building I lived in. That was in May. The magazine was out now; Richardson saw my picture and said to me, "The elbow doesn't seem to bother you when you're having a good time."

"What the hell does that picture have to do with it?" I asked him. "That was taken a month before I was hurt."

The Astros went off on a road trip after this, starting in Pittsburgh. A notice was posted regarding rooming assignments. All of a sudden I had a roommate. Pitcher George Culver, a nice guy, and I were to room together. I went right to Harry Walker, who was in his office in the clubhouse.

"Harry, someone's made a mistake," I told him. "I'm listed to have a roommate on this road trip. I room alone. That's my agreement with Spec Richardson."

"You have no agreement that I know of. You have a roommate: George Culver."

"Harry, I'm rooming *alone.*"

"I said you're getting a roommate."

"No, I'm not."

"What I say goes, and you're getting a roommate."

"What you say is shit. I'm rooming alone. I have an agreement with Richardson. I'm not rooming with anybody."

"You want to bet?"

"You want to bet I'm not?"

"What makes you think so?"

"Because I quit."

I went to my cubicle and packed my personal belongings. George Culver came over and said, "Joe, what's wrong with me?"

"Nothing," I said. "It's not personal. I just don't want to room with anybody."

"Wow, I thought it was me," he said, smiling. "But, Joe, how can you give up the kind of money you're making?"

"They don't give me any choice," I said.

I drove to my apartment, packed all my clothes and personal gear, went right to the airport, and caught a flight to New York. I moved into the apartment above "Joe Pepitone's My Place." Spec Richardson called and asked me to come back. I told him I wasn't going to room with anybody and I wasn't going back to Houston, period. I couldn't stand Harry Walker and all his rules and regulations, I said, and I asked him to put me on waivers. Or trade me to the New York Mets or the Chicago Cubs. I still felt like playing ball. I was in great shape, and I hadn't been hitting too badly: fourteen home runs, thirty-five RBIs, and a .251 batting average in seventy-five games. I was beginning to get used to National League pitching now, and figured to hit a helluva lot better the second half of the season. Richardson said he'd see what he could do, but he couldn't guarantee anything. I was suspended without pay.

I got in touch with a friend in Houston and asked him to check out my apartment a few days later. He called me from the apartment and said it had been cleaned out—everything in it had been stolen. I wondered: Did Harry Walker force me to quit because he wanted all my furniture? It was a pain, though, losing all that new furniture I had charged.

Merv Griffin called and asked me to appear on his television show. Certainly, I said, knowing it would be good publicity for the hairstyling business, and that I'd also enjoy it. Dominic went with me to the taping the next day. Merv said he wanted me to talk about why I'd jumped the Astros. He also said he'd heard that I'd once sung a little on "The Mike Douglas Show," which was true, and asked if I'd sing. I told him I'd sing "Around the World," which was one of about three songs I knew all the words to. Then Merv asked me if I had any funny stories I wanted him to lead me into on the air.

"Joe, tell him about the cap on your tooth," Dominic said, laughing.

I laughed, and told Merv that America was not ready for that story on the airwaves. Then I explained that I had lost the cap on a front tooth, and the temporary one I had on kept coming off. Every time I said a word that began with *F,* in fact, it popped off. But what Dominic was referring to, I said, was the chick I'd been with the day before. When I had gone down on her, I had come up without the cap.

"Don't move!" I'd told her. I'd looked on the bed, on the floor, then checked out the immediate scene of the crime. Yeah, come here, you little rascal.

Merv laughed. But I'll be damned if during the show he didn't say, when I apologized for slurring my *F*s, "Oh, Joe, why don't you tell that funny story about how you lost your cap yesterday?"

"Are you kidding me?" I said, as my face got red.

"Well, one of these days you may be able to tell that on television, Joe."

I sang "Around the World"—"a creditably crooned version," according to *Time* magazine—and Merv asked me to come back on his show the following day, which was a lot more fun than playing baseball for Harry Walker in the world's biggest hair dryer.

At the end of July I got a call from Spec Richardson. Dominic answered the phone in my apartment and said the call was coming from Montreal. Shit, I said to myself, I'm not gonna play in Montreal. I got on the phone and heard Richardson say he wanted me back with the Astros. No way, I told him. He said I had ten hours to make up my mind to come back, or he was suspending me for the season. I told him that was fine with me. Unless I could play for the Mets or the Cubs, I was going to be a full-time hairstyling tycoon.

Richardson called back a few hours later and said Leo Durocher was very interested.

Great!

Then he called back to say he'd sent me to the Cubs for the $20,000 waiver price. Richardson, I decided, wasn't a bad guy after all. The Cubs were in the pennant race, Chicago was among my favorite towns, and Leo Durocher was my kind of manager. He was an older version of me. I'd read about how as a ballplayer Leo spent more than he earned. He'd bought so many nice clothes that he was nicknamed "Fifth Avenue." Later, when he'd been traded to Cincinnati, the team owner paid off all his debts and put him on an allowance, doling him a hundred dollars at a time. Then the other players started calling him "C-Note Leo." Based on my allowance from Bill Sherr, I could have been called "Half-a-C-Note Joe."

I called the Cubs, who were playing in Cincinnati, and Leo told me to join them there the next day. I checked the papers and saw that the Cubs were right behind the Mets and Pirates in the standings. They had terrific personnel: Ernie Banks, Glenn Beckert, Don Kessinger, Ron Santo, Johnny Callison, Jim Hickman, Billy Williams, Randy Hundley—everything except a center fielder. For Leo, I was going to be one helluva center fielder. As I packed my clothes I began singing, "Chicago, Chicago, that wonderful town . . ."

XIX

"We want Pepi!"

On Friday morning, July 31, I joined the Cubs in Cincinnati, where they were to play a twilight doubleheader that evening. I went directly to Durocher's suite at the hotel the club was staying at, and we had a good conversation. I was going to room alone, Leo promised not to bug me as long as I was doing the job on the field, and everything looked lovely.

As I put on my Cub uniform for the first time that afternoon, many of the players came over and welcomed me to the team, which was nice. I had expected a certain amount of coolness until I proved myself, considering my recent record. I told a few funny Yankee stories on myself, and everyone laughed. Then I displayed the three hairpieces I had with me. "This one is special," I said, holding it up. "It's my Gamer. It fits under my baseball cap."

"Maybe you can get a couple of those for Santo and Hundley," said relief pitcher Phil Regan, referring to the most-balding members of the Cubs.

"I was going to send one to Harry Walker for letting me out of his concentration camp," I said, "until I read in the papers what he said about me."

That morning I'd read The Hat's comments on Joe Pepitone: "He can be a good player—when he wants to be. I expect he'll come into Chicago and hustle. He hustled for us in spring training and for the first month or so of the season. Then he got tired and started coming up with a lot of excuses." Fuck you, Hat, I thought, you're not getting one of "Joe Pepitone's My Place" custom-styled hairpieces.

I overheard Chicago writers asking some of the players about their reactions to my joining the team. "It's tremendous, just tremendous," said Santo.

"From what I've seen of him," said pitcher Bill Hands, "he's a player who can do a lot of things. If he comes here in the right frame of mind, he should help us."

"He knows what it takes to win a pennant," said Billy Williams. "He's been on pennant winners. He's got to help us."

I was grooving on the words, totally relaxed. Then the lineup card appeared. I hadn't figured on doing much more than pinch-hitting for the first few days, because I hadn't played ball for a month. But I looked at the lineup card and saw I was listed to start in center field. I rushed outside to take outfield practice, see if my arm was in shape to make the long throws after weeks of working out only in a hairstyling salon. Incredibly, my arm felt strong.

Once the game started, I did fine in the outfield, and I singled in the winning run in the first game. I was tired, but Leo started me in the second game, too, and I singled in another run as we swept the doubleheader from the Reds. Leo finally pulled me out in the bottom of the eighth inning. I got a tremendous hand from the group of Cub fans known as the Bleacher Bums who had made the trip from Chicago to root for us. When I trotted into the dugout, all the players and Leo were lined up to shake my hand and slap me on the back. Man, I thought, I am in love with baseball again.

Three days later we went into New York to play the Mets. We were only two and a half games out of first place, and everyone on the Cubs—who had blown a nine-and-a-half-game lead in August the year before as the Mets won the pennant—was ecstatic. Everyone felt we could win it all this season, and there was a jubilant, confident atmosphere in the locker room that reminded me of my first three years with the Yankees. It was sweet.

I told everyone in the dugout before the game, "Wait'll you hear the fans when they announce my name." You would have thought some ax murderer had been introduced, the booing was so loud and so long. My new teammates thought it was funny,

I thought it was love, the fans thought it was enjoyable, so everyone was happy. We won the game 6–1, and laughed some more in the dressing room afterward.

Santo and Callison tried out my hair dryer, and I offered Ron a hairpiece, which he put on crooked. Then I took one and we ran into Leo's office. I tried to put the rug on his head.

"He's my buffoon," Durocher told the writers who were in talking to him. "But I say that in a complimentary way. He's the warmest, most sociable guy in the world. The greatest thing about him is that he can laugh at himself."

My mother, my brothers and my Uncle Louie had all been at the game, naturally, and I met them in the parking lot. I had to sign about twenty-five autographs, and I did the last few walking to the car. I'd taken care of all of them by the time I climbed into Billy's Pontiac. The windows were up because my brother had the air conditioning on, and just as he started to back out a kid about seven or eight years old suddenly appeared at my window.

"Joe, sign your autograph for me."

I looked at him and pegged him as one of those snotty kids who likes to screw around with you. I'd learned to read every type of autograph-seeker over the years, and I shook my head and told Billy, who was driving, "Let's get out of here."

"Joe," my mother said, "sign that little boy's book."

"Ma, I know these kids, believe me. You open the window and they spit on you. Billy, let's go."

"Joe," my mother said, "Billy's not going to move this car until you sign for that little boy."

"Ma, forget it," I said.

"Joe, please," the kid said, holding out his book. "Sign for me."

"You hear, Joe?" my mother said.

"Ma, all right, for Christ's sake," I said, rolling down the window.

The kid pulled back his autograph book and yelled, "Your mother sucks!"—then turned and ran.

"Ma, you see now?" I said, laughing.

We had a successful road trip, and there was a lot of kidding around on the flight home to Chicago. When we landed, I was sitting up front behind Leo. The steward came up to me and said, "Mr. Pepitone, your chauffeur is waiting for you when you deplane."

Leo's head snapped around. "Your fucking *chauffeur?* What is this shit?"

"I have no idea," I said, which was true. Maybe, I thought, it's a friend playing a gag on me. I went to get my luggage, and standing there was a guy about fifty years old with long gray hair, wearing a black chauffeur's uniform and cap.

"I'll take your luggage, Mr. Pepitone," he said.

"Who sent you here?" I asked him as he picked up my suitcases.

"Follow me, please," he said, walking toward the door. "Where will you be staying, Mr. Pepitone?"

"The Executive House Hotel," I said, following him outside to a sparkling new Cadillac limousine that was obviously custom-made, with special chrome work and a superplush interior. I stopped short, staring at it.

"The horn," said the driver, "plays the theme from 'The Bridge Over the River Kwai.' "

"Splendid," I said, getting in and hitting a button to roll down the glass between the driver and the backseat. "But who the hell are you, and who sent you?"

"I'm Fabulous Howard," he said, smiling, "and I think we can do each other a lot of good." He went on to tell me that he used to own a limousine service in Hollywood and had driven for many movie stars. He had only recently moved to Chicago and was in the process of building a clientele here. He said he would drive me anyplace, anytime I called, at no charge, as long as he didn't have another job. He expected to drive me to and from the ball games daily, and anticipated getting a lot of publicity through me.

"Fabulous," I said, "I like your style. As long as I'm going good on the ball field, this could be a nice arrangement. As soon as I start going bad, we'll have to end it. I won't be able to get away with this shit. In the meantime, drive on."

When we got to the Executive House Hotel, Fabulous opened the door and said, "Just a moment, please, Mr. Pepitone." He had a long red carpet in a cylinder in back, and he unrolled it on the sidewalk leading into the hotel. At the end of the carpet were the words FABULOUS HOWARD.

It was the first time in my life I had ever gotten anything for nothing, and it turned out to be a great arrangement for over a year. Fabulous would come by, hit the horn, and I'd board my limo to the *River Kwai* theme. He'd deliver me to the ball park, then pick me up when the game was over late in the afternoon. Every evening was free in Chicago, because there were no lights in Wrigley Field for night games. What could be better? And Fabulous was always available to ferry me around, or to call for chicks and bring them to my place. I'd phone him at three o'clock in the morning and say, "Fabulous, pick up Miss Donna at such and such address in twenty minutes and deposit her on my doorstep." He'd say, "It's three in the morning!" "Howard," I'd say, "*now*. And use the carpet."

I met this girl I'll call Rachelle the second night I was at the Executive House Hotel, and she was an unbelievable piece of ass. She was barely five feet tall with a perfectly proportioned body and she did it *all*. She was so small I could throw her up in the air and spin her on one finger.

Rachelle was very pretty and very hip. The first time I was balling her, we were really going at it, and suddenly I felt my wig begin to slip. I stopped, reached up, patted it, then resumed. Within two minutes it was slipping again. Again I fixed it. This happened two more times. Finally Rachelle looked up at me and said, "Hold it, you motherfucker. Take off your hat and fuck me right."

I fell off her, roaring, tears running down my cheeks. I thought it was the funniest thing anyone had ever said to me. I saw quite a bit of Rachelle after that. There were some girls who didn't read the sports pages and didn't know I wore a hairpiece. Somehow, I didn't want them to know. I'd go down on them and they'd grab for my head. I was always alert. I'd reach up and hold their hands. But with Rachelle it didn't matter. She knew how to deal with my hat.

Chicago was the best thing that ever happened to me. The first time I went to bat at Wrigley Field, the fans gave me a standing ovation. I'd been averaging an RBI per game since I joined the Cubs, but I had yet to hit a home run for the club and I still got a standing ovation. Sinatra was right: it *was* my kind of town.

Within a month I was getting mentions in Irv Kupcinet's column: "Joe Pepitone, one of the new darlings of the Cubs, dining in elegance at the 95 in the John Hancock Center." I'd always suspected I was one of the beautiful people, but it was nice to see it written down in public.

I dug reading the Chicago papers because I was getting all kinds of good notices. "I don't care what people say about Pepitone," Leo Durocher said for publication, "all I know is what I see. And from what I've seen, he's one helluva ball-player. As a matter of fact, he's an even better ballplayer than I thought he was."

"He's been a great influence on our club," said Don Kessinger. "He keeps the guys laughing and relaxed. But I'll tell you one thing—every time he's walked on that field, he's given us a hundred percent."

I liked to keep them laughing because I wanted them to like me. I'd always wanted people to like me, to enjoy being around me. I didn't pal out with any of the guys in particular, but I always had a lot of foolishness going in the locker room. I took to using the telephone in Durocher's office to make personal calls; you can get away with that—and just about anything else —when you're going well. I was going well, and the Cubs were going well. Leo told the press he didn't mind all that much that I used the phone in his office. "Pepi thinks it's *his* office," he said.

"Pepi is beautiful," said Ernie Banks, whose skills had faded somewhat, but who was still the spiritual leader of the Cubs. "Do you see all those banners hanging from the stands? 'We Want Pepi.' Everyone wants Pepi and *we* have him. He's an inspiration to us all. I even feel like singing my part to-day."

Ernie was one of the most amazing people I ever met in baseball. The '70 season was his seventeenth with the Cubs, he'd hit over five hundred home runs in his major-league career, had been named the National League's Most Valuable Player twice, but he'd never played on a pennant winner. And it didn't diminish his enthusiasm one bit. He was always bubbling over, "singing his part," as he said.

There were mornings when I'd come dragging into the clubhouse, hung over, still half asleep. Ernie would be sitting there and he'd burst into a loud announcer's voice, "Here comes Pepi! What's happening, man? Oh, *look* at those eyes! Open those eyes, Pepi, and see what a beautiful day it is to play baseball in beautiful, ivy-covered Wrigley Field. It's a great day to win two, Pepi! And we're gonna *win two* with you, Pepi! Two for the Cubs! We're gonna win two because we love baseball, don't we, Pepi? Now isn't this a great day to win two for the Cubs, Pepi?"

"Ernie," I'd say, peeling open my eyes with a tongue depressor, "it's a great day for *two more hours' fucking sleep!*"

"Oh, Pepi's got his eyes open! He is *ready!*"

I was ready once the game began, no matter how much partying I did—and I held that down quite a bit—because I had Ernie Banks's kind of enthusiasm for baseball again for the first time in many years. It was really fun.

I batted over .300 through my first five weeks with the Cubs. Then my average plummeted, but not my RBIs. I had 57 hits in 56 games and drove in 44 runs, including 12 homers, and a .268 average. The last home run came on the final day of the season and made us all some money. We were tied with the Mets for second place. That homer won the game and we had second place all to ourselves, which meant we didn't have to split the runner-up money. We finished five games out of first, because we just couldn't keep pace with the Pirates down the stretch. That was a shame.

I really wanted to win a pennant with that great bunch of guys, and for those great Cub fans. So what had started off as a hateful season ended up good, if not good enough. But I personally had no complaints.

XX

"Did she say I was good?"

I went back to Brooklyn after the season and discovered that "Joe Pepitone's My Place" was going bad. Like under. I'd had no inkling. It was as if someone had thrown a light switch, and the bright, shiny salon had gone dark. The sudden death did not smell right to me, but I never found out exactly what had gone wrong. All I knew was that another dream had died.

The hell with it, I said to myself. I'm big in Chicago now and I can live there and get something going that I can keep a closer eye on. I definitely wanted to have a business working for me on the side. I was thirty years old now and I had to think about my future. A business would also help keep me from thinking about my past, which would be nice.

I visited my family, went to see Diane and Lisa, then went out with Dominic for an evening on the town before flying back to Chicago. Dominic Morello had become my best friend in the few years I'd known him. I had more laughs with him than anyone else I knew, and the more I laughed, the better I felt.

Dominic took me to see his father, who had been asking him to bring me by for some time. When I walked in, Mr. Morello yelled, "Giuseppi, Giuseppi! You know my son three year and you no come to meet his father till now. Why you make me wait? You Italian and you no come see your friend's father." Like Dominic, he was a very funny man. "I watch you play ball all the time on the TV," said Mr. Morello. "Sometimes you strike out, and I go to the TV and spit on the screen. But when you make a home run, I wipe it off."

Another close friend with whom I did a lot of partying was

named Alfred. He may be the only man I ever met who was more interested in balling than I was. He was always bragging about the size of his dick—which was rather stupendous—and saying he was a better ball than I was. "Who cares?" I'd say. Of course, I might have cared a little.

I remember one time we had a couple of chicks at my place. We smoked some dope, stripped down, paired off, and started balling on the king-size bed. The girl I was with, whom I'll call Jenny, started groaning and sighing and yipping and screaming. Wow, I said to myself, I must be really great tonight.

"Alfred, you hear her?" I said, glancing over at him.

"Yeah, brother, you really got her going," he said as he started working faster.

Jenny's breathing was becoming heavier and heavier, her groans quicker, deeper, and her head was tossing from side to side. I was really turned on, and I saw that the girl under Alfred wasn't reacting at all no matter how hard he worked.

"Ohhhhh!" Jenny groaned, "Ohohohohhhhhh!" Suddenly her head stopped waggling, she opened her eyes and said, "Joe, would you mind getting off for a minute? I have to take a pee."

Alfred let out a roar and collapsed on his girl. "Oh, you're good," he said. "You're so *good* tonight! She's been putting on an act all this time—and you've been digging it." He rolled off his girl and just lay there, laughing.

I flew back to Chicago and took an apartment in a building a friend of mine owned, the Astor House. It was across the street from the Playboy Mansion, where most of the girls who worked in the Playboy Club lived. I had been dating several of the Bunnies, so my new location figured to be convenient.

Early in November I met another Bunny, Stephanie "Stevie" Deeker, who eventually became my present wife. I totally flipped over her. I asked her for a date, and she said, "Call me at the Mansion." I called the next day. She said she was busy. I called again the day after that, and she was still busy. On my sixth call, Stevie finally said, "Listen, Joe, I've heard about you, and I don't think we'd get along. We have different ideas about things."

It turned out that she had checked on me with her Bunny

friends I had been dating. The reports on me did not appeal to Stevie. Not only that, all of a sudden *none* of the Bunnies would go out with me. Maybe, I thought, Chicago's not my kind of town after all.

But a couple of weeks later I walked into a club called Mothers and saw Stevie sitting at a table with a girl friend named Suzie. I went over and started talking to them. While I was standing there, a guy came by and asked them to dance. They declined. "That's the fourth in the last five minutes," said Stevie, and she asked me to sit with them. They'd just come to listen to the music; neither felt like dancing.

Another guy walked over and asked if either of them wanted to dance. "Listen, sweetie," I lisped, "the girls don't want to be bothered with you."

The next guy who came over asked Stevie to dance, and she said, "I'm with him," pointing to me. So he asked Suzie, who said, "I'm with him," pointing to me. In a few minutes all the single guys in the place seemed to get the message. We weren't bothered any more, and for the first time I really had a chance to rap with Stevie. She went home with me that night, and we started dating.

But she was an independent bitch, and half the time she wouldn't even show up. I'd appear at the club where we were supposed to meet, and she wouldn't. I'd find her across the street at The Gap listening to music. She'd be sitting down front next to the bongo player, and I'd get pissed off. Still, I really dug her, and we began seeing more and more of one another.

I was finally beginning to tire of all the partying, banging around night after night. It was nice to get close to someone and want to be with them most of the time. In a couple of months Stevie began leaving some of her clothes at my apartment. Gradually, more of her things were at my place. One morning in the spring, a steamer trunk arrived. Followed shortly by Stevie. "Joe, I might as well save the fifty-dollars-a-month rent I pay at the Mansion," she said. It was lovely.

I had met Stevie's sister when she was a Bunny at the Playboy Club in Kansas City several years before. We had spent a weekend together. I didn't know it was her sister until Stevie told me, and I couldn't believe it. "It's true," she said.

"Did she say I was good?" I asked.

"Yes, Joe, she said you were good."

"What did she say?"

"She said you started at the toes and worked up," said Stevie. "I told her you *used* to be good."

"I was younger then."

I kept trying to get into the Playboy Mansion after Stevie told me how nice it was. But Hugh Hefner was very careful about who he invited in. Stevie couldn't help at all. One night my cousin Joe Scandora, who is Don Rickles's manager, was in town. He took me into the Mansion, and it was everything that Stevie had said it was. We went there with Rickles and Finest Henderson, who ran the Theatre in the Round in Chicago. Finest and I wandered into a room with a magnificent pool table.

"You shoot a lot of pool growing up in Brooklyn, Joe?" said Finest. "I bet you're a shark."

"I'm good, Finest," I said.

"Well let's play a little straight pool, Joe."

He broke, played safe, but a ball came out of the pack that left me a break shot. I banged in the ball and busted open the rack. Then I started popping the balls in. I ran twelve before I missed. I chalked my cue stick and said, "Finest, you don't know it, but I was *born* on a pool table."

"And that," said Finest, smiling, "is where you're gonna *die.*" He ran fifty balls. *Click, click, click* . . . Game.

My first spring training in Arizona was fun, and productive. After ten years in the major leagues, I was finally beginning to study pitchers, make mental notes of what to expect from them in given situations. In the past I'd always just gone up there swinging, never thinking about what kind of pitch a guy was most likely to throw me. Anticipating sure made hitting a lot easier.

The only problem I had was that Barbara had finally remarried, which helped financially, but her new husband wanted to adopt my children. That was one thing I swore I would never allow—taking my name away from my children. It was bad enough losing my kids without having them bearing somebody else's name. My family felt the same way, particularly my Aunt Fifi, who had raised my brother Billy. She kept telling me, "Never—never give up your kids forever. If they don't carry your name, you lose them forever. You have a son, Joseph Anthony Pepitone, Jr. Let him keep your name." Fifi loved children, having never had any, and I felt the same way she did about my kids and my name.

Barbara's attorney hit me with a subpoena on our first trip to San Francisco to play the Giants. I had to go before a judge regarding the application for adoption, which really broke me up. Stevie had made the trip to the Coast with me, thank goodness. I needed her.

My attorney, Bill Sherr, pushed me to sign the papers. What he said made eminent sense: "Your daughter knows who you are. When she gets older, she'll come to see you if she wants to. She knows you are her father. But her new father is with her and Joseph all the time. You're all the way across the country and almost never see them. It will be better for the children if they take their stepfather's name."

"No way," I told him. "I'm not signing away my daughter and my son to some stranger. To anyone. They are *my* children. I just can't do it."

Sherr kept after me, though, as he engaged in negotiations with Barbara's attorney to make a flat final settlement with her on child support payments. Finally I gave in. Not because of the money. Not because of Sherr's rationale on the benefits to the kids. I gave in because I hoped it would relieve some of the pressure in my head over the children. I did it for *me,* feeling maybe it would get them off my mind.

Late in the spring, Sherr negotiated a settlement figure of $20,000. The Cubs advanced me a check in that amount (to be deducted from my salary, which was now over $50,000 a year). I had to take it to Barbara in person and sign the check in front of her and her attorney. That was it. I no longer owed her anything. I no longer had any children by her. Case closed. I only cried for a week.

For perhaps the first time in my life, though, I didn't come apart in a bad moment. I didn't go berserk. I was feeling together living with Stevie, who understood, who comforted, who was good to be with. She was only a child herself in years, just twenty, but she was so much older intellectually and emotionally.

I had opened the season with a hot bat, and I stayed hot, which helped my head. I saw Billy Williams, a great hitter, studying movies of himself at bat, so every few days I started watching films of myself hitting. It allowed me to pick up any little thing I might be doing differently at the plate and correct the flaw in the game that afternoon. My batting average was over .300, and I was truly enjoying baseball.

Even when Diane hauled me into court to get her support payments raised to $175 a week, I didn't get upset. I told all the guys in the clubhouse, "That's all right, I can be happy on twenty-three dollars a week."

Glenn Beckert, who I liked to kid with, said, "The next time your wife needs a witness, she can call me."

"Which wife?" said Bill Hands.

"Smart aleck," I said. "I'm rid of the first one. The second one, she'll get married someday, too. She's a good-looking woman."

"When are you getting married again?" someone asked.

"The next time I marry, it'll be to a man." I said, "And with my luck, he'll get pregnant."

The one thing that annoyed me was that I chipped a bone in my left elbow making a throw from the outfield on a cold day, and it hurt me all season. The chip irritated a nerve, and the pain got so bad that I couldn't throw a ball across a room. Leo moved me in to first base, which I still liked better than the outfield, but on May 19 I had to go on the disabled list for fifteen days and just rest my arm.

I had always been a streak hitter. When I came off the disabled list I went on a streak that lasted through nineteen games, which even I found incredible. I batted .429 in those nineteen games and raised my average to .350—third best in the National League. Not surprisingly, the writers swarmed around me.

"Man, I'm just a lousy two fifty-nine hitter [my lifetime average]," I told them all. "I'm not a superstar. I'm a stupid star."

Before I went 0-for-4 against John Cumberland of the Giants on June 22, several writers actually asked me if I thought I had a shot at breaking Joe DiMaggio's major-league record of hitting in fifty-six consecutive games. I laughed.

"Joe D's my hero, my all-time idol," I told them. "But let's suppose I did hit in fifty-five games in a row. Now, I know it's not going to happen. But if it did, I'd quit, because there's no way I'd want to break his record." That was bullshit, of course, but it gave the guys something to write. If I had ever hit in fifty-five consecutive games they would have dragged me off to jail, because they would have known I was on something.

The best thing about the streak was that we won thirteen of those nineteen games. Unfortunately, we couldn't come close to that pace the rest of the way. We finished tied with the Mets for third place in the National League's Eastern Division. Although my bad elbow cost me some of my power at the plate and I hit only sixteen home runs, I did bat over .300—.307—for the first time in the majors. If I hadn't missed the last three weeks of the season, I would have had closer to eighty RBIs than the sixty-one I ended up with. About a month after the season, I had the bone chip removed in Wesley Memorial Hospital, where I read rumors that the Cubs were trying to trade me. Christ, I thought, I bat .300 for the first time and my team's trying to trade me?

Then I read a story that quoted John Holland, the Cubs' general manager, to the effect that the rumors were nonsense. "It may come as a surprise to some people, but Pepitone is the best clutch hitter we have," said Holland, which surprised *me*. "We keep statistics on such things and they reveal that Joe has the best percentage, insofar as hitting with men on base is concerned, of anybody on the ball club. As a matter of fact, I believe that our poor showing in the final six weeks would not have happened if Pepitone had been physically sound. We missed his clutch hitting. With him, we might have been in the fight for the division title right down to the end."

Thanks, John, I thought. Remember those words at contract time.

I needed more money because I had decided to open a lounge in Chicago. I had talked to Ron Santo, who, with his business manager-partner, had been very successful in starting businesses in the city. I asked them if they wanted to be partners in my place. They declined, but arranged a forty-thousand-dollar loan for me. It was going to be a nice little saloon which I would call, "Joe Pepitone's Thing." When the team was in town, I could be there nightly to observe what was going on, something I couldn't do with "Joe Pepitone's My Place" after I was traded. I had sure as hell been in enough saloons over the last decade to know what ingredients were necessary to make one a success. And ninety percent of the profits would be mine. For the help Ron and his partner gave me in getting the bank financing, I gave each of them five percent of the club.

"We'll tell all our friends to come and see your thing," said Ron, giggling.

XXI

"Look, the Chicago Zoo
is three blocks away."

John Holland remembered his words. The contract I signed for the '72 season called for a salary of $60,000. I moved into a two-bedroom penthouse apartment and spent all my time getting "Joe Pepitone's Thing" ready to open.

I had no trouble at all getting my liquor license, which is a lengthy, runaround procedure in New York City. My attorney in Chicago, Sam Banks, who knows *everyone* in the city, sent me to see a guy in Mayor Daley's office, and he pushed the whole thing through in a matter of days. The license cost me 217 autographs. I had to pass through every other office in city hall and sign for everyone in them.

I was now kind of sorry that I had fired Fabulous Howard, because he really knew how to get publicity, and a new lounge needs all it can get. One morning during the '71 season, he had called me from downstairs about an hour early. I looked at my watch and said, "Shit, Fabulous, we don't have to leave for the ball park yet."

"Joe, get down here right away," he said. "I've got a surprise for you. You're going to love it."

I got dressed, went down to the lobby, and saw a whole crowd of people gathered by the limousine parked at the curb. About a dozen newspapermen and television reporters. Fabulous saw me and hit the horn. As soon as I stepped out the door, he gave a little flip with his hands and the red carpet he held began unrolling toward me. The carpet tumbled over and over until it flattened at my feet, and written on the end of it were the words THE FANTASTIC PEPITONE.

He was fun, and I hated to fire a guy I wasn't even paying. But I caught his act on a television program one morning, and he made me mad as hell. He said that he was responsible for my having my first good season in years, that he had made me what I was in Chicago. When he came to pick me up that day, I said, "You got some pair of balls."

"You saw the show, Joe?" he said. "Don't let it bother you. No matter what I say, it's good for you, Joe."

"Oh, yeah?" I said, seething. "Well let me hear you say, 'Good-bye.' Because I don't want to see you again."

The press enjoyed his act, and Fabulous would have been an asset in the weeks before I opened the lounge on New Year's Eve. As it turned out, "Joe Pepitone's Thing" didn't need any extra publicity. We were packed opening night, and stayed packed for eight or nine months, often with people lined up outside waiting to get in.

The club was small, long, and narrow, and located on Division Street, just off Rush, in the swingingest section of Chicago. You entered the lounge by walking down a flight of stairs carpeted with Astroturf, opened a door into a little foyer, then another door into the place itself. There was a high-chair bar on one side of the room, and a balcony with tables on the other side. A railing of black baseball bats separated the tables from the main floor. The walls were full of black-and-white photos of me in action, and a large oil painting of your host in a Cub uniform. We had no food and no live music, just a jukebox. The bartenders and waitresses were all attractive girls. They were not burdened by a lot of cumbersome clothing.

We drew a terrific athlete crowd. Most of the guys from the local teams—the Cubs, the White Sox, the Bears, the Bulls, the Black Hawks—as well as visiting players stopped in. And the lounge quickly earned a reputation as a place where stewardesses hung out, which was true. As any innkeeper knows, when you got the girls—you get the guys.

I had a few initial problems, which were to be expected in any business where you served drinks. My manager wasn't up to the task. I fired him and brought Dominic, who was separated from his wife, and my brother Billy, who was accompanied by his wife, in from New York to manage the place for me. Dominic had plenty of experience in running a club, and Billy is very sharp. They did a great job.

We had one night that would have been a total disaster without them. I had been having trouble with the waitresses and bartenders for several weeks. Customers were complaining that they couldn't get service because the girls were spending too much time socializing with certain guys. I saw that the customers were right. I warned the girls that they had to tend to business or they were going to have to go. "Right on, Joe," they said. But the complaints not only continued, they increased. Then one Friday evening I walked into the lounge, and the first four customers I passed said the same thing, "Hey, Joe, what do I have to do to get a drink in here?" I saw that two of the waitresses and one of the bartenders were just standing around talking to guys, while the other customers stood there with empty glasses in their hands and annoyed looks on their faces. I got furious. I yelled for quiet, and said I was sorry but we had just lost all of our waitresses and bartenders. I fired all of them.

That left us with a serious problem, of course, and I asked everyone to please bear with us. Dominic and I went behind the bar, and Billy worked the floor. Dominic knew how to mix drinks. My total drink-mixing repertoire consisted of whiskey and water. I'll be damned if my first customer wasn't a chick who ordered a weird drink.

"What was that you ordered, Miss?" I asked.

"A banshee."

"A what?"

"A banshee."

"Look, do me a favor," I said. "The Chicago Zoo is three blocks away. I think you'll find one of those in cage nineteen."

Then a guy ordered a sloe gin fizz. "Pal," I said, "would you like that beer in a fucking glass?"

For the rest of the night, if anyone ordered anything except a beer, I served the same drink. "What'll you have?"

"One martini, one screwdriver, and two stingers."

"Right."

"Hey, these all taste like Scotch and water."

"We lost all our barmaids this afternoon," I'd say. "You have four or five of those, they'll sting you."

A few people walked out, most laughed and drank up, or squeezed down toward Dominic. But we got through it. The next morning I hired a whole new crew of girls, and everything was fine.

Things were anything but fine with the Cubs. I had a good spring in Arizona, Stevie was with me, the lounge was making money and I felt I was going to have a big season. The Cubs had traded for Rick Monday and Jose Cardenal, both center fielders, so I was being switched back to first base permanently. My arm was strong again, and I was swinging the bat well. Then the Players' Association called a strike and we went out for two weeks. When we came back, the season started, and I had completely lost my timing at the plate. I couldn't hit a goddamn thing. I was coming off a .300 season, I expected to be super, and I couldn't get good wood on the ball no matter what I tried. I started pressing. In the first five games my batting average was .125.

But most of the guys weren't hitting. Everyone's timing was off. I was shocked when we went to New York to play the Mets on April 23 and saw that my name wasn't on the lineup card. It really pissed me off. I wasn't going to start hitting while sitting on the bench. Six guys weren't hitting, and Leo benched me. Why me? I thought. I felt like a scapegoat. Here I'd been happy in Chicago for a year and a half, had really busted my butt trying to do the right thing, to concentrate and play good ball, and I'd succeeded—only to be benched. Suddenly I felt shitty again, because the benching not only seemed unfair, it didn't make any sense at all to me.

This crap kept playing on my mind the next day when I had to stay over in New York to make a court appearance with Diane regarding her alimony payments. The bullshit all seemed to come down at once again, and it made me sick to my stomach. I joined the team in Houston and vomited my guts out before the game. Leo had me back in the starting lineup, but I couldn't play that night or the next one. My stomach was screaming and tearing at me.

When we got back to Chicago, I saw the team physician, Dr. Jacob Suker. But then I felt okay, my stomach had settled down. I seemed to be a little more relaxed at home with Stevie. Then suddenly my stomach started ripping at me again. I didn't report to the ball park on Sunday, April 30. Leo called, and I told him I was sick. He told me to meet Dr. Suker at Wesley Memorial Hospital. The doctor said I had gastritis, which is an inflammation of the stomach lining. I also had an inflammation of the brain. Once again, I hated baseball, hated the shit it was constantly putting me through.

Dr. Suker had given me antacids and told me to see him again on Monday. I didn't show up. I'd had enough baseball bullshit. Ever since I'd been in the game I'd disliked and rebelled against the establishment, against authority, against anyone who put pressure on me. I realized now that the rebelling stemmed from my father, who had smacked me around and forced me to do everything he told me to without allowing me to even begin to question his directives, to tell him how *I* felt about any part of them. Once he died I was free, on my own, and I know now I had needed some strong guidance along the way. I never got any that I respected enough to follow. And it was far too late now to allow myself to be put down by a game I was finally beginning to play properly. It wasn't worth that pain in my gut.

I reported to Wrigley Field on Tuesday, May 2, and was told that vice-president John Holland wanted to see me in his office. He was just the man I wanted to see. Before he could open his mouth, I said, "John, I want you to put me on the voluntary retirement list. I've had it with baseball. I'm not going to play any more." Holland spent half an hour trying to talk me out of it. He pointed out that once my name went on the retired list, I couldn't return to baseball for sixty days even if I decided to. I told him that I understood, but that I didn't plan to come back.

"You'll be welcome, Joe, if you do want to rejoin us," he said.

"Thank you, John," I said.

John Holland was a nice man, but there was no point in trying to fool myself. I wasn't going to help the Cubs or myself in my frame of mind. I was thankful I had my "Thing" to turn to. I liked to fish and there was good fishing in Lake Michigan. I had bought an eighteen-foot powerboat, and I was looking forward to having plenty of time during the summer to use it. I loved toys. I'd also bought a 650cc custom-chopped Triumph motorcycle that Stevie and I cruised around on. It was fun, and we'd be able to do a lot more cruising now. It was really going to be nice not having to go to the ball park every afternoon. I felt as if the driver who had parked his truck on my head ten years ago had finally returned and backed it off.

The lounge was going great. I was clearing as much as eight hundred dollars a week. But even with Dominic and Billy, it was no easy gig. We put in a lot of hours, and there were always problems to deal with. There was a small back room in the place with a horseshoe-shaped bar, a working fireplace, one table, and chairs. When it got too hectic out front, I'd sit in there with a few friends, escape from the crazies. We had plenty of them hanging around. One guy, whom I'll call Kelly, was funny as hell, and he was always carrying great dope. He'd come in, pull out a whole sack of grass, and put it on the bar, yelling, "Heyyyy—here is some super smoke." He was so nutsy, he didn't care who was in the place. I liked him, but I told him if he didn't knock off that stuff, I would bar him. If the police observed his act, they'd take my license. Kelly was funny. I'd get a phone call from him and he'd say, "Joe, you got to come pick me up. My car broke down in Oak Park and I can't get back to Chicago." I'd yell, curse him out, and finally agree to go get him. Then I'd hear a scream of laughter across the room. I'd see Kelly doubled up by the phone on that wall.

One night I was sitting in the back room when Billy came in and said, "Joe, Mrs. Phil Wrigley and her son are out front."

"What?" Who the hell ever expected the wife of the owner of the Cubs to show up at my saloon? I cleared everyone out of the back room and told Billy to show them in. I was a nervous wreck. What if crazy Kelly popped in and laid some grass on the table?

Mrs. Wrigley walked in and said, "Joe, this is a nice little place you have here."

"Thank you, Mrs. Wrigley," I said, as she and her son Bill sat down. "What would you like to drink?"

"A pitcher of beer," she said.

We sat there and drank most of it, had some funny conversation, and they left. Two minutes later Kelly burst into the back room smoking a joint and singing a dirty song.

The lounge wasn't all fun and games, though. I closed the place late one night, locked the doors, and turned up the street for home, when a guy came out of nowhere and hit me in the back of the head. Luckily he didn't catch me solid. I whirled around and knocked him down. "What the fuck is this?" I said.

He sat on the sidewalk rubbing his jaw and explained that his girl had asked me for an autograph earlier in the evening and never got it. I remembered the girl. I'd been called in back by Dominic right at that moment, and I told the girl I'd return in a minute. When I did, she was gone. I thought she had left the place. I'd forgotten about the whole thing until I got hit in the back of the head.

Another night I came in a little late, and there were two cops in the place with a guy whose face was bleeding. The police were questioning my brother. It seemed that the guy had stolen one of the decorative plastic batting helmets we had hanging on a wall. Billy saw him slip it under his jacket, took it back, and told the guy to leave. An hour or so later, the guy was back. Sure enough, he took the same helmet again. Billy caught up to him as the guy was going up the steps. Billy told him to return the helmet and never come back in the lounge again. The guy kicked Billy in the stomach. Billy got up, ran after the guy, and beat hell out of him. I knew one of the cops, and he said he'd take care of the guy without anything going on the records.

But for all the fun I had and all the fishing I got in, after about three and a half weeks of not playing ball, I had to admit to myself that I missed it. Quitting the Cubs had been the stupidest thing I'd ever done. Simply because I'd been benched for one game. I'd acted like a spoiled kid, because that's exactly what I was, what I'd always been. When something went wrong, it was easier to run from it than deal with it. When the fuck, I wondered, was I ever going to learn?

I started going to Cub games, going early so I could stop into the clubhouse, hang around the dugout. When the game started, I had to retreat into the stands, where I'd sit and watch and wish I was out there with the guys. What the hell was I doing in the stands when my team was on the field, when there wasn't a goddamn thing wrong with me physically? Maybe I should have had my psychiatrist go on the road with me, move in with me.

On Saturday, May 27, I was in the dugout talking to a couple of the guys before the game when coach Pete Reiser came over and said, "You're coming back, aren't you?"

"Yes," I said. It just popped out of me. I hadn't planned it. But I meant it. I wanted to come back. John Holland called me and I told him I was serious about what I'd told Reiser. I wanted to start working out with the club. The Cubs put me on a workout program to get into shape by June 30, when I could go back on the active roster, and I even traveled with the club till then. I could be paid meal money, but not salary. I would be out twenty thousand dollars in salary.

The writers thought money was the main reason I was returning. Actually, I was living comfortably on the income from the lounge. I told the writers that my mother, who had visited me over the Memorial Day weekend, was a big factor. She wasn't, even though she had urged me to get into uniform again. The only factor in my return was my head.

I told Phil Pepe of the New York *Daily News* that the reason I was coming back was because the fish had run out. "When the coho stopped running," I said, "there was nothing to do. I love fishing. I've always loved it. I started in the sewers of Brooklyn, and worked my way all the way up to Lake Michigan. Imagine."

Pepe asked me what guarantee was I giving the Cubs that I wouldn't quit and go fishing again before the season ended.

"No guarantee," I told him, honestly. "I don't know what I'm going to do. I was thirty-one in October, but my body is eighty-five, and my mind is sixteen."

Pepe sent me regards from Ralph Houk, who said I was a good guy and that I could have been a great ballplayer.

"I was a great ballplayer last year," I said.

I wanted to find out if I still could be. Durocher was a little cool to me: "What can I say about him?" I heard him tell a writer. "I can't open the man's head." So were most of my teammates. Virtually all of my teammates. One reason was that when I quit we had a 4–10 record, and then the Cubs went on to win sixteen of their next twenty-three games. I knew the guys resented the fact that I'd left them when the club was going bad and that I was rejoining them when they were going well.

I couldn't let the coolness bother me. I couldn't put on any kind of act. I rejoined them as the same loose Joe Pepitone I'd always been. I worked hard to get into shape, which they observed, and I had some fun.

We were all watching Roberto Clemente take batting practice before a game against the Pirates, and he was pure magic at the plate. "Notice how nothing moves when he swings except his arms and hips," I said. "That's the way I want to hit when I grow up."

When I stepped into the cage for my swings, our batting practice pitcher, a young rookie, threw me a scuffed baseball. "It's dirty!" I yelled. "Is that any kind of ball to throw to a former Yankee great?"

Most of the coolness had withered by the time I went back on the active roster. But Durocher put me right into the starting lineup, and the coolness reappeared. I took care of that by hitting good for a couple of weeks. I couldn't sustain it. Whitey Lockman replaced Durocher as manager in late July, and Whitey started platooning me against left-handed pitchers. I kept my mouth shut, because that's all you can do when you're not pounding the ball. I wasn't.

I finished with a .262 batting average, only eight home runs, and a miserable twenty-one RBIs. The team finished in second place, eleven games behind Pittsburgh. I wondered how many of those eleven games I might have won if I had been present. It was apparent that my teammates were wondering, too.

Of course, no one was rooting for me to grow up more than I was. I knew it was getting awfully late in my game. Awfully late.

XXII

"Why are you doing this to me, Whitey?"

I stopped seeing my teammates at the lounge. Ron Santo came by occasionally, not because he had a small piece of the place but because we were friends and he was sympathetic even if he couldn't understand my head. *That* was understandable.

Soon none of the ballplayers could go to "Joe Pepitone's Thing" if they wanted to. A newspaper story reported that all the bars on Division Street were being investigated by the police, who suspected that some of the lounges were employing people with criminal records, particularly drug-related violations. The headline on the story said: JOE PEPITONE'S BAR UNDER DRUG PROBE. Holy shit, I thought, that's not going to do me any good, even though at the end of the story it said that I wasn't implicated. I wasn't worried about turning over my employee records, which I did, because I knew that all my girls were clean.

But the day that headline appeared in the paper, every ball club in Chicago put my place off limits to its players. And where my day business alone had been bringing in between three and five hundred dollars, that afternoon I took in thirty-seven dollars. That night we had less than half our normal crowd.

Brent Musberger came down to do a radio interview with me, and I said, "Look, this probe is on the whole street, but I'm a baseball player and because my name is Joe Pepitone it makes the headlines. Everyone thinks they are investigating only me. And this is just a *check* on employees. There is no proof that any of my people have criminal records or anything like that. Why don't the papers wait until the police prove something before they print this kind of scare headline?"

Then Dominic walked over, and Brent asked him what he thought about the situation. Dominic said, "Let me tell you something. I know this kid and I've known him for years. I know how dedicated to baseball he is. You understand? It's terrible what these newspapers are doing to this kid. If he ever found anybody was doing drugs in this place, he'd break their heads, he'd bust open their faces. You understand? I'm his manager, I run this place with Joe, and I got a daughter, fifteen years old, back in Brooklyn, and if I ever knew she was doing drugs I'd bite her face off. You understand? I love this kid, and I know what he'd do to anyone who did drugs in his place— he'd break their legs and throw them out in the street. He'd *destroy* them. You understand?"

Dominic convinced the radio audience that I hated drugs— but that I was a potential murderer.

Our week's net fell from eight hundred dollars to six hundred; then five hundred, then four hundred, then three hundred, and kept sliding, even after we were cleared by the police. When a bar's "in," you can't keep the people out. Once that appeal is smudged, you can't get people in. You can't make it with an occasional crowd. You've got to have your basic regulars. My brother Billy went back to Brooklyn and joined the police force. I had to let several of the girls go. Dominic and I tried to keep the lounge going all through the fall. Just before New Year's, 1973, I was sitting in my apartment looking over the books and I realized it was hopeless. Where we once regularly cleared over a hundred dollars a night, we were now clearing twenty dollars—on a good night. I called Dominic at the lounge and told him to pack up all the liquor in the place and bring it up to my apartment. Then I called my friend Leroy who ran the garage in the building.

"Leroy," I said, "if you come up to my apartment in about an hour, I have a rare buy on liquor for you and any of the other guys down there who are interested in a one-time-only special. I'm selling every bottle from my lounge at seventy percent off."

I got rid of my entire stock in fourteen minutes and thirty-six seconds, and I was now out of the saloon business. I had earned back my investment, plus a little. But if it hadn't been for the headline in the papers, I could have really done well with the lounge. That was the story of my life, a lot of "I could have done ifs . . ."

I decided the lounge experience was just another pile of shit I had to step in, just like the hairstyling salon, the wives, the treadmill sex. At least I had gotten off that treadmill after I'd been with Stevie a while. I began thinking back on all that screwing, all those different girls, and I realized there was no feeling involved, that there was nothing good about it, really. It was all raw sexless sex—in, out and on to the next. Shit, I couldn't even remember what most of the girls looked like, much less their names. All those names, all those faces.

A girl had come into the lounge during the summer, a pretty redhead with a beautiful smile, gleaming teeth. "Hi, Joe!" she said, and threw her arms around me. "How are you?"

"Fine . . . fine," I said, looking at her closely.

"Don't you remember me?" she said.

"Oh . . . uh."

"The Carriage House in New York three years ago. Sylvia."

"Uh, let me think . . ."

"We spent two weeks together, at your place. Don't you *remember?*"

"I'm sorry. I'm really sorry, Sylvia." I just couldn't remember her, couldn't remember anything about her, and I couldn't lie to her, bullshit her along, fake it, as I would have a few years ago. I had come to realize that virtually all the people who are in charge, the people in authority, are phonies, hypocrites, liars. And that I was just like them. I was the worst phony and biggest liar in the world. As I got older, people began to see through me, through what I thought was a great act. Now I couldn't look anyone in the eye and lie any more. I felt better, being honest with others, and with myself.

It took an incredibly long time for me to get any perspective at all, but I was thankful that it was finally coming. Stevie helped. It was great to really dig somebody, like being with them as much as possible. I thought I loved her, thought about divorcing Diane and marrying Stephanie Deeker. We had such good times together. For the first time, I was happy simply sitting home with a girl, just being with her. But I still had this thing about Diane in the back of my head: maybe I'd want to go back with her some day. It was weird. I had a super relationship going with Stevie, yet I was still hung up on my second wife. Maybe, because I'd mutilated that relationship, it was simply guilt poking at my head, the feeling that I should make it up to Diane eventually.

All I knew for certain was that I loved living with Stevie. She was the most relaxed, together chick I'd ever known. She cared about as much about neatness around the apartment as I did. We liked to live, not straighten up a place every minute. I had Dominic staying with us for a few months, and he's a fanatic for neatness. He drove Stevie crazy with his puttering around. It reached the point where she told me he had to go. We had two dogs, a poodle, and a big sheep dog named Cockeye, one of which he happened to have. Cockeye also had a lot of hair, which he happened to shed constantly. Dominic couldn't stand the dog hairs in his room. One day Dominic hung up a sign on his door that said "No Dogs Allowed," and locked the door from the inside. Our only bathroom was off Dominic's bedroom.

"Get him out of here, Joe," Stevie said. "Because if he doesn't leave, I'm going to."

I picked the lock with a hairpin, opened the door, and Cockeye went bounding in. He jumped right up on Dominic's chest —because he was used to sleeping on that bed when Dom was out—and stood there wagging his tail. With every wag, a dozen hairs fell onto Dominic. When I stopped laughing, I told him he had to find his own place. He took an apartment in a building around the corner that was owned by a woman he knew.

I was still as jealous as ever, and I kept checking up on Stevie at the Playboy Club. Any time she'd go home to Kansas City to visit her mother and stepfather, I'd worry. Her stepfather, Jim Shipley, was a helluva guy. I'd been hunting with him a couple of times and really enjoyed his company. He also liked to go out evenings, and any time Stevie would visit, they'd bounce around. I'd call her at three o'clock in the morning, and her mother would say, "Stevie's not home yet, Joe."

"Not home—at this hour?"

"Well, she's out with her father."

"What do you mean, out with her father? Everything in Kansas City closes at two in the morning. Look, Mrs. Shipley, have her call me when she gets home. I don't care what time it is. It's important."

I'd sit there waiting . . . three-thirty, four o'clock, four-thirty, five o'clock . . . worrying. Who is she really with? At five-thirty, Stevie would call.

"Where the hell have you been?"

"We went to an after-hours place."

"With your *father?* Who are you shitting?"

All of a sudden, Jim would come on the phone. "Joe, she was with me. Be cool."

"Oh, everything's all right, Jim. I wasn't really worried."

In November, when it was apparent that the lounge was on its way out, I called John Holland to find out how I fitted into the Cubs' plans for 1973. If at all. He was noncommittal, but he said that Whitey Lockman would be in the office in a few days and that I could come by and talk to him. I did.

"I was just thirty-two last month," I told Lockman. "I'm in good shape. I don't run around at night any more, my legs feel good. And I can still outhit half the guys in this league. I know it."

"You don't have to sell me on the fact that you can still play baseball, Joe," he said. "I know what you can do. You can help us if you want to. But do you want to? Do you still want to play baseball, Joe? You've got a lot of things to prove to a lot of guys on this club. You've got to convince everyone that you're going to play ball and not quit in the middle of the season."

"Let me show you in spring training," I said. "I'll show you and everyone else what I'm going to do this season. I really want to get back. I really want to play."

I went to spring training to prove that I could still play exceptional baseball. I didn't do any clowning around at the Cubs camp in Scottsdale, Arizona. No kidding at all. Just hustle on the ballfield. When the exhibition games started, Lockman put me with the B team, which was made up entirely of utility men. I hit with this team, trained with it, and traveled with it to road games. It shocked the shit out of me, made me angry. But I held my tongue. I knew Lockman was testing me, and I knew I could hit my way back onto the regular squad.

I ran hard, and hit the ball hard. After three weeks with the B team, though, I couldn't contain myself any longer. I went to Lockman.

"Why are you doing this to me, Whitey?" I said. "What are you trying to prove?"

He stared into my eyes. "I'm getting trouble from you already?" he said.

I turned away. "Just forget about what I said, Whitey. I don't want to get into any arguments."

I kept hitting well, and all of a sudden Lockman started me at first base with the regulars. I got three hits. He kept me with the regulars, and in the next week I got two or three hits every game. I hustled. I kept my mouth shut. I batted .400 in spring training and won the regular job at first base.

Lockman played Jim Hickman at first against most left-handed pitchers, but that was all right. I understood. I planned to hit so well against righties that I'd force the manager to play me against every kind of pitching.

When the season opened, I came out swinging, and the line drives were zinging off my bat. Lockman sat me down against lefties, but I was patient. I felt good. There was plenty of time. I'd show him.

Then, before a game against the Cardinals, the lineup card was posted and I wasn't on it. I checked the Cards' starting pitcher, and saw it was Scipio Spinks, a right-hander. I let out a yell in the clubhouse.

"What the fuck is going on here? I'm swinging good. I'm hitting the ball. What the fuck is this?" I started toward Lockman's office.

Ron Santo grabbed me and said, "Wait a minute, baby. This is what it's all about. This is the true test. You understand?"

"Yeah," I said, heading for my locker. "It's not right, but I get it. I'm okay now."

Another right-handed pitcher started against us the following day. I couldn't wait to see the lineup card. My name was on it. I drove in five runs that day, and in the locker room afterward, Santo came by. He was singing, "What a Difference a Day Makes."

I smiled and said to myself, Up yours, Whitey Lockman. I'll win this job full time whether you know it or not.

A month later I was still being platooned, because I couldn't get in a hitting groove when I was sitting down every second or third game. I had thirty hits in twenty-eight games for a .268 average, three home runs, and eighteen RBIs. Not great, but by no means terrible, either.

The last two of those thirty hits came in Philadelphia on a Saturday afternoon in mid-May. Since I was no longer banging around at night, I had dinner that evening and went back to my hotel room to watch television. About eight o'clock the phone rang. Oh shit, I thought, somebody wants to have a drink or something, and I don't feel like it.

I picked up the phone and said, "Hello."

The guy on the line didn't identify himself, simply said, "You just got traded."

"Go fuck yourself," I said, and hung up on the wise-ass.

The phone rang again. "Joe, this is Whitey Lockman. I wasn't kidding. You've been traded to the Braves. I think it's best for you, best for everyone. The Braves really want you, and I think the change will help you a lot. Eddie Mathews is anxious for you to report to Atlanta as soon as possible. I think he plans to play you regularly at first base."

"Great," I said, and hung up.

But I didn't feel great. The writers came by and told me the Cubs hadn't gotten a lot for me—a minor-league first baseman named Andy Thornton, and an "undisclosed" amount of cash. They asked me how I felt.

"It's all part of baseball," I said. "I'm part of baseball, and I go where the game sends me. I'm disappointed because I like Chicago. I was having a fair year and we were winning. I think the Cubs are going to do it this year."

I just hoped I could beat them every single time they played the Braves. I was hurt and pissed off inside. I felt way down in my gut that this would have been my best year. I finally knew all the pitchers, I concentrated on every pitch, I could make all the plays on the bases and in the field, and I really wanted to prove something. Then the assholes dump me. I'd fucked it up in the past—I'd fucked it up so many times I couldn't count them—but they'd fucked it up this time. The Cubs had a shot at the pennant, and they gave away the only solid first-baseman they had. Fuck them. Fuck me.

I went back to Chicago for a couple of days to be with Stevie, and to think. The Braves' general manager, Eddie Robinson, called. I told him I'd report to Atlanta on Tuesday, that I had to straighten out a few personal things. I talked to Stevie, who was still working at the Playboy Club, and she said she'd go with me to Atlanta if I wanted her to. I sure as hell wanted her to. I told her I'd go first and find us a place to live.

The Atlanta ball park was a nice stadium to hit in, and Eddie Mathews turned out to be a beautiful guy, easy to talk to, honest with you, no bullshit. All the Braves were nice, a good bunch of guys. But in less than a week, I'd had it with major-league baseball. I was hitting all right: four singles in eleven at-bats. I just didn't have any feeling for the game, and I asked myself, What the hell am I doing this for when I'm totally uninvolved? I wanted to be with Stevie. As soon as she got here, though, the team would have to go off on a road trip. Stevie and I wouldn't be together. I'd leave the one person I had tremendous feelings for, to do something I had no feeling for. I had to be crazy to do that.

I went to Mathews and told him it had nothing to do with him or the Braves but I was quitting. He tried to talk me into staying, as did the general manager, Eddie Robinson. He said the club would take care of all my bills if that was what was bugging me. I told him that wasn't it, that I wasn't in much debt now, that I just didn't have any feeling for baseball any more, and I wasn't going to help the club a whole lot if I wasn't motiviated. I also said that if I stayed, I thought I would go out of my mind. I would have to put on one hell of an act to play. And I was getting too old for any more phony bullshit.

I told the press, "My decision is final. I'm tired of the hassle of moving and establishing myself in another town. I'm tired of this kind of baseball, and I want out. I hate the Cubs for trading me the way they did. I busted my ass for them this spring, then they trade me. I just wanted to prove something to those bastards, then I decided proving something wasn't worth the price I'd have to pay."

On the flight to Chicago, I got down, deeply depressed, which wasn't surprising. I was finished with major-league baseball. There was no going back this time. I'd quit before, but every other time I knew that I could return when I wanted to, that some team would want me. I'd put an end to that option this time. Three quits is out. No team would sign me now, because there was no guarantee that I would stay with it, that I wouldn't abruptly take off. I couldn't give any guarantees. But now I wondered, What was I going to do for a living?

When Eddie Robinson had asked me that, I'd told him that I might consider playing in Japan. He'd said that he would make inquiries of the teams there. I started thinking about Japan seriously now. I sure as hell didn't feel like playing any more baseball in the major leagues, even if I was asked to. Hell, the Braves wanted me to. There were just too many bad vibes for me in the majors, vibes that went far beyond all the bullshit in the game, which was bad enough. What was worse—what was the heart of the matter—were all those wasted years that were flashing through my head now. It was just too hard to be around the game, because it only made me think about what I could have been, what I should have been.

In twelve years in the majors, I had hit 219 home runs. I should have hit closer to 400. Much closer. In twelve years in the majors, my batting average was .258. It should have been closer to .298. Much closer. All I had had to do was take care of myself a little bit, have even a minuscule regard for my body, and concentrate about ninety percent of the time, instead of the fifty percent of the time which I did. I had spent most of those twelve years letting talent alone carry me along, making so little real effort myself that now all I was left with was guilt. That seemed to be my only real goal in life: to see just how much guilt I could accumulate, drag around. Escape, escape, escape . . . and pile up the guilt. Well, I'd worked hard at accumulating it.

I'd earned every bit of it. And, after all these years, the bill collector in my head was one very tough dude to dodge.

When I got home, I thought about Clete Boyer, my old Yankee teammate. He had quit the Braves and gone to Japan two or three years ago. He was still playing over there, so it must be a pretty good deal. It gave me something to think about. Getting out of this country might be a damn good thing for my head. I called Eddie Robinson to tell him I was definitely interested in Japan if I could make the right deal.

A few days later he called to tell me the Tokyo Yakult Atoms of Japan's Central Professional League had made me an offer. I thought the salary was low. He called me with a better offer, but I told him I thought we could do better. The third offer I couldn't refuse: a $70,000-a-year contract for two seasons, and the club would pay for my housing in Japan. Wow!

"Stevie, quit your job and pack your bags," I told her. "Your Number One fliend is taking you to a velly fine place. Banzai!"

One sportswriter wondered how long it would take me to get oriented over there. I had my fingers clossed.

XXIII

"Joe no play: shitty in pantsy."

On the way to Japan, Stevie and I stopped in Brooklyn to see my family. Through all the years I'd been playing ball, every time I came home, my grandfather would call me in and give me a lecture. "Hey, Giuseppe," he'd say, "when are you gonna stop fooling around? Your mamma, she worries about you so much. You fool around with all these girls, and you no swinga the bat so good."

"Who do you want me to fool around with—guys?" I'd say.

"Sometimes I think it be better you fool around witha guys," he'd say. "Maybe it make you hit better."

Now Vincent Caiazzo was ninety years old, but he was still incredibly sharp, a truly amazing man. This time when I stopped by, he called me in and said, "I'm not gonna give you no lecture. I just wanna tell you two things. First, I wanna wish you all the good luck in the world, from my heart. I wish you show all the bums that's here, the Yankees and all of them, that you great, that you should be play in this country." He shook his fist.

"The second thing I wanna tell you is to take these," he handed me two dimes. "Before you go to Japan, I wanna you to go down to the butcher shop and buy youself two pounds of brains and put them in you head."

We arrived in Tokyo on June 19. We were met by a delegation from the Yakult Atoms bearing bouquets of roses. "Will you look at this," I said to Stevie. "They know how to treat a star over here!"

I was presented with my own personal interpreter, an Italian-Japanese named Luigi Ferdenza. He took us to our apartment, a nicely furnished two-bedroom place in which I couldn't wear platform shoes without banging my head in the doorways.

We went out to dinner that night, and I discovered that I was going to have all kinds of trouble communicating here. Like, how many times can you say, "Ah so"? And "hari-kari" didn't get me anything in the restaurant except a dirty look. The food was fine, but the bill was not. What seemed like an awful lot of yen written on the bottom of the bill, translated into an awful lot of dollars: eighty-six of 'em. I could see that I was going to lose weight in Japan.

On the way back to our apartment, we stopped for a drink in a typical bar. We had one drink apiece. The bill was eight dollars.

"Stevie," I said as we left, "we're in trouble. We can't afford to eat or drink in this country. We are making seventy thousand dollars a year, and we will have to starve and walk around with dry mouths in order to keep any of it."

Luigi Ferdenza, a nice, pleasant kid, picked me up the next morning and took me to the ball park. He introduced me to the manager and several players, none of whom spoke English. This was going to be a weird experience, I thought. The Japanese teams are allowed to carry only two American ballplayers. Arturo Lopez, a Puerto Rican who was born and raised in New York City and who used to be on the Yankees with me, was the other American. Thank goodness I had someone I could talk to other than Luigi.

The Yakult Atoms were owned by a company that made an orange drink that tasted like the Creamsicles I used to eat as a kid. Thick and sweet. You drank one, and it made you so thirsty you had to have another. The man who owned the company that owned my new team was one very clever businessman. While I changed into my baseball uniform, I drank six of those insidious orange drinks.

When the game started, I felt rumblings in my stomach.

When we came into the dugout for the bottom of the second, I had the runs. "Luigi," I said, "where is the bathroom?"

He led me into the clubhouse and pointed at a door. "Through there."

I went through the door, and all I saw inside was a line of holes in the floor, with rolls of toilet paper set beside each hole. "Luigi," I yelled, "hurry!" He came running in. "Somebody stole all the toilet bowls!"

"Joe," he said, "there are not toilets in Japan. You have to pee in that hole, that's all."

"Luigi, I have to shit. How the hell do I manage that?"

"Just squat over the bowl," he said. "It's not hard. You'll get used to it." He went back into the clubhouse. "Hurry up. I'll wait for you."

I pulled down my pants, squatted, and almost tilted back into the hole. I got my balance and—"Goddamnit!"—I had diarrhea. I had it all over my legs. Those rotten orange drinks. But, Christ, I thought, Luigi said I'll get used to this. Are all Japanese bombardiers, or what?

"Luigi!" I called, and he came hustling back in. At least I liked his style, if not his toilets. "Tell the manager I won't be able to play any more today. I shit all over myself."

"What? What am I supposed to tell the manager?"

"Christ, Luigi, just look at me. You're the interpreter. Say, 'Joe no play: shitty in pantsy.' "

"Be serious, Joe. Clean up and I'll get you new pants. Hurry up."

I hurried, changed, and made it back to first base for the next inning. I made a nice play in the field, but I didn't help the Atoms at bat. I went 0-for-4. I was surprised at how good the Japanese pitching was. As good as a lot of major-league pitchers in America. I was also suprised at how out of shape I was. I sure needed some extra batting practice.

Late that afternoon, Stevie and I went shopping. We had about a hundred little things to pick up for the apartment, which took a couple of hours. Then Stevie had to go to the bathroom. We went into a couple of restaurants and tried to find a bathroom, but we couldn't—and we couldn't make anyone understand what we wanted. So we kept walking until we saw a big sign in English: TOILET. Stevie went in and I waited outside the door. A minute later, a guy walked right through the door Stevie had entered. I heard her shriek. I ran in, saw Stevie squatting down, and standing next to her peeing into the adjacent hole was the guy.

"What the hell are you doing, you sonofabitch!" I yelled.

The guy turned his head and smiled, nodding.

Then I looked around and saw a couple of other guys and a couple of other women going to the bathroom side by side. In Japan, I discovered, the public toilets are unisex. That's the way you had to do it. Stevie wasn't too thrilled.

Within a week, I hated Japan. I didn't have anyone to talk to except Stevie, Luigi, and Arturo Lopez. Arturo was friendly for the first few days, then even he stopped talking to me. I didn't know what was wrong. We went for a couple of drinks after a game, and I asked Arturo what was going on, why he'd grown so distant. Shit, we were the only Americans on the team, and while we didn't have to become bosom buddies, we could at least converse with one another.

"You probably don't remember this," he said, "but one night you and Mantle were going out, and I said, 'Are you guys going to get something to eat?' And you lied to me because you didn't want me along."

Oh, shit, I thought. I did remember. Arturo had been carrying this around in his head all these years. Mickey had said something like, "We got to go someplace, Arturo." Then we did go to dinner and who walked into the restaurant later but Arturo. I remembered it, because I'd felt bad for an instant then. But I said to myself, Tough shit, Arturo—I'm with a star. I was a front-runner and figured I'd rather live in Dallas, Texas, than in Spanish Harlem. Now I felt lousy, because that slight had really hurt Arturo. I'd never given it a second thought, till now, and it was too late to do anything about it.

Stevie didn't like Japan any better than I did. Because of the language problem, we couldn't get around very well, go any place we thought we might want to. It was difficult getting *anything* we wanted. So we ended up just hanging around the apartment and bugging one another. The bad vibes of our circumstances caused bad vibes between us. It was ridiculous. We felt like we'd been shot into another world, and there wasn't a good thing we could say about it.

Within a couple of weeks I received a letter from Diane's lawyer telling me I had to appear in court again. There was no way he could force me to appear. But for the first time I was happy to. Stevie and I flew to New York, and she went on to her folks in Kansas City. She wasn't going back to Japan with me. The whole court deal took less than a week. But I didn't go back to Japan for a month. I almost didn't go at all. Then I figured since there were only a couple of months left in the season, I might as well make the best of it. I was being well paid.

In my second or third game back with the Atoms, I tore some fibers in my ankle running to first base. The ankle swelled up immediately. I told the manager, and he said, "You be okay. You play right field next inning." I played right field and stepped in a drainage hole chasing a ball, and my ankle really blew up. The Atoms didn't seem to think I was actually hurt. I saw several doctors, including an acupuncturist. The ankle didn't get any better. So I flew back to New York and saw a doctor, who put the ankle in a cast to immobilize it. When I got back to Japan, it was obvious that I wouldn't be able to play any more baseball in 1973.

I told the Atoms' management that I didn't like Japan and that I wanted my release. Since I had played in only fourteen games, had managed only seven hits in forty-three times at bat for a .163 average, they were not at all reluctant to part with me. They owed me $10,000 of the $35,000 I was to receive for half a season, and said they'd give me my release for what I had coming to me. I said they could keep the ten grand. I never did get oriented to Japan.

Sayonara.

The only good thing that happened in Japan was that Stevie got pregnant. When she told me, I put her on: "I told you that you were putting those pills in the wrong place. Didn't I keep saying, 'In the mouth'? Well, I won't be finding the pills all over the floor any more."

I couldn't have been happier. I had finally decided to divorce

Diane over a year ago, because I wanted to marry Stevie. The divorce would be final on September 19, 1973. Stevie and I could then get married any time before the baby was due in March. I was really looking forward to this kid. I was going to be around all the time to enjoy this one.

We stayed in Kansas City for a while, and I got in a lot of hunting with Jim Shipley, a great outdoorsman. Then we went back to Chicago for a few months. On January 8, we got married in the Cook County Building. Circuit Court Judge Richard Cuska said, "I've sat on the bench for ten years, and this is the first time my five kids are going to react to a case. When I tell them I married Joe Pepitone, I'll be a hero."

I was glad I didn't marry him. Stevie looked funny enough, with her tummy popping out. She was seven months' pregnant. If we'd waited a month, we could have had the ceremony performed while she was on the delivery table. I was present at the birth of Billy Joe, and it was one of the greatest moments of my life. Stevie had natural childbirth, and right after she delivered, with me standing there watching, they cleaned up my son and handed him to me. He was beautiful.

I didn't have any stupendous financial prospects for the future. But we'd saved enough to live on, simply, for a year or so. I had several job offers. Some friends in Colorado were starting a business and wanted me to go in with them. I didn't have to put up any money and I'd draw a salary of $26,000 a year. The Playboy Clubs offered me the same salary to act as a host, either in New York or Chicago. I decided to wait a while and see what turned up. I preferred to work for myself. I also thought there might be a slight possibility that the Yankees or Mets might take a chance on me. That was a silly thought, considering.

Then I began thinking about baseball and the ridiculous demands it makes. I love baseball, and I hate to see what it's doing to itself. There's so much dead time in it that it's the most boring sport in the world to watch. But it doesn't have to be, it doesn't have to be losing fans in so many cities. Attendance wouldn't decline if fans could go to a ball park and have fun even in the dead time, if they could be allowed to see the players as human beings just like them. But the lords of baseball never allow players to seem human, to bring any fun, any color to the game. When Hawk Harrelson had his act going, the lords of baseball said he was a flake, that he was bad for the game. Yet fans loved him. Jimmy Piersall was another flake, sure, but who came to see the Washington Senators when he was gone? When Dick Allen wrote S-H-I-T in the dirt with his toe, the lords of baseball went crazy. And it was great, because it excited fans. There's not a person in the world who doesn't know what shit means. Seeing one of the greatest hitters in the game write that in the dirt, carving a protest in the base path, stirred up a helluva lot of interest. Shouldn't the game be concerned with stirring up interest in itself, with bringing in more fans?

When I opened my hairstyling place, I brought an extra fifty thousand fags into Yankee Stadium. I did a pregame show with Joe Garagiola before one All-Star Game where the subject was hair care. I showed him the first hair dryer in baseball and talked about my rugs: my Gamer, my Infield rug, my Afro rug for when I wanted to be like a brother. I had a blond rug which I told him I wore when I wanted to be baseball's Golden Boy. Then Garagiola asked me about the two huge combs in my locker. "On damp nights my hair spray gets sticky," I said, picking up the thick-handled comb, "and I use this one. Not only won't it slip out of your hand, but it strengthens your wrist." He asked about the thin-handled comb. "This one's ideal for cool nights," I said. "You can whip it through your hair, and it also loosens up your wrists. So these two combs are the secret for the youth of American who are interested in baseball—the thick-handled and thin-handled models that strengthen and loosen up your wrists."

It was a funny put-on, and I got over two hundred letters from that show. Some of them said things like: "You're a fag, you're wife's a lesbian, and all your kids are fags." I expected some of that. But people came out to see me play. They were interested, or intrigued, by me. They always noticed me. And it's the ballplayers who are noticed who draw the fans. Henry Aaron was a great ballplayer, but for most of his career he wasn't a real gate attraction. He could hit four home runs in a game and people in the stands would hardly react. I *always* got a reaction, because my personal life was always in the papers. A lot of fans identified with me when they read that I was in debt. A lot of them were in debt.

If the Yankees had been smart, they would have released the fact that I was not only in debt—I was seventy thousand dollars in debt. You think people wouldn't have come out to boo and cheer and react to a major-league ballplayer who was in worse financial shape than they? Shit. The commissioner's office would have had a fit if anything near my real story had gotten out. The commissioner, who is a puppet of the owners, had a fit about a lot of the things Charlie Finley did to liven up baseball. But after years of battling with the commissioner and the other owners, Finley finally saw many of his innovations introduced, and fans loved them. Charlie Finley might be a bitch of a man to work for, but he is one of the greatest things ever to happen to baseball. He's colorful, he's unique. What other owner would think of letting a mule shit on the field?

Ralph Houk used to yell at me about the length of my hair. I'd say, "Ralph, do you hit a ball with your hair? Do you catch a ball with your hair?" It was bullshit. Five years later Charlie Finley was paying his players a *bonus* to grow moustaches, to be distinctive. I got fined for having my hair too long. I got fined for not wearing a cap on the field before a game. It was these petty things that bugged me more than the big things in baseball, like the length of the season, the long road trips, the official scorers who made so many bad calls because they were amateurs, sportswriters sitting so far from the play that there was no way they could consistently make accurate judgments.

I played in the Yankees' Old-Timers' Game at Shea Stadium in 1974, and I was sitting on the bench next to Yogi Berra between innings. He asked me if I thought I wanted to play again in 1975. I told him I really didn't know. If I got the right attitude back, if I felt that I could return and really enjoy baseball again without being hassled. . . . It didn't seem likely, unless baseball suddenly named a new commissioner who was about twenty-four years old and smoked grass and encouraged some humanity to enter the game, let the fans see the players having fun out there, being real people.

I knew I was going to miss a lot it. I'd had a lot of good times with a lot of good guys. I'll never forget, in my first full season, walking into the clubhouse one day and finding an original cartoon being hung in my locker by Mickey Mantle. He had been on Phil Linz and me for months about the fact that we tended to use our Yankee affiliation all over town. So Mickey had Murray Olderman, a writer and cartoonist, do a drawing of Phil and I doing our thing around town. The sketch showed me sitting in an open convertible with "JOE PEPITONE AND PHIL LINZ OF THE NEW YORK YANKEES" written on the door. I had my arm around a chick and Phil was in a harness pulling the car and smiling.

Another day Mickey hung a picture of himself in my locker. On the picture he wrote: "To the greatest little Dago blow job in the big leagues. Love, Mickey Mantle."

He could be funny as hell, and he could be moody as hell when he wasn't hitting. He'd sit around the clubhouse with his head down and not talk to anybody. One day during my second season with the Yankees, Mickey was in a mood because he was in a slump, and Roger Maris went over to him.

"Mickey, I hope you don't mind," said Roger, "but can I say something to you?"

"What do you want to say?" said Mickey, barely looking up.

"Well, I know exactly what you're doing wrong at the plate, I can help you."

"Who the fuck are you to tell me what I'm doing wrong?" said Mickey, glaring.

"All right," said Roger, "take it easy. "I'm sorry. I just thought I might help you. But I'll never say another goddamn word to you again."

Our two greatest hitters didn't speak to one another for weeks.

Roger Maris was one of the better people I met in baseball. After hitting those sixty-one home runs in 1961, he never got along with fans or writers. The pressure had been too much for him, and I thought at times that he wished he'd never broken Babe Ruth's record. But Roger was a nice, quiet guy, and a good family man. In all the years I played with him, I never once saw him come on with a chick. All he wanted to do was make money to support his wife and five kids. He went out of his way to help other players. He used to give me tips in batting practice. He was a master of waiting till the last split second before striding into a pitch—something I had trouble with. I tended to stride too soon and hit off my front foot. Roger would stand behind the cage during batting practice and say, "Stay back, Joe, stay back," reminding me to wait. Roger and Wally Moses, the Yankee hitting coach, helped me a lot with this.

The only time I hated to be around Maris was when he was with Clete Boyer and Hal Reniff and they were out drinking. Individually and out of a saloon, they were three of the nicest guys you'd ever want to meet. But almost every time I ran into them with glasses of booze in their hands, they'd start cutting me up so bad I'd want to punch them. After a while, whenever I walked into a bar and saw them there, I'd turn and walk right back out.

I remember one night during spring training in Florida when their mouths really caused trouble. It was in a place called Nick's, and I was sitting with another player and a couple of girls. Maris, Boyer, and Reniff were drinking at a table when a male model walked past them with a pretty girl. Reniff said something to her or made some remark about her. The guy turned to Boyer and told him he expected an apology. Boyer said he hadn't said anything, which he hadn't. They exchanged a few words, and the guy turned away. Then Reniff said something like, "Go fuck yourself." The guy came back and challenged Boyer, who told the guy to beat it, that he hadn't said a word. The guy wouldn't accept that, and the two of them ended up outside. Clete decked the guy, splitting open his mouth. The guy sued Maris, apparently figuring Roger had more money. Boyer had to admit he'd hit the guy.

Johnny Blanchard, the reserve catcher and great pinch-hitter, was the only other Yankee player I hated to run into in a bar. One night Phil Linz and I were on our way to the Tower East, a bar I frequented, when we met Blanchard, who was already smashed. He wanted to go with us. On the drive to the lounge, Blanchard abruptly said to Phil, "Did you ever see a bull in a China shop? That's the way I feel tonight." Phil looked at me like, *What the hell's wrong with him?*

We went into the Tower East and I said hello to Joe the bouncer, a huge friend who was standing by the door. We worked our way to the bar and ordered a drink. Blanchard poured his right down. Then he said to Phil and me; "In two minutes, both of you guys are gonna be on your way to the hospital. Two minutes."

"John," I said, "what're you pissed off about?"

"You guys stay out late every night, and you can't play baseball staying out late every night. You," he said to me, "are the first one going to the hospital, and," he pointed at Phil, "then you."

"That's ridiculous, John," I said, starting to bob a bit. I wanted to glance at the clock to see if my two minutes were up, but I was afraid to take my eyes off Blanchard. He was a big, very strong man.

All of a sudden Joe the bouncer, who was even bigger, stepped in front of John and said, "Listen, pal, there's only one tough guy in this place. That's me. Now you put your hands in your pockets and walk out of this place quietly, or *you'll* be the guy going to the hospital."

Blanchard did exactly as he was told, as Phil and I looked at each other and said, "Whew." The next day I made sure I was the last guy to show up at the clubhouse. I wanted to be sure there were other guys around when I saw Johnny Blanchard. The instant I walked in, Blanchard came right over to me. "Hey, we had a good time last night, didn't we?" he said.

"John," I said, "what the hell was wrong with you last night?"

"What do you mean?" he said, pretending to forget.

When Johnny Blanchard was traded, the big, strong, mean-behind-drink sonofabitch walked around the Yankee clubhouse for an hour crying on everyone's shoulder.

The only two guys I played ball with that I genuinely disliked were Jim Coates and Jim Bouton. Coates was a hard-throwing pitcher with an abrasive personality. I called him "Mummy" because he looked like a mummy, and we were always on one another. He tried to intimidate batters, which was okay, but he'd hit guys and start a fight on the field, then disappear when the punches started flying. When he was traded to Washington, he came up to me after packing his gear and said, "I just hope I pitch against you, because I'm gonna knock you on your ass every time."

"Are you serious, man?" I said. "The first time you hit me,

I'll come out there and hit you with a fucking bat."

Well, the first time I had to face him, I was scared to death. On the first pitch I hit the ground, and I don't even remember what I did that time at the plate, whether I got a hit, walked, or made out. But the next time up, Mantle, batting ahead of me, hit a towering home run off Coates. I pulled my batting helmet down over my ears as I stepped into the box. Just then Gil Hodges, the Senator manager, walked to the mound to take out Coates. What a relief!

I heard Coates say to Hodges, "Just let me pitch to this guy."

Holy shit, I thought, the Mummy really wants to skull me! "Get off the mound, you bum!" I shouted to Coates. "You can't pitch and you never could pitch. You should be a shower monitor."

Coates started in toward me, and I started out toward him. The plate umpire, Larry Napp, grabbed me. "Go fuck yourself, Mummy," I yelled at Coates, brave now that he was out of the game. Fortunately, I never had to bat against him again.

Jim Bouton I disliked from the moment I started playing with him at Amarillo in the Texas League. In my mind he was always a self-centered prick who never cared how he hurt his teammates. If an outfielder dropped a fly ball or an infielder made an error that affected the outcome of a game he was pitching, Bouton always bitched to the writers. He'd say things like, "This club will be all right if we ever get a center fielder." Or, "All this club needs is a second-baseman." He didn't make a lot of friends among his teammates with this kind of comment.

In one of our early years with the Yankees, Bouton and I had a fight on an airplane. We were flying to Denver to play an exhibition game. Bouton had been annoying everyone by crawling around on the floor and trying to give hotfeet. I passed him in the aisle and gave him a little punch in the arm. I forgot that was his sore arm. He jumped up and threw about five punches at me. I blocked them with my arms. Ellie Howard stood up between us, and I lunged over Ellie and rapped Bouton a glancing blow. Then we were both pulled away.

But when we got to the clubhouse in Denver, I was still angry because I hadn't landed a solid punch on Bouton. I started antagonizing him, calling him an asshole and everything else to provoke him into a fight, but he just sat in front of his locker. Yogi Berra came over and grabbed my right wrist and Bouton's right wrist and tried to pull our hands together. "Come on, you two," said Yogi, "make up. Shake hands." Bouton and I were pulling away from Yogi, stretching him until he looked like a crucifixion figure. Yogi tugged our hands closer and closer. The instant they touched, I was still so pissed that I threw a punch at Bouton with my left hand. The great fighter missed again.

The only time I really "got" Bouton was after a game in Detroit. He was in a bar with a chick who kept looking over at Clete Boyer and me. We weren't having much luck in the place, so when Bouton left with the girl, we followed them outside. "Hey," I called to the girl, "where you headed?" She turned and walked right over to us and we started coming on with her. "Jim," she said over her shoulder, "I think I'll go with these guys." We walked off and left Bouton standing there. When we got the girl to the hotel, it turned out she was into weird sex beyond anything even I had imagined. We finally had to throw her out of the room.

Bouton and I were in Houston together when his book, *Ball Four,* came out, and I read it and got mad as hell. Not because of the things he said about me; I couldn't complain about the truth of any of them. What pissed me off was that Bouton didn't reveal any real truths about himself, about any of his sexual interests on the road. He embarrassed other players, but he didn't write anything that embarrassed himself.

Again I tried to provoke him into a fight in the clubhouse. "I hope you choke on the blood money you're making on that book," I told Bouton, and called him every filthy name, said every nasty thing I could think of. Anyone else would have had to hit me. Bouton did the right thing. He just smiled and turned away, saying, "Joe, I got the money."

I wish I had been born ten years later, because I'd have some money, too. Not only have baseball player salaries shot upward, but today guys have their lawyers or agents negotiate their contracts—professionals who know how to get top dollar out of the front office. When I was playing, if you took your lawyer with you to the general manager's office to negotiate your contract, your lawyer had to sit outside. You went in and dealt with the general manager, stepped out to talk to your lawyer, then went back in and got beaten down yourself. If I was playing ball today, I might be a fairly well-to-do individual. Although my wife says that's very debatable.

Stevie and I moved to Brooklyn in the spring of 1974, rented a little house, and settled down to just live. It was nice being close to my family again. Every Sunday there was still a huge dinner for twenty or thirty people at my grandfather's, a two-family house where my mother also lives. After my father died, my mother had gone into a shell, never going out, never having any real fun any more. Something of her died with Willie. But within the last year or so, my mother had finally come out of her shell. She's still a very attractive woman, only fifty-two, and it warmed my heart to see her getting out, doing things, enjoying life again after all those years.

I bought a twenty-foot powerboat and, through the first half of the summer, just went fishing and snorkeling, renewed old friendships with Lemon and all the guys, and relaxed. It was nice, after fifteen years of baseball, to do nothing in the summer. I was keeping my eyes opened for a small business to go into, either alone or with one partner. I definitely wasn't interested in any more lounges or anything elaborate, just something that would be enjoyable to run and bring in a decent income. Having Stevie and Billy Joe, I didn't need a whole bunch of money to be happy.

XXIV

Finally . . . a little perspective.

Beginning with the night my father died, and virtually every night of my life since then, I have had nightmares that scare the hell out of me. Gory, grisly, violent, vicious scenes that follow pretty much the same theme nightly. I'm jumping on some guy —I can't tell who—and I'm throwing punches and kicking and gouging, and nothing is happening. The guy is laughing at me. All of a sudden, he pulls out a knife and slashes me, and I feel the pain, see the blood. Then I want to wake up, and I always do. As soon as I feel the pain, I wake up. When I fall asleep again, I'm right into a similar nightmare. I've become so used to them after all these years that when I don't have a nightmare I worry the next morning. I'm nervous, upset. Something's out of kilter. The nightmares are so much a part of my life, they are like old friends, or old familiar enemies . . . something I am supposed to experience as regularly as breathing. Small wonder.

When I look back on my life, I can't believe how crazed I was. I think I understand what started it all. But I don't understand why I extended the bullshit for so long, why I had to put myself through so much grief for so many years without making some changes. I guess I was too screwed up to change, so I kept turning the screw deeper and deeper and deeper . . .

I think of all the balling I did, and how it gave me good feelings for a while. Then the good feelings started lasting only during the sex itself. When the sex was over, I began to feel miserable. As the years went on, the misery increased, intensified, lasted longer and longer. Yet the misery didn't stop me.

The only thing that even began to change me was getting

older. Not more mature, just older. I couldn't screw as much any more. Then I discovered that I could not only do without it—in those compulsive, frantic, no-feeling terms—but that cutting back on the bullshit sex also cut down my misery cache. Fuck me.

After being with a girl, I used to say, "What a great fuck she was! What a *great* fuck!" Then one day it occurred to me to ask myself, What the hell *is* a great fuck? The best sex of all is easy. When you get right down to it, the best sex of all is provided by your five fingers. They know what your dick likes best, how it likes to move. Only you and your hand know for sure.

The only really great sex partner is someone you care about more than anything. That's why getting to know Stevie was the one thing beyond aging that helped me to change. After I blew the marriage to Diane, I thought I would never find a girl I'd want to be with all the time, a girl that I could sit around with night after night and get off by just being present. I was grasping so hard for love that, until I met Stevie, I never realized that I'd never been in love before, that I didn't have any idea what love was.

When I go to some of the bars I used to hit regularly, the first thing the owner wants to do is fix me up with some girl. "Thanks," I tell them, "but I'm out of that game. Retired." I just drop in to have a couple of drinks, rap, laugh. I like to sit and talk to chicks, to dig into their heads, see what's moving them, what they're into. It's a better, more meaningful game.

I had a falling-out with my best friend, not long ago, because every time we went out together he was trying to get laid. "Look," I'd say, "that's fine for you, but don't try to drag me along. I'm sick of that bullshit." He's over ten years older than I am, and he's never grown up, never tried to change. I'm trying to change, and it doesn't do me any good to pal out with him any more. It's a shame we still can't be close. We had so many laughs together, so many good times. We'd do anything for one another, and I'm sorry we have to go our own ways now. But that's the way it's got to be. I have to think of myself, what's best for me.

I still do some things that are out of line. I have a ways to go. But the improvements I've made in myself—small to some people—are like moonshots to me. I was such a liar, such an asshole for so long, that I came to hate myself, to hate almost everything I did. Now, finally, I really believe I'm a nice guy. I'm concerned about other people. I try never to put down anybody, to hurt anyone. I've hurt too many people . . . so many.

My last year with the Cubs, I visited my children when we played in California. Eileen, who was almost twelve then, was a tall, beautiful girl. Her mother had her dressed like Little Bo Peep: a long dress, curled hair. She didn't like it. I didn't like it because she didn't like it . . . and I heard the words again: "Daddy, don't leave me." Eileen remembered me. Joseph Jr., my first son, who was a big boy for ten years old, didn't know who I was. I didn't cry in front of them.

I haven't done all bad. I've always had a soft heart to go with my crazed head. I don't know how many times I've met a stranger in a bar over the years who started telling me how desperate he was, telling me a horror story that was no worse than mine. But it would touch me so much that I'd reach for my wallet and give him every cent I had on me. I was always in financial trouble, but I was out just fucking around. The hundred dollars or so that I had on me would actually help this guy. He would make better use of it than I would. Of course, I have to admit that at least part of my motivation came from a childhood belief that God would note my generosity when I died.

I remember as a kid, when the March of Dimes collection container was passed in The Itch theater, I'd always put in all the money I had on me. The other guys would put in a dime and save fifteen cents for the candy store later. I'd put in my quarter and think, Maybe God won't let me ever be paralyzed.

Although I don't spend a lot of time in church, I'm still Catholic and I still believe in God. There's nothing wrong with having faith, believing in something. Until it's proven different to me, I'm going to believe. It can't hurt, even if you do have to wonder.

I think about that story I heard when I was growing up in

the Church. About the kid who goes to mass with a pocket full of peanuts. The priest shouts, "God is everywhere!" And the kid freezes, saying to himself, "I hope He's not in my pocket eating my peanuts." Now I wonder, What would it be like to reach in your pocket and pull out God?

One of my greatest regrets is that I wasn't at least semisane about my finances. I made a lot of money playing baseball, particularly in the last years. And I'm still in debt. The only thing good about going to Japan was that my creditors didn't follow me there. When I came back, I was moving around— Kansas City, Chicago, Brooklyn—and it took a while for the bill collectors to run me down. I hadn't seen a process server in so long, I was beginning to feel lonely.

In August of 1974, I opened a little restaurant in Brooklyn: "Joe Pepitone's Italian Dugout." It cost me about nine thousand dollars to convert a luncheonette into a restaurant. I hustled around and lined up the suppliers, got a big stove, a walk-in refrigerator, tables, chairs, and I supervised the remodeling. It was a nice little place, not fancy, a restaurant that served good food, wine, and beer, at inexpensive prices. Perfect for a neighborhood business. Throughout the weeks it took me to get the place ready, I kept saying to Stevie and to my mother, who was helping in the kitchen, "Where are the bill collectors? What are those guys waiting for?"

The night we opened the restaurant, a guy walked in with five other people. "Joe," he said to me, "I've got some good news for you and some bad news."

"Give me the good news first," I said.

"All these people with me are starving, and we're gonna eat everything on your menu."

"Terrific. What's the bad news?"

He handed me a subpoena to appear in court with Diane. "I'm sorry," he said.

"Don't worry about it," I told him. "I've got a whole wall in my house papered with these things, but there's one blank spot. Now I can finish decorating. Thanks."

When Stevie and I had started living together in Chicago, we'd bought three thousand dollars' worth of furniture on time.

For over two years we lived in the same place, and the furniture store never sent us a bill, even when we got married and our address was in the newspapers. We were ecstatic because this was a first—a creditor forgetting about Joe Pepitone. Recently, about three and a half years after I bought that furniture—half of which I sold before we moved from Chicago—I got a post-card in the mail that asked me to call Ray something at a New York phone number. I didn't know Ray something, but I called.

"What number do I have?" I asked.

"You've got the right number," the guy on the line said.

"Well, what does this company do?"

"This is a collection agency."

"Do you know who this is?"

"No."

"Good." I hung up. But I'll hear from him again. I'll hear from all the bill collectors.

I never cared about money until the last few years. All I wanted to do was spend it, live today, screw the future. Everyone I knew worried about money. That was what responsible people did. I rebelled against every single responsibility. All of them. I could have still lived well, more enjoyably, by spending sensibly, not charging everything. I guess I was more interested in bucking the conventional. I never worried about the bills until the collectors caught up with me. But I still don't understand—having lived almost two and a half years on fifty or sixty dollars a week—how I allowed myself to get back into heavy debt again and again. There's still an awful lot I don't understand fully.

I do know that everything happened to me too soon, when I was too young to handle it . . . getting shot, my father dying, being a big star as a child. From the minute I played with the best team in Brooklyn I had everybody trying to grab me, hook into me, praise me, make me think I was something special. Then I signed the bonus contract with the Yankees, made the best team in baseball at age twenty-one, and suddenly bigger, more important people were trying to grab me. All the racket guys who wanted me to hang out with them. They introduced me to dozens of celebrities, and they told everyone, "Hey, look who I got with me—Joe Pepitone, who's gonna be a big star, make us all proud." I became convinced that I *was* special, that I could do no wrong. Things happened so fast, I couldn't put anything in perspective. It would have been difficult for most people. For a baby who was also plagued by guilt and uncertainty, it was impossible.

I've run into some of those racket guys since I've been back in New York, and they all say the same thing, "You coulda made us all proud, Joey, but you got nothin' upstairs. You disgraced us."

"What are you doing to me?" I asked them. "I've shamed you? I didn't *kill* anybody. What did you do to make me proud the last twelve years? What, tell me?"

That kind of talk bugs the shit out of me. I know I should have done things a lot differently. But I hurt myself more than anyone else. I was doing what I had to do then. I thought I was digging it, enjoying it. It turned out otherwise, but that's past. Sure I disappointed a lot of people. And some people disappointed me. But I don't put down anyone for what they did. These people who used to love me and now say I disgraced them, all they're telling me is that they were using me. Over the years, it became clearer and clearer that some people were hanging around me just because of my name, my image.

I know I asked for it, that I used my name to get laid. I didn't give a shit about anything then except getting laid. But when I finally began to have some self-pride—which is the greatest thing in the world—I started wondering, Does this girl really like *me* or does she just dig the world I move in? This is a tough thing for any celebrity to face. When you're a star and you have some money and you like to go out and have a good time, does the chick dig all that alone? What does she think of you? I began to wonder about everyone who hung out with me, even my best friends. Do they really like me, or do they just like what I can provide? It's not a pleasant thought.

This is why I don't think that anybody in the limelight, who's a star, can be completely happy. He has to constantly wonder about his real regard in the eyes of everyone he's close to. I wonder how often Frank Sinatra thinks about this. I wonder,

How many times has he used his name—or wiggled his finger—to get a piece of ass?

I guess I became a celebrity freak because of my father, because he was such a star to me and I wanted to win his approval. The celebrities I admired all gave me approval, so I kept seeking them out. It took me a long time to realize how foolish I was. But I am not alone in being so close to something that I didn't see what I was actually doing.

I see that my own family, without knowing it, is suddenly ignoring my grandfather, and I get so upset I could cry. Vincent Caiazzo is approaching age ninety-two, and when we all assemble at his house for Sunday dinner, I see that everyone shunts him aside, giving him none of the attention he deserves. I say, "What's going on here?" And several members of my family say, "Well, he's getting old. He's getting senile." "Are you crazy?" I say. "He's as hip as he ever was, a wonderful old man."

It kills me that they act this way toward a man who has always taken care of them any time they needed help, who provided housing for everyone, who laid money on everyone when they didn't have it. And now they cast him aside—without even realizing it. I see it because I have been away so much. My family doesn't realize it; they don't mean to discard this man they all love. But they do it.

One day some months ago during a Sunday get-together, my grandfather and I went outside after the meal. We sat and talked for almost an hour, and the tears kept swimming to my eyes when he spoke: "You know, Giuseppe, you people, you aunts and uncles, my daughters and my sons, they think I'm a crazy, that I getta so old I no longer know anything. But, listen now, I wanna tell you. I know more than any of them. I know everything they talk about. I know everything they *thinking*. Before they say, I know."

I hugged him to my chest and kissed him on the cheek. I love my grandfather so. He is a great man, and has always been a great man.

After our talk, I said we should go back inside, rejoin the family. "You go, Giuseppe," he said, waving a hand. "I stay here a while." He smiled and I patted him on the shoulder.

Everyone was still sitting around the table, and I stood in the doorway a minute listening to the conversation. All I heard were people complaining about their health, moaning about the fact that they were getting older, and discussing the dead, running down one member of the family after another who had passed away. It was an Italian habit, this dwelling on the dead, one that my father had never believed in. Any time this kind of talk began when he was alive, he would tell a story, make a joke, have everyone laughing, living in the present. He believed in fun, and as I stood there I pictured him laughing, remembering him just as he was, his head thrown back, his teeth flashing. And, God, I wished he were still with us, wished he were there to turn the conversation. If Willie were there, Vincent Caiazzo would not be sitting out front in the sun alone, smiling and enjoying life by himself.

I sat down at the table next to Stevie, who rolled her eyes upward. I shook my head. Then I pulled out some grass and began rolling a joint.

"Joe," said my mother, "put that away."

"That's not funny, Joe," said my brothers, sounding like a chorus. "That's not funny at all."

"Shut up, all of you," I said. "You do what you gotta do, and I'll do what I gotta do. To put up with you people, I've gotta smoke this shit."

The whole scene was depressing. It's always depressing to see people you love acting stupidly, showing no feeling at all for others. I know my family felt that way about me for years. I gave them ample reason to be concerned about me, about my self-destructiveness, and I'm sorry about that. Truly sorry that I brought them down so many times. I know now that you can't fuck over yourself without messing up the people you care about most, and with that knowledge comes the greatest pain of all. You do what you have to do, and you pay the price—but you pay it doubly when you see how it has hurt others you love.

It's been one helluva long and painful education process. I feel like a guy who was left back in kindergarten twelve times, like I could never get it right no matter how often the lessons were pounded into me.

But for the first time in my memory, I'm happy, really happy. Not for a day or a week or a month—constantly. I love being with Stevie and Billy Joe, worrying about them, taking care of them. In November of 1974, we rented, for only $250 a month, a terrific house on the beach in Queens, and I could hardly wait until the summer came so we could really enjoy it as a family. Stevie is the most relaxed, together girl I have ever known. She lets me go out in the evening if I have to. "Just tell me when you're coming home," she says, "and take care of yourself." So I don't go out often. It's nice just being with her, even though she's quiet, an interior person, and I'm hyper, an extrovert. She'll sit around reading, because she reads everything she can get her eyes on. I'll be watching television or listening to music. But after an hour or so without hearing a word from her, I'll think something's wrong.

"Stevie, what did I do?" I'll say.

"Nothing," she'll say, looking up from her book.

"You talked more when we were going together," I'll say.

"I'm just relaxing, Joe."

"Well, say something once in a while, breathe hard, let me hear the *wind* come out of your nose. Don't make me worry that you've died there."

"Joe, I love you."

Then it's okay. Then everything's okay.

I just wish our restaurant had done better. It started strong. I was able to pay off all of my suppliers within six weeks after we opened. During one of those weeks, a waitress got sick and Stevie filled in for three nights and made eighty dollars in tips. We were on our way, getting ready to expand into the empty store next door, which would double our seating capacity. Then the economy really began to go bad, and the business became up and down. One night packed, the next night empty. After a good night, I always felt fantastic. I'd come home and find that my two dogs—one of which was a Great Dane puppy who tended to go wild—had destroyed the living room. I'd just clean up the mess and yell at them.

After a bad night at the restaurant—when I'd also been hit by another subpoena from Diane—I'd come home in a foul mood. If the dogs had torn up the place, I would beat the hell out of them. I would also be sharp-mouthed with Stevie over nothing things.

"Joe, close the restaurant," Stevie would say. "It's not worth it if owning the place makes you so upset."

"Stevie, don't tell me that," I would say. "I don't want to hear that. I didn't open the restaurant to close it. You've got to stick with me, hon. You gotta keep me going. All I gotta know is that we care for one another, that's all I care about. If I have nothing in the world, as long as I have you and Billy Joe, I'm gonna be feeling pretty good, hon. But you gotta stick with me."

"Joe, you know I'm going to stick with you. I just don't want to see you upset. Just relax. It'll work out."

Things will work out, as long as we're together, even though I finally did have to close the restaurant. I lost nine thousand dollars on it. So it goes. I don't want to be rich. I just want to make enough money to care for my family simply. As long as I can sit around at night and play with my son, yell at my dogs, and be with Stevie—it's beautiful. Making them happy, that's my whole life.

I realize even now that I may get bored with this life, that the pressure to care for my family and try to keep what I have in these difficult times may get to me. When I review my past record, I can't honestly offer any guarantees. I know I still have miles to go before I sleep nightmareless. But now I can look back with at least a little perspective on where I've tramped, and on whom. Could anyone possibly allow himself to go through anything even vaguely resembling that kind of pain again? Knowing full well from this vantage point that it would be even worse one more time? When I get depressed now, I think back on those shudderingly grim years, and no matter what's coming down, the future looks blindingly bright.

Two weeks after we moved into our house at the beach, on Thanksgiving Day, we found that we would never have a chance to walk in the sand and swim in the surf there. We had planned to have Thanksgiving dinner together, just the three of us. We got up early and took the turkey out of the refrigerator, but four hours later it became apparent that we should have left it out all night to defrost. We drove to my mother's for dinner. That evening we got a phone call from the lady who lived next door to us in Queens. Her voice was choked. Our house had burned to the ground. An electrical fire had flashed through the house and destroyed everything we owned—all our clothes, furniture, appliances, and the dogs. Our fire insurance had not yet been transferred.

Stevie was so strong, composed. Until we went to bed that night. Then she began thinking about the dogs, and she started crying and couldn't stop. I held her, tried to comfort her. But she was hysterical, she had held it in for hours, and had to let it out.

"Go ahead, hon," I said. "It's all right. Get it all out, and everything will be all right. Maybe it's New York, maybe this place is a jinx. Most of the pain in my life has happened here. Maybe we should move. Maybe it's just as well that everything's gone, that we can just pick up and go, start fresh someplace else. We have each other and Billy Joe, and nothing else means a damn thing."

I hugged her to me as hard as I could without cracking her ribs, and we went to sleep like that. I had a supergory nightmare.

The next morning, Stevie was together and I was depressed at breakfast. My mother saw my head down and said, "Now, Joe, don't you start doing that stuff all day," and she drew on an imaginary cigarette without letting any imaginary smoke out. I smiled. My mother, this incredible woman, she knows me, knows my escapes so well. I guess that's why I feel that in the long run I really don't have anything to worry about. I wish to God that Willie Pepitone were still alive. I wish it with all my heart and soul. But as long as Angelina Pepitone is present, she will take care of me: feed me and clothe me, and give me a dime every day.